World Politics

at the Edge of Chaos

SUNY series, James N. Rosenau series in Global Politics

—————————

David C. Earnest, editor

World Politics
at the Edge of Chaos

Reflections on Complexity and Global Life

Edited by

Emilian Kavalski

SUNY
PRESS

Published by State University of New York Press, Albany

© 2015 State University of New York

SPONSORED BY THE

Federal Ministry
of Education
and Research

Rachel
Carson
Center

ENVIRONMENT AND SOCIETY

For information, contact State University of New York Press, Albany, NY
www.sunypress.edu

Production, Diane Ganeles
Marketing, Kate R. Seburyamo

Library of Congress Cataloging-in-Publication Data

World politics at the edge of chaos : reflections on complexity and global life / edited
    by Emilian Kavalski.
        pages cm. — (SUNY series, James N. Rosenau series in global politics)
    Includes bibliographical references and index.
    ISBN 978-1-4384-5607-2 (hc : alk. paper)—978-1-4384-5608-9 (pb : alk paper)
    ISBN 978-1-4384-5609-6 (ebook)
    1. World politics.   2. International relations.   3. Globalization. I. Kavalski, Emilian.

JZ1310.W675 2015
327—dc23   2014020303

10 9 8 7 6 5 4 3 2 1

*Dedicated to the memory and inspiration
of James N. Rosenau
(1924–2011)*

We dance to the rhythms of the universe.
We dance sometimes alone; sometimes in groups,
Each sensing and responding to a slightly different beat in the chaotic
rumble;
Each encompassing the whole, yet remaining unique.
Not random error, or noise,
The out-of-step footsteps
follow a path charted in the infinity of time, rational and beautiful,
if only we could see it from outside ourselves.
We live and celebrate life
Made possible in the violent death of stars so long ago—
lost to human memory.
Can we comprehend the reasons and the patterns with our puny minds?
If we can't, is truth then less true?
Can we deny the meaning in complexity because we haven't been able to
reduce it to our size?
Can we learn to see the universe without confining it inside borders of
our own creation and the accepted meters of our times?
We look for revealed truth and discard what doesn't fit our craving for
certainty.
Yet, life is uncertainty—surprise and adventure, the unexpected.
We dance to the rhythms of the universe.
If one dance is lost, all our science can't replace it.
We all are pieces of a puzzle,
our bends and straight lines mesh to make a picture—
a whole.
Are our footsteps set for us by some mad choreographer?
Can we deconstruct, then reconstruct, the dance?
Do we truly want to?
Perhaps—
Only if we can learn to visualize, to internalize, life in
multiple dimensions, drawn through time.
In a brilliant burst of light and energy—
long since dissipated—
we are born to dance to the rhythms of the universe.

—Karen G. Evans (1998, v–vi)

Contents

PART I
COMPLEXITY THINKING AND
ANTHROPOCENTRIC INTERNATIONAL RELATIONS

List of Illustrations

Figures

Tables

Acknowledgments

I wish to thank the contributors to this volume for their cooperation and collaboration. Without their support and encouragement this book would have never "self-organized" into its current shape. The initial conditions of possibility emerged during two workshops in early 2011—the first one from 19 to 20 January in Sydney (Australia) and the second one from 11 to 12 February in Munich (Germany). The Sydney workshop was made possible by support from the International Workshop Grant program of the Academy for the Social Sciences in Australia, the Center for Citizenship and Public Policy (especially, its director—Anna Yeatman), and the University of Western Sydney. The Munich workshop was funded by the Rachel Carson Center for Environment and Society (RCC). I am deeply grateful to Christof Mauch and Helmuth Trischler for their support and the generous subvention assistance as well as for creating the RCC "research haven" in the first place. It was at these two workshops that the idea of this volume was first conceived. A huge thank you is also owed to the discussants and participants at these workshops for their feedback and insight, especially to Brett Bowden, Christine Brachthäuser, Walter C. Clemens, Andreas Duit, Sarah Graham, Sean Hays, Dylan Kissane, Kai Lehmann, Jonathon Louth, Klaus Mainzer, Tony Rivera, Gerda Roelvnik, Chris Roberts, Dennis J. D. Sandole, Nick Srnicek, Gordon Winder, and Magdalena Zolkos. Last, but not least, I would like to thank all my colleagues at the Institute for Social Justice at the Australian Catholic University (Sydney) for the stimulating intellectual exchanges and whose insights left a mark on the final shape of this volume. The usual caveat applies.

Introduction

Inside/Outside and Around

Observing the Complexity of Global Life

Emilian Kavalski

> And so he [the student of world politics] embarks on a search for certainty, only to find that it lies in such phrases as "apparently," "presumably," and "it would seem as if."
>
> —James N. Rosenau (1960, 21)

Introduction

"Apparently," to use James Rosenau's suggestion in the epigraph, uncertainty has always been a defining feature of world affairs. So why then are policy makers, international relations (IR) scholars, and we—the news-thirsty public—so surprised when the world turns out to be unpredictable? After all, depending on how far back one is willing to look, the discipline (at least in its "Eurocentric" form) has gone a long way since the first department of international politics opened its doors at Aberystwyth or since Thucydides scripted his account of the Peloponnesian wars. In either case, the veritable age of IR should have "presumably" provided it with enough experience to expect—if not necessarily be prepared for—the unexpected. Yet, as Rosenau (1980) reminds us, IR is anything but prepared for uncertainty (and has been so for a while). According to him, "it would seem as if" the mainstream has lost its "playfulness." Thus, instead of allowing "one's mind to run freely, to be playful, to toy around with what might seem absurd, to posit seemingly unrealistic circumstances and speculate what would follow if they ever were to come to pass," the IR mainstream has sidelined its mischievous nature in favor of stiff parsimonious models simplifying the contingent nature of most that passes in world affairs. Therefore, for Rosenau, it is no wonder that IR has consistently failed to "imagine the unimaginable" (Rosenau 1980, 19–31).

It is for this reason that he pioneered nonlinear approaches "to toy around" with the complex patterns of world politics (Rosenau 1990). Subsequently, the propagation of complexity thinking (CT) concepts and ideas across the IR domain has become one of the most fascinating trends in the discipline. Complex challenges emerging from the interconnectedness between local and transnational realities, between financial markets and population movements, and between pandemics, a looming energy crisis, and climate change have tested IR's ability to address convincingly their turbulent dynamics. The contention of this volume is that such complex challenges intimate a pattern of interactions marked by sharp discontinuities. Modern, large-scale actors—such as states and international organizations—have become vulnerable to unexpected shocks. However, IR, with its tradition of state-based analysis, has difficulties with the cross-cutting and intersecting character of many complex challenges. In fact, the emergence of such qualitative uncertainties demands a different type of thought process capable of addressing the multitude of forces and random processes that animate the dynamism of global life (Bernstein et al. 2000).

The need for a new vocabulary reflects the twin tendency in IR to think in paradigms and to return to familiar concepts. This is a perplexing trend, bearing in mind that the topography of IR theory—especially following the end of the Cold War—has developed into a multicolored matrix of perspectives and frameworks on the appropriate ways for studying world affairs. Motivated by the failure to anticipate the demise of Soviet superpower, the discipline embarked on an unprecedented widening and deepening of its outlook. It appears, however, that two-and-a-half decades later the innovative spark that invigorated this proliferation of views has petered out. Instead, what used to be a liberating tearing up of conceptual straitjackets seems itself to have oscillated into the very "paradigmatic imperialism" that it sought to displace. As J. Samuel Barkin cogently demonstrates, the discipline is plagued by a "castle syndrome"—proponents of different IR schools engage in defending and reinforcing the bulwarks of their analytical castles, while bombarding the claims of everybody else (Barkin 2010).

The contention is that the discipline has increasingly immersed itself in debates on the substantiation of particular paradigms rather than engaging with the reality of global life. To put it bluntly, the turbulence of world affairs appears to have relevance (primarily) to the extent that it can validate (or disprove) the proposition of a particular IR school. Such contention should not be misunderstood as a condemnation of the field, or as a suggestion that it lacks sophistication. On the contrary, post–Cold War developments have challenged the discipline to venture into intellectual terrains that it previously did not deem necessary, important, or worthwhile. The suggestion here is that while this has been going on, IR scholars failed to break from the leftover mode of thinking in paradigms—probably one of the most palpable Cold War legacies of the discipline. Thus, despite the "new challenges," IR has not abandoned its "old habits" (Waltz 2002). Such a proclivity has recently been termed as "returnism"—IR's predilection for traditional conceptual signposts that provide intellectual comfort zones but are "simply images of old concepts" decontextualized from (and, therefore, inapplicable to) current realities (Heng 2010).

Such a mentality has hindered the interaction between the different IR paradigms, between IR and the advances in other social and natural sciences, as well as the development of qualitatively new intellectual platforms for engaging the complexity of world affairs. This volume addresses this shortcoming by bringing together distinct readings of international patterns developed by proponents of CT. The claim here is that while IR scholars often employ the metaphor of complexity, the potential theoretical and policy contributions emerging from the analytical principles of CT have largely been neglected. The marginalization of CT proponents within the discipline reflects both their refusal to think in paradigms and the espousal of a new vocabulary both for the study of IR and for the explanation and understanding of global life, which very often has its origins in the natural rather than the social sciences.

However, one question that needs to be addressed at the outset is: Why complexity thinking? The answer offered by the contributors to this volume is that IR needs new forms of knowledge to respond to emerging complex challenges, in particular knowledge coming from a different epistemological, ontological, and ethical place than the conventional repertoire of IR (Ang 2011; Murphy 2000). CT offers such a point of departure. In particular, CT endeavors a form of argument that illuminates that the development of sophisticated and sustainable responses to current challenges requires the recognition of complexity—not for complexity's own sake, but because simplistic solutions are unsustainable and counterproductive (Kavalski 2012b). What IR can gain from such a move are useful analytical and policy-making concepts and ways of thinking about the dynamism of a fragile and unpredictable global life.

The use of the notion of "global life" is not coincidental here. It allows the contributors to this volume to explore the full spectrum of CT's contributions to IR. As it will soon become apparent, CT has a (potentially) transformative impact both on the established anthropocentric IR and on the emerging nonanthropocentric one. Having its roots in the Latin word *complexus*—describing "that which is woven together" as well as something that has "embraced," "plaited" several elements—the complexity perspective infers the *interwovenness* of life (both as an inherent quality and a systemic condition). The recognition of such interwovenness between human and natural systems defines *global life* not merely as international politics, but as coexistent "worlds," "domains," "projects," or "texts" of ongoing and over-lapping interconnections (Rosenau 1988). Global life consists of more than just political communities and the polities that they inhabit—that is, it is not only about what happens "inside/outside" the state, but also about what happens "around" the state. It also reveals that the "international system" is embedded within wider structural conditions and interactions located within the environment "around" the conventional focus on interstate relations, an environment which conceptually constitutes as well as causally conditions (although not in a mono-causal and linear fashion) states *and* other actors (Kurki 2008, 255–261).

It has to be stated from the outset that such engagement with the "around" of global life is much less radical than it might appear at first sight. In fact, it merely recollects the central place that the agency of nature used to be accorded in the study of IR. The term "nature" is not used here in an essentialized sense, but meaning "an independent domain that both enables and constrains human activities, and [that] will not prove endlessly adaptable on the demands made on it by human beings" (Soper 2010, 223). Such encounters with the "around" of world politics should not be new to IR. For instance, by the 1920s, the discipline acknowledged that the natural environment is one of the key actors on the international stage. As Raymond Garfield Gettell insisted, despite "man's best efforts to bring the world in which he lives under his control, the influence of the natural environment upon political evolution has been throughout all human history an important and, in many instances a decisive, factor . . . Battles, upon whose outcome the fate of nations has depended, have been decided by natural phenomena such as wind, rain, fog or snow, beyond human control" (Gettell 1922, 322). In particular, the significance of the "around" of global life to the study and practice of international affairs has been stressed by the suggestion that "the dominant factor which determines the survival of a group is suitability to the environment" (Heath 1919, 143).

In this sense, already from its outset, IR has acknowledged that nature's agency—even if unintentional—plays an important role in the unfolding of world affairs (and should therefore not be discarded). For instance, it is often overlooked that with his emphasis on the "geographic causation [behind] the competing forces in current international politics," Halford Mackinder, the so-called father of geopolitics, intended not only to draw attention to the crucial role played by geography, but rather "to exhibit human history as part of the life of the world organism" (a statement which can be read as Mackinder's version of the notion of the "around" of global life). From this point of view, the dynamics of world affairs demonstrate that "man and not nature initiates, but nature in large measure controls [the outcomes]" (Mackinder 1904, 422). This ontological commitment is echoed by Harlan and Margaret Sprout in their outline of "ecological viewpoints, concepts, and theories in connection with politics in general and international politics in particular." The Sprouts defined world politics as a turbulent set of "man-milieu relationships," which includes "both tangible objects, non-human and human, at rest and in motion, and the whole complex of social patterns, some embodied in formal enactments, others manifest in more or less stereotyped expectations regarding the behaviour of human beings and the movements and mutations of non-human phenomena" (Sprout and Sprout 1956). Consequently, such recognition of and confrontation with the "around" of global life calls for

> a major revision of our understanding of international relations: politics among and above nations is recognised as a part of a vast natural system, a biosystem. Therefore, all past units we [have] become accustomed to—territorial units and functional relationship—are subsumed under the biosystemic perspective. All units and all relationships become relevant. (Haas 1975, 842)

Thus, the emphasis on the notion of global life intends to resuscitate IR's interest in the ossified knowledge about the embeddedness of world affairs in the "around" that provides the context for what has and makes possible its interactions. Human societies and their international interactions are just "one component in a package of interdependent life forms that continue to adapt to each other" (Clark 2000, 4). The suggestion is that the "inside/outside" and the "around" aspects of the study of world politics are not in contradiction, but part of the same spectrum of dynamics embedded in the patterns of global life. The notion of global life therefore elicits that all human interactions are embedded in and made possible by complex global interconnections. The claim is that in contrast to the conventional distinction between subjects (humans) and the objects (the world around them) (Rosenow 2012), the emphasis on the concomitance of the "inside/

outside and around" allows for acknowledging the agency and subjectivity of human and nonhuman actors on the global stage.

As the contributors to this collection aptly demonstrate, the reference to global life should not be misunderstood as an insistence on the similarity of human and nonhuman systems (be they biophysical or technological). On the contrary, the notion of global life does not deny the qualitative differences between human and nonhuman systems. Instead, it underscores that the two are mutually implicated and interdependent. In other words, the emphasis on the global life proffers a "human-in-ecosystem" perspective on the study and practice of IR, which recognizes "the mutual influence of ecological and social processes, instead of treating social and ecological systems as linked but separate domains" (Davidson-Hunt and Berkes 2003, 54). Thus, while this volume does not want to brandish CT as a panacea for the crises plaguing the global condition, it nevertheless suggests that CT offers unique opportunities (if not for blurring the dichotomy between anthropocentric and nonanthropocentric IR) for a thorough reconsideration of the explanation and understanding purveyed by representatives of both anthropocentric and nonanthropocentric IR.

The confrontation with the radical reality of global life—namely (to use Emmanuel Adler's term), its "cognitive punch"—seems to suggest that existing analytical frameworks, institutions, and types of political behavior have become "dysfunctional and can no longer deal with the situation in the old ways" (Adler 2005, 75). The intention of this collection is to offer a glimpse into CT's potential to generate new ideas and new arguments for tracking the evolution of global life through periods of discontinuous change, in ways that promise to better over time both understanding and action (Geyer and Rihani 2010). The following sections provide a brief overview of the "complexifying" trends in IR and the contributions to this volume.

Complexifying IR

As the contributions to this volume demonstrate, the applications of CT to the study of world politics offer perhaps the best confirmation of the insistence that "the value of complexity exists in the eye of its beholder" (Manson 2001, 412). As a referent for the intricacy of international processes, "complexity" has become an integral part of IR discourses as is instanced by the notions of "complex interdependence" (Nye 1993, 169), "complex learning" (Wendt 1999, 170), "complex political emergencies" (Goodhand and Hulme 1999), "complex security" (Booth 2005, 275), "complex socialization"

(Flockhart 2006), and "complex political victims" (Bouris 2007)—to name only a few. Yet, despite their sophistication, such uses of the term fall short of suggesting the analytical paradox of the complexity of global life—"the less foreseeable the future, the more is foresight required; the less we understand, the more is insight needed; the fewer the conditions which permit planning, the greater is the necessity to plan" (Ruggie 1975, 136).

In this respect, the proponents of a CT approach to world politics insist that IR scholars are unaware of the built-in limitations of the mainstream agenda (Cederman 1997, 20). In order to address these shortcomings, the application of CT research to IR has cut across the intellectual purview of the discipline:

- *revision of IR paradigms* (Bousquet and Curtis 2011; Clemens 2013; Cudworth and Hobden 2011a; Geyer and Cairney 2015; Harrison 2006; Kavalski 2007; 2011; 2012a; Keating 2013; Lehmann 2012; Morçöl 2012; Rosenow 2012);

  - *rationalism/realism* (Axelrod 1997; Brown 1995; Byrne 1998; Friedman 2014; Gunitsky 2013; Jervis 1997; Kissane 2011; Özel 2003; Zolo 1992);

  - *constructivism* (Adler 2005; Cederman 1997; Hoffman 2005);

  - *postmodernism* (Cilliers 1998; Coetzee 2013; Deuchars 2010; Dillon 2000; 2005; Lenco 2012; Popolo 2011);

  - *eclecticism*—synthesizing rationalist and reflectivist approaches (Cooksey 2001; Dittmer 2013; Geyer 2003b; Cîndea 2006);

- *international history* (Beaumont 1994; Brunk 2002; DeLanda 1997; Dobuzinskis 1987; Hoffman and Riley 2002; Jervis 1997; Khalil and Boulding 1996; Ma 2011; Richards 2000; Rosenau 1990);

- *globalization* (Boardman 2010; Chandler 2014; Chesters 2004; Clark 2000; Cole 2003; Geyer 2003c; Grove 2011; O'Riordan and Lenton 2013; Ramalingam 2013; Rosenau 2003; Urry 2003; Walby 2007; Whitman 2005);

- *European integration* (Barry and Walters 2003; Clemens 2001; Connolly 2011a; Geyer 2003b);

- *conflict resolution* (Azis 2009; Beech 2004; Bueno de Mesquita 1998; Burt 2010; Davis 2004; De Coning 2012; Hendrick 2009;

Little 2008; Mesjasz 2006; Pil-Rhee 1996; 1999; Raphael 1982; Sandole 1999; 2010; Suedfeld and Tetlock 1977);

- *development* (Boardman 2010; Coetzee 2013; Cole 2003; Dimitrov and Hodge 2002; Farrell 2004; Özel 2003; Longstaff 2005; Loorbach 2010; Parfitt 2006; Ramalingam 2013; Rihani 2002; Sassen 2014; Whiteside 1998);

- *security studies* (Alberts and Czerwinski 1997; Ayson 2006; Bousquet 2009; 2012; Coetzee 2013; Cudworth and Hobden 2011b; Dillon and Wright 2006; Dunn Cavelty 2007; Elhefnawy 2004; Grove 2011; Kavalski 2008; 2009; Little 2008; Longstaff 2005; Martinás et al. 2010; O'Riordan and Lenton 2013; Ramsden and Kervalishvili 2008; Scheffran 2008a);

- *state-building* (Cederman 1997; Coghill 2004; Dobuzinskis 1987; Little 2008; Matthews 2013; Zolo 1992);

- *policy-making/strategy* (Cairney 2012; Chandler 2014; Comfort 2000; Dennard et al. 2008; Dobuzinskis 1987; Duit and Galaz 2008; Elliott and Kiel 1999; Feder 2002; Geyer and Cairney 2015; Geyer and Rihani 2010; Hoffman 2003; Kavalski 2012b; Kiel 1992; Kuah 2012; Lane and Maxfield 1996; Lehmann 2011; Longstaff 2005; Loorbach 2010; Morçöl 2012; Özer and Şeker 2013; Ramo 2009; Richards 2000; Room 2011; Rosenow 2012; Teisman and Klijn 2008; Wallace and Suedfeld 1988; Whiteside 1998; Zolo 1992).

The breadth and scope of this literature corroborate the suggestion of a "paradigm shift" in the study of world politics (Harrison 2006; Rihani 2002). At the same time, Adler (2005, 32) insists that the application of CT to IR proffers images and sets of perceptions about causality, which are broader and more profound than the concept of "paradigm" would suggest. Without wishing to comment on the nuances of these claims, the suggestion of this volume is that there is not one single CT approach to IR, nor even an emergent complex international relations theory—if anything, there is a multitude of contending complex IR theories. Thus, the proposition of this volume is that the cross-over between complexity research and the study of international affairs suggests a nascent complexification of IR.

On a theoretical level, the application of CT to the study of world affairs proffers "new ways of thinking about how global politics unfold" in an environment where "uncertainty is the norm and apprehension the mood"

(Rosenau 2003, 208). Thus, while most IR scholars would agree that the world of their investigations is complex, they still insist that the proper way for acquiring knowledge about it is through the modeling of linear relationships with homogeneous independent variables that discern between discreet stochastic and systemic effects (Hoffmann and Riley 2002, 308; Johnston 2005). The value from the complexification of IR is to *start thinking* about the interconnections of global life in terms of complex systems. The application of CT to IR asserts that uncertainty and unanticipated consequences should be expected (Beaumont 1994, 155; Cioffi-Revilla 1998, 25). Although this might seem like a truism, it is surprising how little attention mainstream IR theory spares for the study of contingency and contradictions. Ruggie's assertion that the leitmotif of international politics is "better orderly error than complex truth" still appears to hold true (in LaPorte 1975, 145). In translating the jargon of complexity to the vocabulary of IR, Rosenau (2003, 11) has substituted it with the term "fragmegration." His intention is to suggest "the pervasive interaction between fragmenting and integrating dynamics." As such, fragmegration

> serves as a constant reminder that the world has moved beyond the condition of being "post" its predecessor to an era in which the foundations of daily life have settled into new and unique rhythms of their own. Equally important, the fragmegration label captures in a single word the large degree to which these rhythms consist of localizing, decentralizing, or fragmenting dynamics that are interactively and causally linked to globalizing, centralizing, and integrating dynamics. (Rosenau 2003, 11)

Yet, the point of this volume is not to suggest *the one way* for studying global life, but (by acknowledging that there are many possible avenues for observing global life) to provide a conceptual framework within which IR theory can learn, adapt, and interact "to maximize its own local interactions and complexity to find its own way" (Geyer 2003a, 254).

Outline of the Volume

How important is complexity? This is an important question which the blossoming literature with the word "complexity" in its titles does very little to address. The contributors to this volume answer this query in their analyses of the causes, characteristics, and consequences of complexity. The intention is not to produce a unified response on the content and practices of complexity, but to bridge some of the gaps between the different discussions of CT. The aim is to encourage the development of new questions and ideas in IR. With these objectives in mind, the contributors to the volume offer their own distinct responses to the questions: What can CT add to our understanding of the challenges posed by global life? How can CT improve the study of IR? In what ways can CT assist IR to suggest ethical modes for navigating the complex challenges of our time? Can CT prepare institutions, organizations, and communities to be surprised?

While focusing the conversation, such queries allow for transcending the paradigmatic bulwarks of IR by engaging with the very concepts that the discipline uses in its explanation and understanding of global life. At the same time, the diversity of responses engendered in the contributions to this collection outline two distinct trends in the complexification of IR—an anthropocentric and a nonanthropocentric one. While neither of these labels is envisaged as a value judgment, the emphasis on this bifurcation is probably the key contribution of this volume to the emerging literature on complexified IR. Moreover, distinguishing between these trends assists the development of new questions and ideas in IR. In this respect, part 1 of the volume explores CT's contribution to IR's preoccupation with relations between human subjects (and their anthropomorphized effects such as states). The anthropocentric perspective frames IR as a study of how humans engage one another independent of the environments that they inhabit. The contributors to this section offer a panoply of approaches for the explanation and understanding the discontinuities of global life. Part 2 investigates CT's contribution to IR's consideration of relations between human and various nonhuman subjects. The contributors suggest that there appear to be two key relationships at stake—between sociopolitical and biophysical systems and between sociopolitical and technological systems. In both these instances, the IR mainstream lacks the language and concepts to account for and engage human metabolism with nonhuman systems (Ahmed 2012, 348).

It needs to be acknowledged at the outset that the bifurcation between anthropocentric and nonanthropocentric approaches is somewhat forced upon the contributions. Admittedly, the intention is to distinguish the volume from existing attempts to bring CT ideas to bear on the study of IR. At the same time, such a division offers productive ways for focusing the conversation and allows the opportunity to make a comprehensive overview of the current state of the art on CT's contribution to IR. As the following chapters will demonstrate, the contributors tend to agree that the CT vocabulary of complex adaptive system, nonlinear patterns, emergence, coevolution and endemic change, and so on provide pertinent and novel ways for the explanation and understanding of global life. Yet, this agreement notwithstanding, the contributors offer distinct (and, admittedly, sometimes contradictory) ways for applying CT to the challenges posed by the fragility and unpredictability of global life.

The divergent viewpoints reflect the eclectic research program of the volume. On the one hand, the demand for eclecticism arises from the study of "unobservable wholes"—such as the complexity of global life—which reveal "considerable uncertainty about whether the parts observed are actually elements of the wholes inferred" (Puchala 2003, 21–22). On the other hand, the diverse perspectives presented in the volume intend to suggest that IR—especially, in its complexified form—is not an exact and homogenous science, but a field of ongoing contestation and struggle. Such analytical reflects the inherent desire of complexity research to encourage the transcendence of dogmatic representations by discouraging understandings grounded in any *one* particular perspective (Cooksey 2001). At the same time, eclectic inquiry allows for encountering the infinite messiness of global life without reducing its complexity (Sil and Katzenstein 2010)—that is, "in a period of rapid, discontinuous, fundamental, global, multicultural change, coherent belief systems are an obstacle to the effective structuring of comprehension and action" (Allenby and Sarewitz 2011, 121). Thus, while consistency might be at stake, the eclecticism adopted by this collection aims to suggest that it does not intend to provide a uniform, grand-narrative-style account of a singular complexity theory/complexity science of IR (hence the emphasis on complexity thinking by the contributors to this volume). Instead the volume aims to explore the various "alliances" forged between CT and IR and allow IR to develop the skills, frameworks, and governance mechanism to "think the unthinkable" dynamics of the future (Connolly 2011b).

Part I: Complexity Thinking and Anthropocentric IR

Perhaps one of the key challenges of CT to IR is the insistence on the endemic nature of change. CT draws attention to "variation, change, surprise and unpredictability to the center of the knowledge process" (Baker 1993, 123–24). At the same time, it offers analytical and policy "antidotes" to the anxiety that randomness engenders in traditional IR (Feder 2002, 117). In other words, a key aspect of the complexification of IR is the insistence that we need to learn to live with uncertainty (Morin 2008, 97). This challenges what many perceive to be the central tenets of the IR mainstream. Yet, even the founders of the discipline stressed that "[t]he first lesson the student of

international politics must learn and never forget is that the complexities
of international affairs make simple solutions and trustworthy prophecies
impossible" (Morgenthau 1973, 4–6).

CT suggests that the uncertainty associated with unforeseen events and
random changes not only is an intrinsic condition of all phenomena animating global life but also a crucial feature of all knowledge. This inference
brings us back to James Rosenau's complexity research and, in particular, his
insistence that the student of IR "must be tolerant of ambiguity, concerned
about probabilities, and distrustful of absolutes." Thus, by stressing the need
to be "genuinely puzzled about international phenomena," Rosenau suggests
that the IR scholar "must be constantly ready to be proven wrong" (Rosenau
1980, 19–31). In other words, the acceptance to live *in* and *with* change opens
the potential for coming to terms with the turbulence of global life. The
recognition of uncertainty as a *normal* condition of existence (as opposed to
something which is exceptional, out of the ordinary, and different) informs
a new repertoire of IR responses to "anticipate the unexpected as the norm"
(Fowler 2008). The contention of this volume is that the abstractions of CT
offer relevant cognitive frameworks to address problems not merely difficult
to prevent, but also difficult to foresee.

In this setting, the sense of insecurity pervading popular and policy
attitudes reflects the contingency of complexity that is subject not only to
vast past and future influences, structural reflexivity, and amplification, but
also to the rise of *simultaneity*—both as a feeling of time according to which
an individual can be and participate at any spatial location simultaneously
and as the sense that others are doing at the same time things that are
meaningfully related to one's own experience (Kütting 2001, 350). It is not
surprising, therefore, that the first part of the volume opens with David
C. Earnest's provocative question: "Why is global life complex"? While a
straightforward one, such a query lends itself to no simple answers. The
nonlinearity of interactions and the recursivity of causes and effects demand
analyses that break the reductionist scientific explanations underpinning the
IR mainstream. Paving the way for such interpretative journeys, Earnest
outlines four different types of complexity—interaction, strategic, ecological,
and reflexive.

While the first three have been previously mentioned in the literature,
Earnest's exploration does not merely update the validity of these terms; he
also reinstates the enhanced relevance of such typology to the explanation
and understanding of global life. As he poignantly demonstrates, many of the
most pressing challenges of world politics today—the 2008 financial crisis,
accelerating climate change, the resource curse, and others—share a common

feature: the interaction of political institutions with physical, technological, biological, or ecological systems. Thus, the patterns of global life are made unpredictable by the contingent interactions between these four different types of complexity. Earnest points out that as actors interact with physical, technological, or natural systems, they alter not only the system but also the incentives, payoffs, and strategies of future actors. For him, therefore, CT provides both the analytical frameworks and the scholarly tools to engage meaningfully with the complexity of global life.

A similar motivation informs Colin Wight's exploration of CT's contribution to IR. His point of departure is the relationship between theoretical pluralism, science, and democracy. The intention is to demonstrate that while in democratic societies diversity and the tolerance for alternative opinions are seen as inherent good and rarely questioned, in the social sciences theoretical pluralism is encouraged only to the extent that it complies with the accepted scientific methodology. Wight refers to this trend as the unity-through-pluralism (UtP) position. It is this UtP position that provides the basis for the reductionism dominating most of mainstream IR. Wight's call therefore is that the discipline needs to develop an unconditional acceptance of pluralism regardless of the methodological commitments of individual perspectives. In other words, his investigation questions why it is that we do not question the necessity of pluralism to democracies, while putting preconditions to its existence in science. Wright therefore proposes an "integrative pluralism" approach relying on the notions of emergence and organized complexity. His suggestion is that if IR persists in its UtP ways, not just the discipline will lose its relevance, but the viability of the very institutions and structures will be severely undermined.

The latter point is developed further by Christopher A. Ford in chapter 3. In particular, his investigation draws attention to some of the challenges that CT presents for public policy making by seeming to explode the very idea that the complex adaptive social systems of the human world may be purposefully manipulated in order to bring about specific desired situational outcomes. Ford suggests that it may be possible—consistent with our emerging understandings of CT—to argue that some types of policy input are more likely to have significant effects upon operational behavior and longer-term systemic patterns than others, and that some of these inputs may indeed also operate in ways that are less stubbornly "unpredictable" than CT might at first seem to indicate. Specifically, Ford demonstrates the importance of ideational inputs for complex adaptive social systems—in particular, that subset of complex adaptive systems the unit-level constituents of which happen to be sentient humans. Inputs at the level of conceptual organizing frameworks, narratives that structure people's understandings and expectations of the world around them, are to some degree purposefully manipulable by members of the policymaking community and are perhaps unusually likely to affect systems in ways that are "predictable" at least to the extent that such inputs will tend to exert recognizable patterning influences over time.

To that end, Ford discusses whether and to what degree it is possible to speak of political ideologies as being themselves systems that may usefully be understood through the lens of CT and perhaps subjected to purposive manipulation (for good or ill) by policy elites. Ford indicates that a CT-informed analysis of ideologies is possible and outlines a tentative program for further work aimed at understanding the internal dynamics, feedback loops, stabilities and instabilities, and morphogenic processes of ideologies. In this way, Ford stresses that CT-informed dynamical analysis offers a way to conceptualize ideologies and their evolution over time that avoids at least some of the pitfalls and incoherencies of past efforts to theorize about ideology and that may offer some hope of better informing public policy analysis and formulation in operationally useful (as opposed to merely post hoc and descriptive) ways.

One of the complex issues plaguing IR scholars and practitioners is ensuring the security and safety of the growing number of refugees around the world. In chapter 4, Erika Frydenlund and David C. Earnest use a CT-reading of the Mugunga III refugee camp in the Democratic Republic of Congo. With the help of agent-based modeling (ABM), they examine how cell phone networks can improve the security of refugee camps. At its core, ABM constructs models of how communities, social institutions, and values arise "bottom-up," from the interactions between individuals. Crowd sourcing has been gaining prominence in the social sciences in recent years, but the IR mainstream has kept aloof from its implications. In this respect, Frydenlund and Earnest offer one of the first detailed treatments of the potential and shortcomings of "human sensor networks" in IR. They evidence that social networks can play an important role in the provision of collective security and safety to vulnerable individuals. They also indicate that ABM analysis in this nascent field of IR, while not without its limitations, illuminates a novel understanding of a self-organizing form of governance without government.

In this context, the final contribution to part 1 of the volume subscribes to Frydenlund and Earnest's intentions but takes issues with their ABM approach. As Mark Olssen insists ABM misses what is distinctive about CT. His suggestions that ABM tends to confine research to a narrow positivist-imitating style typical of the North American IR environment in which it was developed. The concern is that ABM approaches ignore the normative aspects of the complexification of IR, especially as it relates to the analysis of political authority, institutionalization, and the political ethics of cooperation. Thus, drawing from continental contributions to CT, Olssen suggests that the complexification of IR opens possibilities for a richer conception of complexity-based historical materialism which have far reaching implications for research in politics, international relations, and indeed the social sciences in general. In short, the aim of his chapter is therefore to reorient the complexifaction of IR away from ABM approaches and toward what Olssen considers to be the "richer" research promise of CT.

Part II: Complexity Thinking and Nonanthropocentric IR

The terrorist attacks of September 11, 2001, were perceived by some as an epochal event that quite literally changed overnight the study and practice of IR. Others, however, while acknowledging that the violence and trauma of that day produced unique experiences and responses, have suggested that the events of September 11 provided one of the clearest confrontations with the complexity of world affairs—a complexity that reflects the underlying unpredictability and uncontrollability of global patterns as a result of the bewildering synergies between various systems. In the subsequent decade the threat (and fear) of terrorism produced profound changes in security discourses and practices intent on enhancing our feeling of safety. The ensuing "security theater" of the biometric border, the color-coded threat-level system of the Department of Homeland Security, and the full-body scanners at airport terminals provides the parameters of the new normal for our "orderly" lives (Schneier 2003). Yet, despite this hankering after predictability and certainty, these security measures have been unable to provide protection against (let alone reduce the anxiety from) the growing scale and frequency of natural disasters and other forms of biophysical insecurity.

Offering clear indications of the self-organizing pervasiveness of "episodic patterns" (as opposed to regularized orders) in global life (Dunn Cavelty 2007), such vulnerabilities to environmental degradation and technological interconnectivity attest to the potential for exponential transformations triggered by incremental changes. Such recognition, however, does not make the confrontation with complexity any less frustrating. For instance, the U.S. Congressman Roy D. Blunt (2008) from Missouri remarked in exasperation: "We do not need any more of this stuff! This area has been hit in the last twenty-four months with one disaster over another—ice storms, floods, tornados . . . Enough is enough!" In this respect, "global warming" has become convenient (albeit incongruous) shorthand for the enveloping uncertainty of the post–Cold War climate of international interactions.

The problems associated with the dynamic patterns of climate change and their unintended consequences continue to challenge the capacities for comprehension and tend to evince the fickleness of established models for their management. The growing impact of environmental contingencies on everyday lives has demanded a reconsideration of the relationship between sociopolitical and biophysical systems. While a pressing concern, the environment is not a new preoccupation for IR. By the 1970s Ernst Haas has commented that "international politics . . . is becoming synonymous with man's efforts to carve out a pattern of coexistence with his biological and physical environment. *International politics becomes ecopolitics*. No wonder things are complex." This statement offers a surprisingly contemporary (if not prophetic) description of global affairs at the start of the twenty-first century. It could be argued that Haas' statement offers a useful point of departure for exploring the dynamics of global life under (what he labels as) "complexity"—both as a descriptor of global dynamics and an analytical perspective for their comprehension. As Haas points out, the reference to complexity in IR: (i) acknowledges that global life is characterized by "the condition of turbulence" (which "can be visualized as a giant simultaneous chess match over which the judges have lost control"), and (ii) interrogates the conceptual frameworks for "coping with complexity"—namely, it "calls for clearer understanding of why we want to cope" (Haas 1975, 861; 1976, 175).

The portrayal of such "ecopolitics" queries the ontological underpinnings of IR and its interpretation of political action in an environment where "complexity" arises from the "interconnected parts" between human/sociopolitical and natural/biophysical systems. In this setting, the engagement with the "around" of global life gains its significance to the theory and practice of IR, because it is only when "environmental factors [are] being perceived and taken into account in the policy-forming process" (Sprout and Sprout 1965) that there can be hope for ethical adaptation to the challenges of the anthropocene. It must be acknowledged, however, that Haas was not particularly sanguine about IR's capacity to tackle this challenge. As he indicated, "the existence of this complexity is not matched with a political recognition of the problem. The knowledge to bring about recognition exists. But the political institutions for acting on the knowledge do not. Hence, we are headed toward ecological catastrophe" (Haas 1975, 861). Thus, the contributions to part 2 of the volume propose that in order to cope with the escalating complexity of global life, IR has to abandon its predilection for linear models, accept unpredictability, respect (and utilize) autonomy and creativity, and respond flexibly to emerging patterns and opportunities.

Obviously, not all IR scholars are (or have been) enthralled by the orderly paradigm of the discipline; however, the contention is that despite the commonsensical complexity of politics and the undeniable evidence of divisions within the discipline, it still remains dominated by an empiricist vision of an orderly Newtonian framework. As a result the mainstream ontological purview of IR has been underpinned by the perception that human/sociopolitical systems (such as civil society, states, international organizations, etc.) are both *detached from* (not only conceptually, but in practice) and *in control of* the "nonhuman" natural/biophysical systems. Not surprisingly, therefore, IR has been concerned *only* with "the human subject" (and its anthropomorphized effects such as states). Thus, while human subjectivity in IR has been largely emancipated from the restrictions imposed by class, race, gender, and religious affiliation, nature remains subject to the same hegemonic jackboot discourse.

The assertion here is that the relative stability of the Cold War "geohistorical context" (Thompson 1992)—*when* and *in response* to which majority of conventional IR discourse has been articulated—has obfuscated the realization that human societies inhabit complex spaces. The opening chapter of part 2 aims to rectify this. In it, Erika Cudworth and Stephen Hobden sketch out a prolegomenon for a posthuman IR. Posthumanism represents a significant new research direction for both IR and the social sciences. As Cudworth and Hobden indicate, posthumanism emerges from questions about interspecies relations which challenge dominant perceptions of what it means to be human. Such an approach mounts a fundamental epistemological and ontological challenge to the IR mainstream. However, with the help of CT, Cudworth and Hobden offer a radical revision of the "complex ecologism" of IR. Theorizations of the political in general, and world affairs in particular, have been little concerned with the vast variety of other, nonhuman populations of species and "things." The chapter therefore advocates a differentiated complexity that views the social world as embedded in a diversity of nonsocial systems. A logical conclusion of the differentiated complexity approach is the significance of human systems as embedded in a wide range of animate and nonanimate systems. These systems intersect, overlap, and coevolve. Hence a CT approach provides a means of analyzing these relations which so far has eluded mainstream IR. This implies a move to a posthuman IR, seeing human systems as "of nature" rather than "in nature"; and it fundamentally reorients our notion of "the political." Cudworth and

Hobden demonstrate that this view has profound implications for the means and purposes of the study of IR.

In chapter 7, Antoine Bousquet concurs with such assessment. In fact, his contribution stresses that CT offers unique opportunities for addressing IR's shortcomings. Nevertheless, he is quick to acknowledge that this theoretical export from the natural to the social sciences while promising has not been without difficulties. In this respect, Bousquet's installment to the postanthropocentric reinvention of IR reconsiders some of the key conceptual and analytical hurdles of such an endeavor. However, unlike the posthuman IR of Cudworth and Hobden, which focuses primarily on the relations between human and various biological systems, Bousquet's postanthropocentric IR details the full spectrum of human embeddedness in both the biosphere and the technosphere.

Such an approach suggests that CT makes available a much-needed vocabulary to engage the emergence, practices, and dynamics that cut across the turbulent domains of natural and technological environment. Bousquet's complexification of IR proposes a radical reconsideration of the anthropocentric certainties dominating the purview of the discipline. At the same time, he is clear that CT is far from perfect, yet it seems to offer some of the more pertinent responses to the challenges defining the complex ecologies—be they natural or technological—that we inhabit, interact with, and coconstitute.

The risks and challenges emerging from the complex interactions between human and nonhuman systems are the focus of the Myriam Dunn Cavelty and Jennifer Giroux's analysis. To deploy Bousquet's term, their investigation explores the technospheric aspects of nonantrhopocentric life. For them, the notion of complexity occupies a special and multifaceted place in the discussion about risks in international security. On the one hand, complexity is conceptualized as a key characteristic of new security challenges, and therefore viewed as a threat. On the other hand, scientific observations regarding the behavior of complex systems have become a powerful driver for conceptualizing new modes of security governance to tackle increasingly complex phenomena. This conceptual duality of "the complex"—and the interrelationships between the two—is explored in this chapter via a salient subissue of the current security debate: vital systems security/critical infrastructure protection. In other words, complexity is a property of technological, biophysical, and sociopolitical systems. In this setting, Dunn Cavelty and Giroux demonstrate that CT-inspired approaches can construct capabilities to cope with vulnerabilities, defy adversity, and construct new proficiency in response to the uncertainty, cognitive challenges, and complex unbounded risks of global life.

Finally, in chapter 10, Jürgen Scheffran draws attention to environmental degradation. In particular, the complex interactions between climate stress, environmental change, human responses and social conflicts that could significantly shape the future landscape of global life. As he points out, depending on vulnerability, environmental changes will stress basic human needs and values (such as the availability of water, food, energy, health and wealth) which may lead to social disruption through instability events (such as migration, riots, insurgencies, urban violence or war). The analysis suggests that the stability of this interaction depends on the sensitivities between crucial variables which determine how events spread in the network of interconnections. Scheffran suggests that as a result of non-linear effects, an increase in global temperature above a certain threshold may trigger instabilities, tipping points and cascading sequences that could exceed the viability of natural and social systems. In this respect, a key challenge for policy-making is to develop new approaches that stabilize the interaction. Scheffran argues that it is with the help of concepts such as adaptive complexity and stability that policy-makers can develop relevant skills and responses to deal with complex challenges.

The dominant theme of the contributions to this part of the volume is the inability of IR to grapple convincingly with the challenges posed by the natural and technological ecosystems that form the fibers of global life, of which anthropocentric world affairs is only one aspect. The claim therefore is not that mainstream approaches are *blind* to the complexity of global life, but that they chose to ignore it (not least because of their focus on *willed* human/sociopolitical phenomena). Thus, despite the intellectual challenges posed by the growing interdependence and connectedness between human and nonhuman systems, the mainstream of IR research has been, on the one hand, dominated by the deterministic and parsimonious tools of the traditional reductionist mode of investigation and, on the other hand, underpinned by an inherent antibiologism (if not biophobia).

In this respect, the contemporary criticism leveled at the constructs of IR emanates not because of their truncated representation of the reality of world affairs, but because of IR's failure to acknowledge that this truncation is only one facet of a much more complex field of observation. The contributors to part 2 of the volume demonstrate that the application of CT to the study of world politics disrupts the entrenched human-centered purview of the discipline and urges it to account for the interactions between sociopolitical systems and the ecologies that they inhabit. The contention is that the recognition of the unpredictability and randomness of such sociopolitical, technological, and biophysical interdependence remove the constraints on

IR's imagination. Such inference echoes James Rosenau's intuition that IR has to get comfortable with the power of the contingent and chaotic forces of the fast-changing and complex global life. The key to IR's coping in such a dynamic context is its willingness to change (that is, abandon existing assumptions), its "being able to adjust to the unexpected in creative and appropriate ways" (Rosenau 2001, 149; Rosenau 1970). The hope is that the contributions included in this collection make a meaningful, if small, step in this direction.

Bibliography

Adler, E. (2005). *Communitarian international relations.* Cambridge: Cambridge University Press.

Alberts, D., and Czerwinski, T. J. (1997). Preface. In D. Alberts and T. Czerwinski. (Eds.).Washington, DC: National Defense University.

Allenby, B. R., and Sarewitz, D. (2011). *The techno-human condition.* Cambridge, MA: MIT Press.

Ang, I. (2011). Navigating complexity: From cultural critique to cultural intelligence. *Continuum* 25(6), 779–794.

Axelrod, R. (1997). The complexity of cooperation: Agent-based models of competition and collaboration. Princeton: Princeton University Press.

Ayson, R. (2006). Stability and complexity in Asia-Pacific security affairs. *Asian Perspectives* 30(3), 179–192.

Azis, I. J. (2009). *Crisis, complexity, and conflict.* Bingley: Emerald Publishing.

Barkin, J. S. (2010). *Realist constructivism: Rethinking international relations theory.* Cambridge: Cambridge University Press.

Barry, A., and Walters, W. (2003). From EURATOM to "complex systems." *Alternatives,* 28(2), 305–329.

Beaumont, R. (1994). *War, chaos and history.* Westport, CT: Praeger.

Beech, M. F. (2004). Observing Al Qaeda through the lens of complexity theory: Recommendations for the national strategy to defeat terrorism. *Center for strategic leadership sudent issue paper,* S04–01.

Bernstein, S., Lebow, R. N., Stein, J. G., and Weber, S. (2000). God gave physics the easy problems: Adapting social science to an unpredictable world. *European Journal of International Relations* 6(1), 43–76.

Blunt, R. D. (2008). Interview with KCRW's "To the Point" program (12 May), available: http://www.kcrw.com/news/programs/tp.

Boardman, R. (2010). *Governance of earth systems: Science and its uses.* Basingstoke: Palgrave Macmillan.

Booth, K. (1979). *Strategy and ethnocentrism.* New York: Holmes and Meier.

Booth, K. (Ed.). (2005). *Critical security studies and world politics.* Boulder, CO: Lynne Rienner.

Bouris, E. (2007). *Complex political victims*. Bloomfield, CT: Kumarian Press.

Bousquet, A., and Curtis, S. (2011). Beyond models and metaphors: Complexity theory, systems thinking and international relations. *Cambridge Review of International Affairs*, 24(1) March, 43–62.

Bousquet, A. (2009). The scientific way of warfare: Order and chaos on the battlefields of modernity. London: Hurst Publishers.

Bousquet, A. (2012). Complexity theory and the War on Terror: Understanding the self-organizing dynamics of leaderless Jihad. *Journal of International Relations and Development* 15(2), 345–369.

Brown, C. (1995). Serpents in the sand: Essays on the nonlinear nature of politics and human destiny. Ann Arbor: University of Michigan Press.

Brunk, G. G. (2002). Why do societies collapse? A theory based on self-organized criticality. *Journal of Politics* 14(2), 195–230.

Bueno de Mesquita, B. (1998). The end of the cold war. *Journal of Conflict Resolution*, 42(2), 131–155.

Burt, G. (Ed.) (2010). *Conflict, complexity, and mathematical social science*. Bingley: Emerald Publishing.

Byrne, D. (1998). Complexity theory and the social sciences. London: Routledge.

Cairney, P. (2012). Complexity theory in political science and public policy. *Political Studies Review*, 10(3), 346–358.

Chandler, D. (2014). *Resilience: The governance of complexity*. Abingdon: Routledge.

Chesters, G. (2004). Global complexity and global civil society. *Voluntas*, 15(4), 323–342.

Cilliers, P. (1998). Complexity and postmodernism: Understanding complex systems. London: Routledge.

Cîndea, I. (2006). Complex systems: New conceptual tools for international relations. *Central European Review of International Affairs*, 26, 64–88.

Cioffi-Revilla, C. (1998). *Politics and uncertainty*. Cambridge: Cambridge University Press.

Cederman, L-E. (1997). Emergent actors in world politics: How states and nations develop and dissolve. Princeton, NJ: Princeton University Press.

Clark, R. P. (2000). Global life systems: Population, food, and disease in the process of globalization. Lanham, MD: Rowman and Littlefield.

Clemens, W. (2001). *Complexity theory and european security*. Lanham, MD: Rowman and Littlefield.

Clemens, W. (2013). *Complexity science and world affairs*. Albany: State University of New York Press.

Coetzee, W. S. (2013). Rethinking the theoretical foundation of the security-development nexus: Does a hybrid complexity-postmodern model contribute? *Academic Journal of Interdisciplinary Studies* 2(9), 295–303.

Coghill, K. (2004). Federalism: Fuzzy global trends. *Australian Journal of Politics and History*, 50(4), 41–56.

Cole, K. (2003). Globalization: understanding complexity. *Progress in Development Studies*, 3(4), 323–338.

Comfort, L. (2000). Disaster. *Cambridge Review of International Affairs*, 14(1), 277–294.

Connolly, W. E. (2011a). *A world of becoming*. Durham, NC: Duke University Press.

Connolly, W. E. (2011b). Complexity and relevance. *European Political Science* 10(2), 210–219.

Cooksey, R. W. (2001). What is complexity science? A contextually grounded tapestry of systemic dynamism, paradigm diversity, theoretical eclecticism, and organizational learning. *Emergence* 3(1), 77–103.

Cudworth, E., and Hobden, S. (2011a). *Posthuman international relations: Complexity, ecologism and global politics*. London: Zed Books.

Cudworth, E., and Hobden, S. (2011b). Beyond environmental security: Complex systems, multiple inequalities and environmental risks. *Environmental Politics* 20(1), 42–59.

Davidson-Hunt, I. J., and Berkes, F. (2003). Nature and society through the lens of resilience: Toward a human-in-ecosystem perspective. In F. Berkes, J. Colding, and C. Folke (Eds.), *Navigating social-ecological systems: Building resilience for complexity and change*. Cambridge: Cambridge University Press, 53–82.

Davis, L. (2004). *Education and conflict: Complexity and chaos*. London: Routledge.

De Coning, C. H. (2012). *Complexity, peacebuilding and coherence: Implications of complexity for the peacebuilding coherence dilemma*. Unpublished Doctoral Dissertation. University of Stellenbosch.

DeLanda, M. (1997). *A thousand years of nonlinear history*. New York: Swerve.

Dennard, L. F., Richardson, K. A., and Morçöl, G. (2008). *Complexity and policy analysis: Tools and concepts for designing robust policies in a complex world*. Goodyear, AZ: ISCE Publishing.

Deuchars, R. (2010). Deleuze, DeLanda and social complexity: Implications for the "international." *Journal of International Political Theory* 6(2), 161–187.

Dillon, M. (2000). Poststructuralism, Complexity and Poetics. *Theory Culture & Society*, 17(5), 1–26.

Dillon, M. (2005). Global security in the 21st century: Circulation, complexity, and contingency. *ISP/NSC Briefing Paper*, 05:02, 2–3.

Dillon, M., and Wright, C. (Eds.). (2006). *Complexity, networks and resilience*. London: Chatham House.

Dimitrov, V. and Hodge, B. (2002). Social fuzziology: Study of fuzziness of social complexity. Berlin: Springer.

Dittmer, J. (2013). Geopolitical assemblages and complexity. *Progress in Human Geography*, 38(3), 385–401.

Dobuzinskis, L. (1987). *The self-organizing polity: An epistemological analysis of political life*. Boulder, CO: Westview Press.

Duit, A., and Galaz, V. (2008). Governance and complexity: Emerging issues for governance theory. *Governance and International Journal of Policy, Administration and Institutions*, 21(3), 311–335.

Dunn Cavelty, M. (2007). Securing the digital age: The challenges of complexity and ir theory. In J. Eriksson and G. Giacomello (Eds.), *International Relations and Security in the Digital Age* (85–105). London: Routledge.

Elhefnawy, N. (2004). Societal complexity and diminishing returns in security. *International Security*, 29(1), 152–174.

Elliott, E., and Kiel, L. D. (1999). *Nonlinear dynamics, complexity, and public policy*. Commack, NY: Nova Science Publishers.

Evans, K. G. (1998). *Governance, citizenship, and the new sciences*. Unpublished PhD Thesis: Virginia Polytechnic.

Farrell, K. (2004). Epistemology, complexity and democracy. *Local Environment*, 9(5), 469–479.

Feder, S. (2002). Forecasting for policy-making. *Annual Review of Political Science*, 5, 111–125.

Flockhart, T. (2006). Complex socialisation, *European Journal of International Relations*, 12(1), 89–118.

Friedman, J. (Ed.) (2014). *Societal complexity: System effects and the problem of prediction*. Abingdon: Routledge.

Gettell, R. G. (1922). Influences on World Politics. *The Journal of International Relations*, 12(3), 320–330.

Geyer, R. (2003a). Beyond the third way. *British Journal of Politics and International Relations*, 5(2), 237–257.

Geyer, R. (2003b). European integration, the problem of complexity and the revision of theory. *Journal of Common Market Studies*, 41(1), 15–35.

Geyer, R. (2003c). Globalisation, europeanisation, complexity, *Governance*, 16(4), 559–576.

Geyer, R., and Cairney, P. A. (Eds.). (2015). *Handbook of Complexity Theory and Public Policy*. London: Edward Elgar.

Geyer, R., and Pickering, S. (2011). Applying the tools of complexity to the international realm: From fitness landscapes to complexity cascades. *Cambridge Review of International Affairs*, 24(1), 5–26.

Geyer, R., and Rihani, S. (2010). *Complexity and Public Policy*. London: Routledge.

Grove, J. V. (2011). *Becoming war: Steps to an ecology of global security*. Unpublished PhD dissertation: John Hopkins University.

Goodhand, J., and Hulme, D. (1999). From wars to complex political emergencies. *Third World Quarterly*, 20(1), 13–26.

Gunitsky, S. (2013). Complexity and theories of change in international politics. *International Theory*, 5(1), 35–63.

Haas, E. (1975). Is there a hole in the whole? *International Organization*, 29(3), 827–876.

Haas, E. (1976). Turbulent Fields and the Theory of Regional Integration. *International Organization* 30(2), 173–212.

Harrison, N. E. (Ed.). (2006). *Complexity in World Politics: Concepts and methods of a new paradigm*. Albany: State University of New York Press.

Heath, A. E. (1919). International politics and the concept of world sections. *International Journals of Ethics* 29(2), 125–144.

Hendrick, D. (2009). Complexity theory and conflict transformation. *CCR Working Paper* 17.

Heng, Y-K. (2010). Ghosts in the machine: Is IR eternally haunted by the specter of old concepts? *International Relations* 47(5): 535–556.

Hoffman, M., and Johnson, D. (1998). Change and process in a complex world: Using complexity theory to understand world politics. *Annual Meetings of the International Studies Association*, Minneapolis, MN.

Hoffman, M., and Riley, J. (2002). The science of political science. *New Political Science*, 24(4), 303–320.

Hoffman, M. (2003). Constructing a complex world: The frontiers of international relations theory and foreign policy-making. *Asian Journal of Political Science* 11(3), 37–57.

Hoffman, M. (2005). *Ozone depletion and climate change*. Albany: SUNY Press.

Hornborg, A. (Ed.). (2007). *World-system history*. Lanham, MD: AltaMira Press.

Kavalski, E. (2007). The fifth debate and the emergence of complex international relations theory. *Cambridge Review of International Affairs* 20(3), 435–54.

Kavalski, E. (2008). The complexity of global security governance. *Global Society* 22(4), 423–43.

Kavalski, E. (2009). Timescapes of security: Clocks, clouds, and the complexity of security governance. *World Futures*, 65(7), 537–551.

Kavalski, E. (2011). From Cold War to global warming: Observing complexity in global life. *Political Science Review* 9(1), 1–12.

Kavalski, E. (2012a). Waking ir up from its "deep newtonian slumber." *Millennium* 41(1), 137–150.

Kavalski, E. (2012b). Acting politically in global life: Security and its logic of resilience. In D. Walton and M. Frazier (Eds.). *Contending views on international security*. (87–102). New York: Nova Science.

Keating, J. (2013). Can chaos theory teach us anything about international relations? *Foreign Policy*, May 23.

Khalil, E. L., and Boulding, K. E. (1996). *Evolution, Order, and Complexity*. London: Routledge.

Kiel, L. D. (1992). The nonlinear paradigm. *Systems Research*, 9(2), 27–42.

Kissane, D. (2011). *Beyond anarchy: The complex and chaotic dynamics of international politics*. Stuttgart: Ibidem.

Kuah, A.W. J. (2012). Complexity science and public policy: Wither the policy maker? *RSIS Commentaries* 120.

Kurki, M. (2008). *Causation in international relations: Reclaiming causal analysis*. Cambridge: Cambridge University Press.

Lane, D., and Maxfield, R. (1996). Strategy under complexity: Fostering Generative Relationships. *Long Range Planning* 29 (2), 215–231.

LaPorte, T. (Ed.). (1975). *Organised social complexity: challenge to politics and policy*. Princeton, NJ: Princeton University Press.

Lehmann, K. (2011). Crisis foreign policy as a process of self-organisation. *Cambridge Review of International Affairs*, 24(1), 27–42.

Lehmann, K. (2012). Unfinished Transformation: The Three Phases of Complexity's Emergence in International Relations and Foreign Policy. *Cooperation and Conflict* 47(3), 404–413.

Lenco, P. (2012). *Deleuze and world politics: Alter-globalizations and nomad science.* Abingdon: Routledge.

Little, A. (2008). *Democratic Piety: Complexity, Conflict, and Violence.* Edinburgh: Edinburgh University Press.

Longstaff, P. H. (2005). *Security, resilience, and communication in unpredictable environments such as terrorism, natural disasters, and complex technology.* Cambridge, MA: Center for Information Policy Research.

Loorbach, D. (2010). Transition-management for sustainable development: A prescriptive, complexity-based governance framework. *Governance,* 23(1), 161–183.

Ma, S-Y. (2007). Political science at the edge of chaos? The paradigmatic implications of historical institutionalism. *International Political Science Review,* 28(1), 57–78.

Mackinder, H. J. (1904). The Geographical Pivot of History. *The Geographical Journal* 23 (4), 421–437.

Manson, S. M. (2001). Simplifying Complexity: a Review of Complexity Theory. *Geoforum,* 32(3), 405–414.

Martinás, K., Matika, D., and Srbljinović, A. (Eds.). (2010). *Complex Societal Dynamics: Security Challenges and Opportunities.* Amsterdam: IOS Press.

Matthews, F. (2013). *Complexity, fragmentation, and uncertainty: Government capacity in an evolving state.* Oxford: Oxford University Press.

Mesjasz, C. (2006). Complex Systems Studies and the Concepts of Security, *Kybernetes* 35(1), 3–4.

Morçöl, G. (2012). *A Complexity Theory for Public Policy.* London: Routledge.

Morgenthau, H. (1973 [1948]). *Politics among nations: The struggle for power and peace.* New York: Knopf.

Murphy, P. (2000). Symmetry, contingency, complexity: Accommodating uncertainty in public relations theory. *Public Relations Review* 26 (4), 447–462.

Nye, J. (1993). *Understanding international conflict.* New York: HarperCollins.

O'Riordan, T., and Lenton. T. (2013). *Addressing tipping points for a precarious future.* Oxford: Oxford University Press.

Özel, H. (2003). Closing Open Systems: Two Examples of the "Double Hermeneutic" in Economics. *METU Studies in Development* 30(2), 223–248.

Özer, B., and Şeker, G. (2013). Complexity theory and public policy. *SDU Journal of Faculty of Economics & Administrative Sciences* 18(1), 89–102

Parfitt, T. (2006). Hylomorphism, complexity and development. *Third World Quarterly,* 27(3), 421–441

Pil-Rhee, Y. (1999). *The dynamics and complexity of political systems.* Seoul: Ingansarang Press.

Pil-Rhee, Y. (Ed). (1996). *Complex systems model of South–North Korean integration.* Seoul: National University Press.

Popolo, D. (2011). *A new science of international relations: Modernity, complexity and the Kosovo conflict.* Farnham: Ashgate.

Puchala, D. (2003). *Theory and history in international relations.* London: Routledge.

Ramalingam, B. (2013). *Aid on the edge of chaos: Rethinking international cooperation in a complex world.* Oxford: Oxford University Press.

Ramo, J. C. (2009). *The age of the unthinkable: Why the new world disorder constantly surprises us and what to do about it.* London: Little, Brown.

Ramsden, J. J., and Kervalishvili, P. K. (2008). *Complexity and security.* Amsterdam: IOS Press.

Raphael, T. (1982). Integrative complexity theory. *Journal of Conflict Resolution,* 26(3), 423–450.

Rihani, S. (2002). *Complex systems theory and development practice.* London: Zed Books.

Richards, D. (Ed.). (2000). *Political complexity: Non linear models of politics.* Ann Arbor: University of Michigan Press.

Richardson, K., and Cilliers, P. (Eds.). (2007). *Explorations in complexity thinking.* Mahwah, NJ: ISCE Publishing.

Room, G. (2011). *Compexity, institutions, and public policy: Agile decision-making in a turbulent world.* Cheltenham: Edward Egar.

Rosenau, J. N. (1960). The birth of a political scientist. *American Behavioral Scientist* 3(1), 19–21.

Rosenau, J. N. (1970). Foreign policy as adaptive behavior: Some preliminary notes for a theoretical model. *Comparative Politics* 2(3), 365–387.

Rosenau, J. N. (1980). *The scientific study of foreign policy.* London: Frances Pinter.

Rosenau, J. N. (1988). Patterned chaos in global life. *International Political Science Review* 9(4), 335–340.

Rosenau, J. N. (1990). *Turbulence in world politics.* Princeton, NJ: Princeton University Press.

Rosenau, J. N. (1997). Many damn things simultaneously: Complexity theory and world affairs. In D. Alberts and T. Czerwinski (Eds.), *Complexity, global politics, and national security.* Washington, DC: National Defense University.

Rosenau, J. N. (2001). Stability, stasis, and change: A fragmenting world. In R. L. Kugler and E. L. Frost (Eds.), *The Global Century: Globalization and National Security* (127–153). Washington, DC: National Defense University Press.

Rosenau, J. N. (2003). *Distant proximities: Dynamics beyond globalization.* Princeton: Princeton University Press.

Rosenow, D. (2012). Dancing life into being: Genetics, resilience, and the challenge of complexity theory. *Security Dialogue* 43(6), 531–547.

Ruggie, J. G. (1975). Complexity, planning, and public order. In Todd LaPorte (Ed.), *Organised social complexity: Challenge to politics and policy* (119–150). Princeton: Princeton University Press.

Sandole, D. J. D. (1999). *Capturing the complexity of conflict: Dealing with Violent ethnic conflicts of the post-Cold War era.* New York: Pinter.

Sandole, D. J. D. (2010). *Peacebuilding: Preventing violent conflict in complex world.* Cambridge: Polity.

Sassen, S. (2014). *Expulsions: Brutality and complexity in the global economy.* Harvard, MA: Harvard University Press.

Scheffran, J. (2008a). The complexity of security. *Complexity.* 14(1), 13–21.

Schneier, B. (2003). *Beyond fear: Thinking sensibly about security in an uncertain world*. New York: Copernicus Books.

Sil, R., and Katzenstein, P. (2010). *Beyond paradigms: Analytical eclecticism in the study of world politics*. New York: Palgrave Macmillan.

Soper, K. (2010). Unnatural times? The social imaginary and the future of nature. In B. Carter and N. Charles (Eds.), *Nature, Society, and Environmental Crisis* (225–235). London: Wiley-Blackwell.

Sprout, H., and Sprout, M. (1956). *Man-milieu relationship: Hypotheses in the context of international politics*. Princeton: Princeton University Press.

Sprout, H., and Sprout, M. (1965). *The ecological perspective of human affairs with special reference to international relations*. Princeton: Princeton University Press.

Suedfeld, P., and Tetlock, P. (1977). Integrative complexity. *Journal of Conflict Resolution*, 21(1), 169–184.

Teisman, G., and Klijn, E. (2008). Complexity theory and public management. *Public Management Review*, 10(3), 287–297.

Thompson, W. (1992). Geohistorical context of structural transition. *World Politics* 45(1), 127–152.

Urry, J. (2003). *Global complexity*. Cambridge: Polity.

Walby, S. (2007). Complexity theory, systems theory, and multiple intersecting social inequalities. *Philosophy of the Social Sciences*, 37(4), 449–470.

Wallace, M., and Suedfeld, P. (1988). Leadership performance in crisis: The longevity–complexity link. *International Studies Quarterly*, 32(4), 439–451.

Waltz, K. N. (2002). The continuity of international politics. In Ken Booth and Tim Dunne (Eds.), *Worlds in collision* (Palgrave Macmillan).

Wendt, A. (1999). *Social theory of international politics*. Cambridge: Cambridge University Press.

Whiteside, K. H. (1998). Systems theory. *Policy Studies Journal*, 26(4), 636–656.

Whitman, J. (2005). *The limits of global governance*. London: Routledge.

Zolo, D. (1992). *Democracy and complexity: A realist approach*. University Park: Pennsylvania State University Press.

Part I

Complexity Thinking and
Anthropocentric International Relations

Chapter 1

The Gardener and the Craftsman

Four Types of Complexity in Global Life

David C. Earnest

> If man is not to do more harm than good in his efforts to improve the
> social order, he will have to learn that in this, as in all other fields where
> essential complexity of an organized kind prevails, he cannot acquire the
> full knowledge which would make mastery of the events possible. He
> will therefore have to use what knowledge he can achieve, not to shape
> the results as the craftsman shapes his handiwork, but rather to cultivate
> a growth by providing the appropriate environment, in the manner in
> which the gardener does this for his plants.
>
> —Friedrich Hayek (1975, 442)

In his acceptance speech for the 1974 Nobel Prize in Economics, Friedrich
Hayek noted several essential features of societies that help us understand
why global life is "complex." It is no insight to observe that global life today is
full of surprises, from seemingly irresoluble financial crises to waves of revolution cascading across the Middle East and North Africa. Yet increasingly,
social scientists and policy makers alike seem to recognize that not only are
these events *unforeseen*, but they also are *unforeseeable*, a point that chaos
theory has demonstrated (Lorenz 1963; Saperstein 1997). Hayek's speech
emphasized this very point. Although many hope that "our increasing power
of prediction and control, generally regarded as the characteristic result of
scientific advance . . . would soon enable us to mould society entirely to our
liking," Hayek instead argued that "to act on the belief that we possess the

knowledge and the power which enable us to shape the processes of society entirely to our liking, knowledge which in fact we do not possess, is likely to make us do much harm" (Hayek 1975, 439, 441). More than simply noting the dangers of intellectual hubris, Hayek observed that because social life is complex, our incomplete understanding of this complexity necessarily limits society's ability to govern global life. The best we can hope for is to cultivate beneficial conditions.

Why is global life complex? This question defies ready answers, due in no small part to the absence of a consensus among researchers about how to define "complexity" (Mitchell 2010, 894–911). For purposes of this chapter, I define complexity as a condition of nonlinear and/or recursive relationships between causes and effects, which consequently "limits the ability of individuals to identify the full set of possible outcomes or assign probabilities to particular outcomes of specific actions" (Poteete et al. 2010, 58). Complexity is not the same as "complication." As Miller and Page (2007, 9) suggest, a complicated system may contain many parts, but because those parts maintain a substantial degree of independence, "removing one such element (which reduces the level of complication) does not fundamentally alter the system's behavior." In other words, a complicated system is amenable to scientific reductionism: one can understand the system by disaggregating the whole into its constituent parts, studying them and their interrelationships. If global life were merely complicated, we could understand it by undertaking such reductive analysis. Observers could have predicted, for example, the Egyptian revolution of 2010 if they simply had enough information about the preferences of Egyptian citizens. Yet global life is not merely complicated; it is also complex. Because of nonlinear cause-effect relationships and recursive endogeneity, scientific reductionism is not possible. Complex social systems produce "emergent" phenomena, defined as systemic "properties or behaviors that are different from those of the parts" (Jervis 1997, 6). One cannot explain the Egyptian revolution merely by reducing it to the preferences of the Egyptian people precisely because these preferences themselves were interdependent—any individual's choice to participate in the protests in Tahrir Square likely depended considerably on her estimate of the anonymity afforded by the presence of other protesters. Likewise, one cannot understand the events in Egypt without understanding the contagious revolution in Tunisia. In other words, emergent phenomena occur in specific locations and specific historical contexts—spatiotemporal dimensions without which one cannot explain important global events.

Emergent phenomena are interesting not merely because they surprise us, but also because they are intrinsic to globalization. I borrow Scholte's definition of globalization as the set of commercial, demographic, techno-logical and ideational processes through which social relations assume a transplanetary configuration that transcends geographic boundaries (Scholte 2005). Due to the transplanetary scope and nearly instantaneous speed of social relations today, surprises in global life seem to emerge faster than we can react. Government officials, scholars, and the public now share a "widespread understanding that unexpected events are commonplace, that anomalies are normal occurrences, that minor incidents can mushroom into major outcomes" (Rosenau 2003, 209). The ubiquity of emergence in global life today suggests that Hayek was correct: a purposive mastery of events simply is not possible.

For all the surprises of global life, paradoxically complex social systems may also produce robust social structures that are resilient and stable. Con-sider the Westphalian system as a whole. Miller and Page note that some international relations theorists "would like to be able to develop a theory that helps us understand how states of the world (composed of lower-level entities and interaction rules) are transformed into higher-level entities" (Miller and Page 2007, 42). This argument closely parallels Wight's discus-sion of the agent-structure debate: "[W]hat appears as a structure on one level becomes an agent on another. Hence . . . the international system plays the role of structure with the nation state as an agent" (Wight 2006, 107). Wendt makes a very similar argument about anarchy in the international system: though in an important way states have "made" anarchy, this social structure in turn is robust and conditions the preferences of states such that actors and structures reproduce each other (Wendt 1992, 181–85). The conception of social structure put forth by these theorists is very similar to complexity theorists' concept of emergence: while the actions and choices of actors produce the emergent behavior of complex systems, such emergent properties in turn constrain the actions and choices of actors. A primary challenge to observers of global life, then, is to understand when complex-ity produces sudden surprises and when it produces robust and enduring social structures.

To make these arguments, the following pages identify four types of complexity in global life: interaction complexity, strategic complexity, eco-logical complexity, and reflexive complexity. The argument owes much of its thinking to the seminal work of Robert Jervis, who identified three of these sources of complexity in his 1997 book *System Effects*. Jervis called these three types "interactions" to convey both the interrelationships among vari-ables as well as the interdependence among actors' strategies and rewards. Jervis's "first interactions" roughly correspond to interaction complexity;

"second interactions" are strategic complexity; and "third interactions" are ecological complexity. The chapter updates Jervis's argument both with contemporary examples and with the addition of a fourth category, reflexive complexity—a source of complexity in global life that arguably distinguishes complex social systems from their natural and physical counterparts. I use "complexity" instead of Jervis's preferred "interactions" because the latter term often has specific statistical connotations that correspond roughly to what Jervis called first interactions and what this chapter terms interaction complexity. The decade and a half since Jervis wrote has only validated his insights, and for this reason they deserve reconsideration. The knowledgeable reader will quickly recognize the intellectual debt this chapter owes to Jervis.

Interaction Complexity

The first source of complexity in global life today is what one might call interaction complexity. A rough definition for interaction complexity is a condition in which the extent of a factor's effect on a social system depends upon the state of other factors. A trivial example of interaction complexity illustrates the idea. When I flip on a light switch, it almost invariably produces a system behavior that I anticipate, recognize, and can predict with reliability—the light comes on thanks to a current running through an electrical circuit that the switch closes. But on the rare occasions when the light does not come on, I naturally think about how the light switch interacts with other factors. Has the filament in the bulb burned out? Has the circuit breaker tripped? Did I pay my electric bill this month? This example shows that, in a world of interaction complexity, what seems like a normal and reproducible cause-effect relationship may break down in surprising and often counterintuitive ways. Interaction complexity helps explain, for example, differences in public opinion in the United States about climate change. Democrats tend to express greater concern about climate change than Republicans, while more educated people generally express greater concern than less educated ones. One recent study found, however, that education has opposite effects on Democrats and Republicans. More educated Democrats express greater concern than less educated Democrats, but the effect reverses among Republicans: those who are more educated are *less* concerned about climate change than less educated Republicans (Hamilton 2011). This interaction complexity between education and political orientation helps explain why the politics of climate change in the United States has become so polarized. Because education has opposite effects, additional information about climate change through traditional and social media only hardens opposing positions. This structure of disagreement seems quite stable.

Sociologist Charles Perrow was among the first to appreciate the implications of interaction complexity for organizations seeking purposive control of systems, whether they are bureaucracies, firms, or governments. In *Normal Accidents*, Perrow noted that in many systems, the isolated failure of components usually is harmless but failures in combination can be catastrophic. The question that interested Perrow is whether effects in systems are isolated or whether they spread to other components. In the latter type of system, which he called "tightly coupled," risks are inherently a property of the ordering and interrelationship of components rather than a property of the components themselves. By definition, one cannot eliminate interrelationships in a system. One can only manage whether the system is tightly or loosely coupled. For this reason, Perrow argues, not only do accidents occur, but they are inevitable (Perrow 1984). Interaction complexity arises not only from the interrelationship of elements of a system in space, but also from the sequence of interaction. "Path dependence" of occurrences explains in part whether effects produce normal or surprising outcomes. The nuclear disaster at the Fukushima Daiichi nuclear power plant illustrates the importance of both the temporal and spatial forms of interaction complexity. If isolated, the earthquake, power outage, or tsunami alone likely would not have caused the partial meltdowns Fukushima experienced, but in combination and in sequence they produced a horrific accident (Perrow 2011).

There are numerous examples of interaction complexity in global life, but few have received as much attention as the financial crisis of 2008. Though the subprime mortgage market was a relatively small portion of the U.S. financial services industry, interaction complexity caused its distress to spread to the global financial system. The market's use of "tranches" sought to partition the risk of subprime mortgages among investors by bundling together risky mortgages. This practice assumes, however, that the risk of default in one mortgage in the tranche is independent of the risk of default for the others. Under most historical conditions, this assumption was sound—usually, my neighbor's inability to pay his mortgage has no effect on my ability to pay. But in 2008, this assumption no longer held. As a growing number of mortgages failed, homeowners who already were overleveraged suddenly found their principle asset (their homes) depreciating dramatically. Whereas the probabilities of mortgage default once were uncorrelated, they had become interdependent. Two other features compounded the crisis. One was the interaction between housing prices and insurance: credit default swaps tied the mortgage market to the insurance industry, precisely the

tight coupling that gives rise to normal accidents. The other was the failure
of regulators to appreciate the problems of interaction complexity. Recent
efforts at reforming finance also have ignored the interaction complexity of
the industry:

> The proposals also betray a desire to ring-fence deposit-taking
> firms and let everything else fry. However understandable, the
> reality is that investment banks, credit-card operators, insurers and
> even carmakers' finance arms had to be bailed out. The system
> was too interconnected. (*The Economist* 2008)

This regulatory failure is not a one-off occurrence. Institutions often fail to
manage the edge-of-chaos dynamics of global life precisely because their
focus on the components (whether people, banks, firms or others) commit
a fallacy of composition: safe components do not necessarily make for safe
systems, particularly when such social systems are tightly coupled. Writing
about the failure of banking regulators in 2008, *The Economist* noted, "The
assumption was that if each institution was safe, then the system as a whole
would be too" (*The Economist* 2008; see also Salmon and Johnson 2009).
As economic and technological processes of globalization create modern
marvels and conveniences—that is, as they create ever-more tightly coupled
global financial, communications, transportation, and social networks—
interaction complexity actually increases.

Interaction complexity affects the behaviors of individuals as well as
organizations. One of the more promising areas of recent research is the
study of genetics and political behavior. Traditionally, social science has
assumed that social structural factors do not affect an individual's genes,
and likewise that genes do not interact with social structures. For much of
the history of social science, this was a convenient simplifying assumption
because we lacked the technology to observe and measure the structure of
genes. With the mapping of the human genome, however, social scientists
are investigating how genetics interact with behaviors. For example, researchers have found that entrepreneurial activities are significantly "heritable,"
passed genetically from parents to children. By studying the differences in
entrepreneurial activities of twins, researchers have found significantly stron-
ger correlations among identical twins (who share a genome) than among
fraternal twins, even when controlling for an individual's family upbringing
and socialization (Nicolau et al. 2008). Genetic factors also shape how people
evaluate risk and assign values among risky choices, a finding that questions the validity of the assumption of people as rational utility maximizers

(Cesarini et al. 2009; Frydman et al. 2011). Thus genetic factors may help explain one of the important findings of cognitive psychology: that people tend to assign probabilities differently to prospective gains and losses (Levy 1997). Other researchers have found that genetic factors significantly affect a person's political orientations (Alford et al. 2005); voting behavior (Fowler and Dawes 2008); and party affiliation (Dawes and Fowler 2009). These findings help explain why parents and children often have similar strengths of party affiliation that are stable and enduring. This is not to suggest, however, that biology alone affects political behavior. A study of adult Australian twins has found, for example, that although identical twins are significantly more likely to either *both vote* or *both not vote* than fraternal twins, when one controls for social structural factors there is no significant correlation of the *vote choices* of identical twins (Hatemi et al. 2007). In other words, biology may help explain why people participate in entrepreneurial activities or political behaviors, but social structural factors may help explain the choices they make when they do participate. This suggests social factors and genetic ones exhibit interaction complexity: social structural factors may have strong effects on some people but not others, depending in part on their genetics. This has profound implications for our understanding of global life, from people's voting behavior and their consumption choices to how leaders innovate and evaluate risk.

One might object that "interaction complexity" simply captures the idea that monocausal explanations for social phenomena rarely suffice. After all, intuitively we know that both familial and social factors shape political behavior. Yet such an objection relies upon the assumption that causal processes are decomposable into constituent "parts." One need not review arguments against reductionism in science to understand the fallacy of this objection. If we assume that causal processes are decomposable, then we cannot explain why causes usually have some effects, but on rare occasions have none or even opposite effects. We cannot explain why mortgage tranching usually reduces risks but sometimes makes the risks much greater, why political socialization affects some children but not their siblings, or why education about climate change persuades Democrats but not Republicans. Precisely because social behavior is not decomposable, at least one researcher has argued:

> Even the difficulty of constructing comprehensive models in the biological sciences pales in comparison to that of modeling the workings of human brains and societies. By these measures, the social sciences are the hard disciplines, because the subject

matter is orders of magnitude more complex and multifaceted. (Shermer 2007, 44–46)

Strategic Complexity

Global life is complex because interdependent payoffs characterize many social choices. "Strategic complexity" arises because these interdependencies encourage actors to anticipate each other's decisions, or as Jervis stated, "actors consciously react to others and anticipate what others will do" (Jervis 1997, 44). In global life, people learn about, adapt to, and coevolve with each other in ways that produce perpetual novelty and surprises. This interdependency of actors' choices means that one cannot simply extrapolate from the individual to the aggregate level (Schelling 1978, 14). The "minority game" illustrates how strategic complexity gives rise to rich social behavior. In these choice problems, actors face strong incentives to behave in unpredictable ways (Arthur 1994a; Challet and Zang 1998). The classic example is a day at the beach. Although I enjoy the ocean, my dislike of crowds encourages me to find days when everyone else stays home. Of course, many other people probably follow the same reasoning. If so, a deterministic choice will lead us all to overcrowd the beach or to stay home, neither of which improves our welfare as a group. Social welfare is improved, however, if some people behave probabilistically, pursuing different choices with some element of chance. As long as some people sometimes head to a crowded beach, or simply act without thinking about others' choices, we end up using the beach more efficiently. Counterintuitively, in situations of strategic complexity the unpredictability of actors is a good thing, making everyone better off. This intrinsic unpredictability of strategic complexity explains in part why so many events in global life today not only are unforeseen but also are unforeseeable.

Consider the suddenness and surprise of the recent revolutions and civil wars in Tunisia, Egypt, Libya, and Syria. In his analysis of the East German revolution of 1989, Kuran noted that in authoritarian states people have strong incentives to disguise their true preferences—that is, sincere critics of the regime often find themselves in jail. While this insincerity abets the regime's stability in normal conditions, such "preference falsification" makes popular opinion brittle and subject to rapid shifts. An individual protestor's revelation of her true preferences for change can cause others to join protests and reveal their true preferences. These positive feedbacks—dynamics in which a person's choice increases the likelihood of others making the same choice—give rise to sudden shifts in popular opinion that are intrinsically unpredictable (Kuran 1991). This is because very small historical accidents, such as the weekly peace prayers at the Nikolai church in Leipzig in 1988, can trigger cascades of information that help actors coordinate their choices even if none of them set out to do so (Lohmann 1994).

Arguably, strategic complexity characterizes many democratic societies. In parliamentary systems, voters' anticipation of others' vote choices may produce surprising elections. In the United Kingdom, for example, Liberal-Democrat voters have a long history of insincerely voting for Labor candidates to prevent Tory gains (Fieldhouse et al. 1996). Such tactical voters try to anticipate who other voters are likely to support and react by voting against a third party rather than for their first-choice candidate. One consequence of this form of strategic complexity may be preference cycles, in which individual preferences remain relatively constant but add up to intransitive social choices that change regularly and unpredictably. Research suggests that such preference cycles exist in public polling data (Gaubatz 1995), opinions of the U.S. Supreme Court (Stearns 1999), and shareholder votes in publicly traded firms (DeMarzo 1993). In general, strategic complexity creates social choices that are inherently unstable and unpredictable (DeMarzo 1993, 725).

More recently, the Euro-area financial crisis has exhibited complex strategizing between states, banks, and bondholders. Counterintuitively, the IMF's infusion of cash into the European Financial Stability Facility (EFSF) may actually induce investors to sell rather than hold their bonds. Because the EFSF would receive preferred creditor status, holders of sovereign bonds are less likely to get paid in the event of a default (*The Economist* 2012). In this respect, the EFSF actually increases the risks to bondholders. However, recalcitrant bondholders may choose to hold troubled bonds rather than settle for a reduced payout, knowing that either the potential severity of sovereign default would force the EU to settle on terms favorable to bond holders or that they would likely receive better payouts from their insurers (Jones 2012). Of course, in all likelihood holders of Euro-denominated bonds are heterogeneous: some may sell despite IMF assistance while others may refuse to sell no matter what. This strategizing greatly complicates the choices for EU leaders: cash infusions may provoke an unintended flight from troubled bonds, increasing the likelihood of the sovereign default that only encourages holders of swaps to sit tight for a better payout. Yet EU leaders simply cannot allow Italy, Greece, or other states to default.

In general, conditions of strategic complexity explain two fallacies that tempt social scientists: the ecological fallacy and the fallacy of composition. The latter clearly has plagued financial regulation, as already noted.

Conversely, the examples of tactical voting illustrate the ecological fallacy—
the error of inferring the interests of actors in a complex social system based
on observations of the system as a whole. A complex system may exhibit
macrolevel stability even while actors constantly strategize against each other.
For example, polling data may exhibit consistency in the aggregate even
when individuals frequently change their opinions (Gaubatz 1995). Conversely, revolutions and civil wars may occur even though no one wants
this. The challenge for observers of global life is to understand whether the
adaptation and learning among actors produces macrolevel stability or sudden, surprising changes. Strategic complexity reminds us to observe both
actors and emergent structures of social systems as a whole.

Ecological Complexity

Global life is complex because people and organizations constantly change
their environments, both deliberately and without intention. By changing
their environment, they also change the rewards or payoffs they receive
for their choices. One might call this "ecological complexity." An example
from nature—the introduction of the Nassau grouper to a Caribbean fish
reserve—helps illustrate the basic idea. The grouper's primary diet is the
parrotfish, which in turn grazes on algae growing on coral reefs. Ecologists
were concerned that the grouper's predation on the parrotfish would lead
to excessive growth of algae and the destruction of the reserve's coral reefs.
In fact the opposite happened. The grouper did indeed thin the parrotfish
population, but the surviving parrotfish were larger and more capable grazers
who doubled the grazing of algae and reduced algae coverage of the reefs
by four times (Mumby 2006). Ecologists recognize that in general predation
improves the welfare of the population of prey, a paradox which ecological
complexity helps us understand. Jervis quotes a Maasai proverb that captures
this type of complexity: "Cows grow trees, elephants grow grass" (Jervis
1997, 49).
    With anthropogenic climate change a growing challenge, scientists
increasingly have examined how people change their natural environments.
Consider the challenge of preserving common pool resources, or natural
resources like fisheries or forests that tend to suffer from overharvesting
(Ostrom 1990). Because no one can be excluded from consuming a common pool resource, individuals have strong incentives to consume the good
without paying for it. Such free riding diminishes the supply and eventually
exhaustion of the good—what Hardin characterized as the "tragedy of the

commons" (Hardin 1968). While actors may design institutions to solve such collective action problems, often these institutions fail to account for the dynamics arising from ecological complexity. For one, Wilson argues that conventional approaches to managing common pool resources have tended to focus on a single species, in effect ignoring interactions among species (or other systems) within an ecosystem (Wilson 2002). Such conventional views about the management of ecological complexity assume that scientific investigations can reduce uncertainty arising from exogenous disturbances and from our lack of knowledge of cause and effect in such systems. In essence, conventional management has adopted a reductionist scientific approach that assumes causal relationships remain stable. Yet ecosystems are so complex—due to "their size, spatial distributions, multiple scales, large number of components, continuous change, and other factors" (Wilson 2002, 340)—that no individual or group is likely to understand completely the relationships governing the system. Both extreme uncertainty and ecological complexity give rise, then, to surprises, some beneficial (like the improvement of the Caribbean reefs) and others harmful (such as food shortages).

Ecological complexity does not merely arise from the interrelationships between human and natural systems. Within social systems, people and groups learn how to change the social environment to improve their rewards. W. Brian Arthur's seminal work on increasing returns helps us understand how high-tech firms compete for a market share in today's global economy (Arthur, 1994b). It is no coincidence that many of the world's largest, wealthiest, and most innovative firms are those that produce technologies with network externalities. These are products whose value to consumers grows (sometimes exponentially) as the number of users of the product grows. Another simple example illustrates this phenomenon. If I buy an orange, the utility I derive from that choice does not change irrespective of the number of other consumers of oranges. If I buy a mobile phone, however, my utility greatly depends upon others' choices. I would find my phone useless if I owned the only one in the world; it would be marginally more useful if 1,000 owned mobile phones; and it would be transformative if I could call a billion other subscribers. For this reason, the decisions of early adopters of a product will strongly condition the choices that subsequent consumers make. In this way consumers produce robust emergent structures like oligopolistic competition.

Although such technological "lock-in" was originally a historical accident (Arthur 1994b), today firms deliberately try to create such market lock-in. For example, manufacturers of aircraft engines are willing to sell their product at a loss to some airlines so that the airlines will invest in engine

maintenance and overhaul facilities. This in turn makes it more economical
for other airlines in the region to purchase the same engine. Manufacturers of the next generation of electric and hybrid automobiles similarly have
competed to capture early adopters, whose choices will shape the infrastructure that lowers costs for future consumers. The smart phone and tablet
computer industries achieve similar increasing returns using proprietary
technical standards, operating systems, and "apps." Tablets like Apple's iPad
and Amazon's Kindle Fire not only lock consumers into a particular set of
hardware but also into a particular distribution channel for music, films,
e-books, and other media, assuring Apple and Amazon of many years of
steady income. This corporate strategy of creating lock-in helps explain why
firms' fortunes may rise and fall with breathtaking suddenness. For example,
Finnish communications firm Nokia once was the largest manufacturer of
mobile phones in the world but saw its profits fall 49 percent in the three
years following Apple's introduction of the iPhone (Lynn 2010). Stephen
Elop, Nokia's chief executive, recognized the power of ecological complexity
in a 2011 memo to employees:

> The battle of devices has now become a war of ecosystems, where
> ecosystems include not only the hardware and software of the
> device, but developers, applications, ecommerce, advertising,
> search, social applications, location-based services, unified com-
> munications and many other things. Our competitors aren't taking
> our market share with devices; they are taking our market share
> with an entire ecosystem. This means we're going to have to decide
> how we either build, catalyse or join an ecosystem. (Ziegler 2011)

Such competition among product ecosystems is an increasingly important
feature of global business.

Arthur's insights about increasing returns and positive feedback help
explain several other surprising features of the global economy. For example,
despite neoclassical economics' expectation that factor prices will equalize,
in technologies characterized by increasing returns, investment tends to concentrate in geographic clusters rather than seek low-cost areas. Competitors
tend to locate near each other in part because they benefit from a shared pool
of highly trained, specialized labor, and in part because for many technologies, firms cannot capture the full monopoly rents of their innovation. These
spillovers in turn incentivize new investment, thus creating a virtuous cycle
of technological growth. These increasing returns more than offset a firm's
increased costs in labor and land. This is why high-tech firms concentrate

in Silicon Valley and film studios cluster in Hollywood or Mumbai: co-located firms capture some of the benefits of their competitors' creativity. Not only do increasing returns affect global patterns of investment, but they also explain the persistent trade advantages some states enjoy. Strategic trade theory suggests that governments can exploit oligopolistic competition to shift production from foreign to domestic competitors (Gilpin 2001, 108–48). Ecological complexity helps explain why global life today creates persistent core-periphery structures in the economy. The "product ecosystems" that Stephen Elop identified explain why firms in some industries enjoy oligopolistic pricing power, immense size, and enormous profits. As I write this, less than a week after the release of the third-generation iPad—arguably the most sophisticated example of product lock-in yet devised—Apple's stock price trades at nearly $600 per share and its market capitalization is about $560 billion in U.S. dollars. In a similar form of lock-in, the internet brings news, culture and ideas to all corners of the globe, but the United States nonetheless enjoys a privileged position in terms of both bandwidth and hyperlinks—information flows through the United States (Barnett and Park 2005). Once firms and states create these initial advantages, furthermore, they become self-reinforcing. The costs to actors of switching to alternative technologies, standards, or product ecosystems become prohibitive. As actors in global life change their environments, they create robust structures of advantage, concentration, and power that challenge the capacity of states, international organizations, and civil society to create a more equitable world.

Reflexive Complexity

Global life is complex because people recognize and understand complexity. This is not a circular argument because the recognition of emergent phenomena in social systems fundamentally changes peoples' behavior. Although similar to strategic complexity, this "reflexive complexity" arguably distinguishes complexity in social life from the physical and natural worlds. The coevolution of predator and prey is a form of strategic complexity, but species do not recognize emergent conditions like symbiosis, homeostasis, and biodiversity. By contrast, equity traders may bet against trading partners—a form of strategic complexity—but also may buy swaps, derivatives, and short-sell contracts, all of which reflect an understanding of emergent price dynamics in equity markets. Gilbert and Troitzsch define this as "second order emergence": "Not only can we as social scientists distinguish patterns of collective action, but the agents themselves can also do so and therefore their actions can be affected by the existence of these patterns" (Gilbert and Troitzsch 2005, 12). This second-order emergence makes global life inordinately dynamic and unpredictable. One general consequence of reflexive complexity is what sociologist Anthony Giddens called the double hermeneutic: people understand social knowledge and respond to it. "Sociological knowledge spirals in and out of the universe of social life, reconstructing both itself and that universe as an integral part of that process" (Giddens 1990, 15). For this reason, our knowledge of global life is intrinsically temporal and unstable. That is, our understanding of global complexity in finance, politics, and culture gives rise to the very social behaviors that may invalidate our understanding of global complexity.

Nowhere is reflexive complexity more apparent than in global finance. Alan Greenspan, then chairman of the Federal Reserve of the United States, noted in 1996 that "irrational exuberance" among investors might be inflating asset values beyond their intrinsic worth (Greenspan 1996). The phrase found new salience after the collapse of the dot-com bubble in 2000 and the U.S. real-estate market bubble in 2006. Yet the phrase "irrational exuberance" belies what is a reflexive strategy among investors: even if the market overvalues an asset, one can nevertheless make money by anticipating that other investors will keep bidding up the price—in effect betting on the exuberance of others. To investors, what matters is the behavior of other investors, not what economic theory or market research suggests should be the market value of an asset. Interestingly, one could make a similar claim about the current economic recovery: a persistent "unjustified pessimism" slows economic growth because consumers remain pessimistic about other consumers despite the theoretical indicators of macroeconomic growth. Together, the phenomena of irrational exuberance and unjustified pessimism suggest that the cycles of the global economy become a self-fulfilling prophesy of instability, producing bigger asset bubbles and more destructive market crashes than market "fundamentals" would suggest (Graham 2003, xiii).

"Signaling" is another important example of reflexive complexity. Actors are aware that their actions provide cues to others and can use this knowledge to shape emergent structures. During the fall of 2008, U.S. Secretary of the Treasury Henry Paulson understood the perils of signaling as he sought to manage the consequences of the Lehman Brothers bankruptcy. The Bush administration had created the Troubled Asset Relief Program (TARP) to provide immediate liquidity for distressed commercial and investment banks. Yet Paulson and his advisers quickly realized that channeling assistance to specific banks would signal to investors that the chosen banks were in trouble. Such a signal would cause investors to flee the banks' stocks, thus creating the very crisis the Treasury wished to avoid. Paulson's solution was to use TARP funds for all banks, including those that were adequately capitalized and did not want government investment. This blanket approach would prevent the market from discerning which banks were distressed and which were healthy (Sorkin 2010, 527–28).

People's capacity for recognizing signals produces surprising emergent phenomena. Actors' responses to signals from other actors may weaken over time. The well-known phenomenon of "alert fatigue" helps explain why decision makers often ignore signals. Betts argues, for example, that the Soviet Union ignored the threat from Nazi Germany after March 1941 because frequent reports of impending German aggression initially proved false, while frequent alarms reduced the readiness of frontline Soviet troops (Betts 1980/1981). In political campaigns, voters become inured to once provocative advertisements and the outrageous claims of candidates. This suggests that reflexive complexity gives rise to path-dependent social processes. Initially, actors' recognition of emergent phenomena causes them to adapt and learn. Yet this causal relationship breaks down in two ways: actors become habituated to complexity, or their adaptation changes the system enough that the emergent phenomenon itself disappears. For example, asset bubbles "burst" as enough investors flee the asset to change the dynamics of price appreciation. At the same time, actors adapt so that a new "normal" structure emerges: short sellers have learned to profit from declining asset values; major exchanges impose trading curbs on stocks exhibiting extreme volatility; and trading firms create high-volume automated trade algorithms to capture profits from small but sudden movements in asset prices. Thus, reflexive complexity exhibits dialectic properties: emergent phenomena create actor adaptations that in turn introduce new surprises, such as the so-called "flash crash" of the New York Stock Exchange on May 6, 2010. In this respect, Giddens is prescient: our recognition of the complexity of global life produces the very conditions that introduce new, unanticipated complexities.

This suggests that governance is at best an exercise in minimizing the consequences of complexity—if we cannot predict it, purposive governance seems impossible. Best that we just learn to manage and adapt quickly to the complexities of global life. Yet the idea of reflexive complexity helps us understand an intriguing possibility suggested by Christopher Ford in this volume. He argues that unlike in natural and physical complex adaptive systems, actors in complex adaptive social systems respond to ideas. The capacity of people to recognize ideas and respond to them reintroduces the possibility of purposive governance. Decision-makers and others can introduce ideas that help actors structure their understandings of global life and to coordinate their collective action. As Ford writes, "the deliberate shaping of *ideas* seems to offer us a chance to affect behavior within complex systems in ways that are not utterly unpredictable, at least to the extent that such inputs will tend to exert recognizable patterning influences over time" (Ford 2011). In this respect, the reflexive capacities of social actors allow for the possibility of governance in the form of ideas, paradigms, and conceptual frames. How such ideas and conceptual paradigms interact with social actors is itself an important source of complexity in global life.

Understanding Cause and Effect in a Complex World

One consequence of the four types of complexity is that social systems exhibit chaotic dynamics. That is, for much of the time social systems exhibit stable cause-effect relationships, but on rare occasions the linearity of these relationships breaks down. Most of the time, capital flows to geographic locations where costs are lowest and returns are greatest, but on rare occasions capital concentrates in a Silicon Valley or Bollywood. Most of the time, people choose to vote for their preferred candidate, but on rare occasions they will vote against a despised third candidate. For this reason observers of world politics face a double challenge: to understand the four types of complexity and to understand when and where such complexity might occur. Discussing the collapse of fisheries, Wilson explains that it is difficult to understand such complex systems

> because the relative intensity of causal relationships in the system changes from time to time. Extreme examples are the regime shifts such as have occurred in response to fishing and environmental changes in many places around the world. . . . Under these circumstances, similar species may be present, but in such radically altered proportions that predictions based on past relationships would be far off the mark. Certainly, if one were in a position to compare the entirety of the two systems (before and after the shift) as if they were stable systems, one probably would find strong dissimilarities in the intensity and relative importance of the interactions among components. (Wilson 2002, 334)

In effect, the presence of complexity means that causality itself—its presence, intensity, and direction—is not stable over time, or even within parts of the same system.

As the contributors to this volume demonstrate, complexity researchers use different methods to understand complexity in global life. Empirical methods such as process-tracing and case research are important techniques: We can learn from the real world. Nevertheless, the four types of complexity impose some practical limits on what we can hope to learn from empirical data (Lustick et al. 2004, 211–12). Because many complex phenomena are more or less rare (revolutions, secessionism, or market crashes, for example), the scarcity of events creates a paucity of empirical data. For similar reasons, researchers face considerable costs, both practical and ethical, to the collection of empirical data. Consequently, social scientists often rely on aggregate data collected by governments to make inferences about the behavior of individuals, which risks the ecological fallacy. Even if we could gather high-quality empirical data about individuals, however, interaction complexity in particular and chaotic dynamics in general confound statistical tools like regression analysis which assume the linearity of cause-effect relationships. In effect, empirical analysis of complexity becomes a drunkard's search. We look for answers in the "light" of convenient empirical methods and strong assumptions, rather than with those methods that are most likely to help us understand the complexities that characterize global life.

In my view, the method of agent-based modeling (ABM) offers an invaluable complement to empirical research about global life. Briefly, an ABM is a computational model of the microlevel behavior of autonomous actors who produce interesting macrolevel phenomena. To understand such emergent features of social life, the model represents actors in a social system as an "agent," or a small computer program that represents a real-world actor's abilities, cognition, and decision-making procedures as a set of instructions ("algorithms" in programming parlance) (Miller and Page 2007; Gilbert 2008). The computer then replicates each agent as many times as necessary to represent a complete system. Although early ABM researchers created "artificial societies," or abstract representations that eschewed external validity for generality and simplicity, recently they have used empirical methods to inform and validate their models (Bousquet et al. 1999; Geller and Moss 2008). This evidence-driven modeling suggests an emerging synergy between the empirical and simulation traditions of complexity researchers. ABM not only has lower costs, but also allows for quasitrue experimentation. That is, unlike in natural experiments, in an agent-based model the researcher can manipulate the values of the parameters of theoretical interest. Of course, the researcher is experimenting with a model, not a real world complex system. Nevertheless, quasitrue experimentation reintroduces scholars to a scientific method that does not rely upon reductionism.

None of this is to suggest that our understanding of the four sources of complexity allows us to control them or to foresee the next financial crisis, revolution, or technology boom. To put it simply, just because we understand complexity does not mean we can control it. Hayek's distinction between the craftsman and the gardener makes this very point. "The recognition of the insuperable limits to his knowledge ought indeed to teach the student of society a lesson of humility which should guard him against becoming an accomplice in men's fatal striving to control society," he wrote. Much like a gardener, we can manage and nurture complexity in global life, but we cannot build solutions to it as a craftsman would. The relationship between scholarship and policy, then, is itself a complicated one. Hayek concluded his Nobel acceptance speech by articulating a view of governance that resonates with contemporary complexity thinking. Purposeful control is "a striving which makes [the social scientist] not only a tyrant over his fellows, but which may well make him the destroyer of a civilization which no brain has designed but which has grown from the free efforts of millions of individuals" (Hayek 1975, 442). Whether our striving to understand the edge of chaos is tyrannical or liberating depends, in the end, on our capacity to recognize the core paradox of the sciences of complexity: that we now understand our knowledge has insurmountable limits.

Bibliography

Alford, J., Funk, C., and Hibbing, J. (2005). Are political orientations genetically transmitted? *American Political Science Review*, 99(2), 153–167.

Arthur, W. B. (1994a). Inductive reasoning and bounded rationality. *The American Economic Review*, 84(2), 406–411.

Arthur, W. B. (1994b). *Increasing returns and path dependence in the economy*. Ann Arbor: University of Michigan Press.

Barnett, G. A., and Park, H. W. (2005). The structure of international Internet hyperlinks and bilateral bandwidth. *Annals of Telecommunications*, 60(9–10), 1115–1132.

Betts, R. K. (1980). Surprise despite warning: Why sudden attacks succeed. *Political Science Quarterly*, 95(4), 559.

Bousquet, F., Barreteau, O., Le Page, C., Mullon, C., and Weber, J. (1999). An environmental modelling approach. The use of multi-agent simulations. In F. Blasco and A. Weill (Eds.), *Advances in Environmental and Ecological Modelling* (113–122). Paris: Elsevier.

Cesarini, D., Dawes, C., Johannesson, M., Lichtenstein, P., and Wallace, B. (2009). Genetic variation in preferences for giving and risk taking. *The Quarterly Journal of Economics*, 124(2), 809–842.

Challet, D., and Zang, Y. (1998). On the minority game: Analytical and numerical studies. *Physica A: Statistical mechanics and its applications*, 256(3–4), 514–532.

Dawes, C., and Fowler, J. (2009). Partisanship, voting, and the dopamine D2 receptor gene. *Journal of Politics*, 71(3), 1157–1171.

DeMarzo, P. M. (1993). Majority voting and corporate control: The rule of the dominant shareholder. *The Review of Economic Studies* 60, 713–734.

Fieldhouse, E. A., Pattie, C. J., and Johnson, R. J. (1996). Tactical voting and party constituency campaigning at the 1992 general election in England. *British Journal of Political Science*, 26(3), 403–418.

Ford, C. A. (2011). Policymaking at the edge of chaos: Musings on political ideology through the lens of complexity. Paper presented at the Conference on "Is Complexity the New Framework for the Study of Global Life?" University of Western Sydney, Australia.

Fowler, J., and Dawes, C. (2008). Two genes predict voter turnout. *Journal of Politics*, 70(3), 579–594.

Frydman, C., Camerer, C., Bossaerts, P., and Rangel, A. (2011). MAOA-L carriers are better at making optimal financial decisions under risk. *Proceedings of the Royal Society B* 278, 2053–2059.

Gaubatz, K. T. (1995). Intervention and intransitivity: Public opinion, social choice, and the use of military force abroad. *World Politics*, 47 (4), 534–554.

Giddens, A. (1990). *The consequences of modernity*. Stanford, CA: Stanford University Press.

Gilbert, N. (2008). *Agent based models (quantitative applications in the social sciences)*. Thousand Oaks, CA: Sage Publications.

Gilbert, N. and Troitzsch, K. G. (2005). *Simulation for the social scientist* (2nd ed.). New York: Open University Press.

Gilpin, R. (2001). *Global political economy: Understanding the international economic order*. Princeton, NJ: Princeton University Press.

Graham, B. (2003). *The intelligent investor* (Revised Edition). New York: HarperCollins.

Greenspan, A. (1996). *The challenge of central banking in a democratic society*. Washington, DC: American Enterprise Institute. Retrieved March 23, 2012, from http://www.federalreserve.gov/boarddocs/speeches/1996/19961205.htm.

Hamilton, L. (2011). Education, politics and opinions about climate change: Evidence for interaction effects. *Climatic Change*, 104(2), 379–422.

Hardin, G. (1968). The tragedy of the commons. *Science* 162, 1243–1248.

Hatemi, P. K., Medland, S. E., Morley, K. I., Heath, A. C., and Martin, N. G. (2007). The genetics of voting: An Australian twin study. *Behavioral Genetics*, 37, 435–448.

Hayek, F. A. (1975). The pretence of knowledge. *The Swedish Journal of Economics*, 77(4), 433–442.

Jervis, R. (1997). *System effects: Complexity in political and social life*. Princeton, NJ: Princeton University Press.

Jones, S. (2012). Bondholders in stand-off with Athens. *Financial Times* (London). March 7.

Kuran, T. (1991). Now out of never: The element of surprise in the East European revolution of 1989. *World Politics*, 44(1), 7–48.

Levy, J. S. (1997). Prospect theory, rational choice, and international relations. *International Studies Quarterly*, 41(1), 87–112.

Lohmann, S. (1994). The dynamics of information cascades: The Monday demonstrations in Leipzig, East Germany, 1989–1991. *World Politics*, 47(1), 42–101.

Lorenz, E. (1963). Deterministic nonperiodic flow. *Journal of Atmospheric Sciences* 20, 130–141.

Lustick, I., Miodownik, D., and Eidelson, R. J. (2004). Secessionism in multicultural states: Does sharing power prevent or encourage it? *American Political Science Review*, 98(2), 211–12.

Lynn, M. (2010). The fallen king of Finland. *Bloomberg BusinessWeek* 4196, 7–8.

Miller, J., and Page, S. (2007). *Complex adaptive systems: An introduction to computational models of social life*. Princeton, NJ: Princeton University Press.

Mitchell, M. (2010). *Complexity: A guided tour*. New York: Oxford University Press.

Mumby, P. J. (2006). Fishing, trophic cascades, and the process of grazing on coral reefs. *Science*, 311, 98–101.

Nicolau, N., Shane, S., Cherkas, L., Hunkin, J., and Spector, T. (2008). Is the tendency to engage in entrepreneurship genetic? *Management Science*, 54(1), 167–179.

Perrow, C. (1984). *Normal accidents: Living with high risk technologies*. New York: Basic Books.

Perrow, C. (2011). Fukushima and the inevitability of accidents. *Bulletin of the Atomic Scientists*, 67(6), 44–52.

Poteete, A., Janssen, M., and Ostrom, E. (2010). *Working together: Collective action, the commons, and multiple methods in practice*. Princeton, NJ: Princeton University Press.

Rosenau, J. N. (2003). *Distant proximities: Dynamics beyond globalization*. Princeton, NJ: Princeton University Press.

Salmon, F., and Johnson, D. (2009). A formula for disaster. *Wired*, 17(3), 74.

Saperstein, A. (1997a). The prediction of unpredictability: Applications of the new paradigm of chaos in dynamical systems to the old problem of stability of a system of hostile nations. In L. D. Kiel and E. Elliott (Eds.), *Chaos theory in the social sciences: foundations and applications* (139–164). Ann Arbor: University of Michigan Press.

Schelling, T. (1978). *Micromotives and macrobehavior*. New York: W. W. Norton.

Scholte, J. A. (2005). *Globalization: A critical introduction*. New York: Palgrave Macmillan.

Shermer, M. (2007). The really hard science. *Scientific American*, 297(4), 44–46.

Sorkin, A. R. (2010). *Too big to fail: The inside story of how Wall Street and Washington fought to save the financial system—and themselves*. New York: Penguin.

Stearns, M. L. (1999). Should justices ever switch votes? Miller v. Albright in social choice perspective. *The Supreme Court Economic Review*, 7, 87–156.

The Economist (2008). After the fall. November 13, 29–32.

The Economist (2012). The Euro crisis: The Eurozone's rescue strategy still does not add up. March 3, 12–14.

Wendt, A. (1992). Levels of analysis vs. agents and structures: part III. *Review of International Studies*, 18(1), 181–195.

Wight, C. (2006). *Agents, structures, and international relations: Politics as ontology.* New York: Cambridge University Press.

Wilson, J. (2002). Scientific uncertainty, complex systems, and the design of common-pool institutions. In E. Ostrom (Ed.), *The Drama of the Commons* (327–59). Washington, DC: National Academy Press.

Ziegler, C. (2011). Nokia CEO Stephen Elop rallies troops in brutally honest "burning platform" memo. Retrieved August 12, 2012, from http://www.engadget.com/2011/02/08/nokia-ceo-stephen-elop-rallies-troops-in-brutally-honest-burnin/.

Chapter 2

Theorizing International Relations

Emergence, Organized Complexity, and Integrative Pluralism

Colin Wight

Introduction

Since its inception at the end of World War I, the discipline of international relations (IR) has seen a steady increase in the number of competing theoretical perspectives. Such has been the pace of this growth in recent years that it is probably an impossible task to catalog them all, let alone possess a comprehensive understanding of them. There are almost as many approaches as there are theorists. Theoretical diversity is not necessarily a problem. Indeed, a commitment to theoretical pluralism is often assumed to be integral to all science. The growth of scientific knowledge requires the operation of an open-ended market in ideas. Thomas Kuhn (1962), of course, challenged this idea and argued that what enabled scientific progress was a dominant paradigm around which research revolved. Despite the widespread influence of Kuhn's ideas, the incipient conservativism at the heart of his model of science was always likely to prove a problem for the social sciences (Fuller 2000; 2003). Unlike the natural sciences, the social sciences are unable to construct decisive test situations that can settle theoretical disputes, to the general satisfaction of a majority of the research community. Given this epistemological uncertainty, accepting some theoretical diversity seems the rational choice.

The commitment to theoretical pluralism can also be defended on the basis of a supposed relationship between democracy and science (Popper

1952). Scientific progress, it is argued, is best achieved under conditions that foster debate and allow the challenging of conventional wisdom. Likewise, there is a widely held belief within the scientific community that the values of science—honesty, objectivity, and a respect for the intrinsic merit of a wide range of ideas and opinions—are essential to a democratic culture. In democracies, diversity and the safeguarding of minority opinions are seen as inherent goods. Any attempt to stifle alternative views, or underrepresented groups, is tantamount to giving up the democratic ideal.

Yet, as with contemporary debates surrounding the limits of free speech in democratic societies, pluralism in the social sciences poses problems. One aim of any science is to sift through knowledge claims in the hope of discarding those that fail to provide a valuable contribution to the overall stock of knowledge. Science is a competitive environment, and many social scientists are concerned that an open-ended commitment to pluralism may lead to a debilitating relativism and the loss of all critical standards. An alternative view presents theoretical pluralism in an altogether differing light. According to this view, pluralism is tolerated only because it represents a temporary phenomenon. Eventually, the social sciences will mature and develop a consistent scientific methodology such that theoretical disputes can be settled. Theoretical pluralism can be tolerated, but only on the basis of methodological unity. What the social sciences need is a rigorous, and clearly defined, set of scientific methods that constitute the framework through which theoretical disputes can be settled. The unity of method will eventually lead to theoretical unity. As King and colleagues (1994, 9) put it, the "unity of all science consists alone in its method." The steady accumulation of knowledge generated through the application of scientific methods will eventually place the social sciences on as secure an epistemological footing as the natural sciences. This position is still committed to pluralism, but pluralism is now a means and not an end. Pluralism is tolerated because it exists within a horizon of unity. It is a pluralism that serves the purposes of unity; unity-through-pluralism (UtP).

The UtP position is often linked to reductionist views of science (Mitchell 2003). According to reductionists the various scientific disciplines are necessary only insofar as the overall stock of scientific knowledge is incomplete. Ultimately, reductionists believe that there will eventually emerge a set of explanations at the most basic level that will explain all other levels. Typically, physics has been portrayed as the master science, which will, in due course, provide a "grand theory of everything" (Weinberg 1992). Extreme reductionist views are not common in international relations and political science. One notable exception is Hans Morgenthau's version of political realism. According to Morgenthau, objective laws rooted in human nature govern politics (Morgenthau 1973). This locates the real causes of political conduct in biology and portrays the political science disciplines as forms of social engineering or technology-based kinds of knowledge.

Although Morgenthau's is a radical version, other less extreme forms of reductionism are common. Methodological individualism, for example, suggests that the ultimate explanatory variable in any social theory should be the individual (Bhargava 1993). Methodological individualism underpins many theories and approaches to political science, most notably rational choice theory (Green and Shapiro 1994). Irrespective of their theoretical orientations, many international relations scholars have suggested that theories be grounded in microlevel phenomena. Although theoretically diverse, these claims can be understood as reactions to various modes of structural theory within the discipline. Liberals and neoclassical realists, for example, proceed by translating individual preferences into collective political phenomena in an effort to analyze international politics (Moravcsik 1997; Schweller 2003). Even contemporary neoliberals (or institutionalists as they are often termed), who, despite a sharing neorealist structuralist assumptions, argue that institutionalist theory is moving "farther from its neorealist roots, putting more emphasis on agency" (Keohane and Martin 2003, 83). Likewise, many constructivists have attempted to distance themselves from Wendt's structuralist constructivism and develop an account of international relations based on microphenomena. As Jeffrey Checkel (1998, 342) puts it, the problem for constructivists is "how to get from microfoundations to outcomes." When viewed in this context it may be that methodological individualism is undergoing something of a renaissance in international relations (Leon 2006).

Methodological individualism and theoretical pluralism, however, are not incompatible positions. It is possible to agree that the individual is the ultimate source of explanation in the human sciences, but disagree about what explains this behavior, or what the most important aspects of it are. This suggests that reductionism and the UtP position are not as closely related as some philosophers of science seem to suggest (Mitchell 2003, 1). We can, however, contrast the UtP position to the alternative view, which sees little or no prospect of any type of theoretical unification. Given the limited prospects of settling theoretical disputes at the epistemological level, the social sciences should embrace an open-ended commitment to all theoretical approaches. According to advocates of this view, we should embrace a strategy of letting "a thousand theoretical flowers bloom." This position can be defended on two grounds. First, it is suggested that since theoretical diversity is itself a necessary component in the growth of knowledge, we should embrace a plurality of differing perspectives (Feyerabend 1975). For the committed pluralist, unity is neither possible nor desirable; but rather, it is the intrinsic good of pluralism itself which is to be defended. Pluralism here is an end, not a means. Only pluralism can deal with a multifaceted and complex reality.

An alternative defense of pluralism rests on the belief that the epistemological uncertainty at the heart of all social science requires an acceptance of all theoretical perspectives. According to this view, pluralism does not lead to more and better knowledge, but rather, given the lack of agreed epistemological standards for assessing competing knowledge claims, we should embrace all perspectives. Theoretical perspectives according to this view are likened to political positions, with "right" and "wrong" functioning as ethical or aesthetic values (Campbell 1998).

Neither the UtP viewpoint nor the various defenses of pluralism seem attractive positions for any science to adopt. Given the history of scientific progress, it would seem inappropriate for any science to adopt theoretical conformity as a goal. Epistemologically, how would we know when we had reached a point where theoretical pluralism is no longer required? The history of science is replete with examples of well-established bodies of knowledge being overturned. Competing visions of science mean that there are no agreed standards for arriving at a unity of method (Chalmers 1999; Godfrey-Smith 2003). Pluralism for the sake of pluralism, however, seems to lead to an incapacitating relativism, or what Yosef Lapid (2003) calls a "flabby pluralism." A better term might be disengaged pluralism. No claim or viewpoint would seem to be invalid, and theorists are free to pursue their own agenda with little or no contact with alternative views. This is a disengaged pluralism because there is no attempt to specify the relationships between theories or to examine one's own theoretical position in the light of alternative views. The absence of an agreed unity of method would also entail that the standards by which the various theories are to be judged would be internal to the theory (Smith 2003). This would be a disengaged form of pluralism with each theoretical perspective legitimating its claims solely on its own terms and with little reason to engage in conversations with alternative approaches. It is the kind of pluralism that finds its political expression in apartheid.

Despite these problems IR theory has taken a pluralist turn in recent years. Rudra Sil and Peter Katzenstein have articulated an influential argument that outlines an approach to knowledge generation predicated on what they call "analytical eclecticism" (Sil and Katzenstein 2010). Likewise, Patrick Jackson (2011) also attempts to construct a framework to guide inquiry in

IR that can help foster the cause of pluralism. Going even further, David Lake (2011) has argued that "isms are evil." While laudable in their aims, what is often missing from these attempts to construct a pluralist approach to IR is an examination of the conditions of possibility for fragmentation. Why is the discipline so fragmented?

In this chapter, I want to explore an approach called "integrative pluralism" (Mitchell 2003). Integrative pluralism is the most appropriate strategy for IR to adopt for two reasons. First, at the level of ontology, I argue that the international political system is best understood through the related concepts of "emergence" and "organized complexity." Because all human systems have this form, they require a plurality of explanations to deal with phenomena at differing levels and the complex differentiation of causal mechanisms within levels. But equally, at the epistemological level, the nature of theorizing itself, and the fact that no one theory could hope to grasp the complexity of global life, entails a commitment to integrative pluralism. However, even though there are sound ontological and epistemological grounds for pursuing integrative pluralism, there are two related factors that impede its development. First is the academic division of labor, which compartmentalizes knowledge into zones of expertise, which in turn, structurally impedes the development of interdisciplinary research needed to explain complex systems. Second is the structure of IR as an academic discipline, which, using a framework developed by Richard Whitley (2000), I will characterize as a fragmented adhocracy. A fragmented adhocracy is characterized by a low degree of reputational interdependency between competing research groups, with few organizational restrictions regarding the choice of theoretical framework or research methodology. It typically displays a relatively fragmented knowledge structure and an almost complete lack of agreement concerning the relative importance of different problems to be solved. As a consequence, the research activity within the field proceeds in an ad hoc, arbitrary, and incoherent manner, with limited attempts to integrate new solutions with the existing structure of knowledge. In such an intellectual structure the potential for integrated pluralism is low.

This chapter is structured in the following manner. First, I explain the properties possessed by systems that exhibit organized complexity and display emergent properties. Complexity thinking (CT) has already been discussed in the discipline and throughout the wider social sciences (Ablert and Hilkermeier 2004; Cilliers 1998; Cudworth and Hobden, 2011; Jervis 1997b; Rosenau 1990; Snyder and Jervis 1993). In general, however, these attempts have tended to take the formal characteristics of CT as given and apply them directly to political phenomena. The analysis of political systems through CT, however, requires some modification. Hence, while political systems are self-organizing, they are also subject to various forms of control and direction. Second, I discuss the notion of integrated pluralism drawing on Sandra Mitchell's distinction between theory as the abstract identification of causal mechanisms and explanation of open systems in concrete situations where multiple mechanisms are at play (Mitchell 2003). In this section I also examine some of the barriers to the development of integrative pluralism as a result of the intellectual structure of the field. Finally, I briefly discuss the problems surrounding the theorization of the international political system indicating both some general guidelines for the implementation of integrative pluralism, as well as sounding some words of warning about the possibility of producing knowledge of complex systems that might then be deployed in practice.

Properties of Complex Systems

It is important to distinguish complex systems from merely complicated ones. CT refers to systems that have a specific set of properties. Complicated systems, on the other hand, might appear to be complex, but unless they possess particular properties they would not be susceptible to analysis through CT. If political systems were complicated rather than complex, then an all-embracing theory of international politics might be possible. Many complicated systems have been accurately modeled by science. However, a complex system can never be modeled in a manner that accurately captures its dynamic diversity and modes of interaction. The key properties that mark out complex systems are their irreducible open nature, emergence, self-organization, nonlinearity, and feedback.

All natural and social systems are open systems, and this presents particular problems in terms of their theorization. In simple terms, a closed system is one that has no interactions with its environment. A closed system does not rely on external inputs from its environment or produce outputs into that environment. Its behavioral characteristics are self-contained, and its logics are internally determined. Closed systems do not occur spontaneously in nature and require human intervention. A good example here are laboratory experiments which are explicit attempts by scientists to isolate some or other mechanism from external influence in order to study its behavior (Hacking 1983). Once isolated the behavioral dynamics of the mechanism can be formulated safe in the knowledge that it is the isolated mechanism producing the observed effects. In practice no system can be totally isolated in terms of interaction with its environment. In closed systems laws have uniform/linear effects. This means that it is possible to use the responses to a small set of inputs to predict the response to any possible input. This makes it possible, in theory at least, to characterize the system completely. If a system is closed, then the energy contained within the system is also finite. Once the total sum of energy within the system has dissipated, the system is said to have reached equilibrium. A system that has reached equilibrium is a system that is dead; it is a system in which no change occurs. As Erwin Shroedinger (1944) argued, when a system is isolated, life will eventually come to an end. In a system that reaches this state no observable events occur. This is known as the state of thermodynamical equilibrium, or of "maximum entropy." An organism lives because it absorbs energy from the external world and processes it in order to maintain itself and avoid falling into a state of equilibrium. Although we talk in terms of social systems reaching states of equilibrium, they never actually achieve this state. Social systems are always undergoing change.

An open system, on the other hand, interacts with its environment. Biological and social systems are "open" systems in this sense. As W. Koehler (1981, 73) puts it, "no organism is detached from the rest of the world to an extent that would make our [closed-system] principles directly applicable to living systems." The behavioral dynamics of open systems cannot be explained solely in terms of their internal logics, but rather, depend upon a specification of their relationships with their environment. This requires a consideration of the mechanisms and rules determining their regulation of, and adaptation to, external influences and a consideration of how that external environment structures the internal dynamic of the system under study. Given this, theories of open systems must take into account the external environment not merely as a complicating factor, but rather as an intrinsic aspect of the system itself. Open systems inevitably require multidimensional and holistic forms of theory.

A sophisticated attempt to lessen the impact of open systems on social theorizing comes in the form of autopoesis, or what are known as self-producing systems (Mingers 1995). This is a variation on the distinction between open and closed systems and was originally developed from the work of Maturana and Varela (1980; 1987). The theory originates in biology, where it was initially formulated to explain the difference between living and nonliving systems. Living systems are in a constant state of self-production, using the individual components that constitute them in the first place to restructure the system in the on-going process that we call life. According to Maturana and Varela, systems such as this are self-referential and organizationally closed. It is important to be clear on what this claim entails. Maturana and Varela distinguish between structure and organization. Structure refers to the actual configuration of systems (the components, relations, and processes), while organization is a subset of the relations that apply to all systems of a similar type. Organization specifies the formal characteristics of a system that make it the type of system it is, whereas structure refers to the actual dynamic development of systems in concrete situations. Thus all living systems share an autopoietic organization, but this organization can be realized in a multitude of different structures. Such systems are "organizationally closed" in terms of the relations of self-production, but "structurally open" in that actual systems interact with their environment through their components.

The most sophisticated application of this idea in a social context is that of Niklas Luhmann (1995). Luhmann's theory can be understood as an attempt at restricting the level of complexity in open systems. The core mechanism of Luhmann's social theory is communication. Social systems are theorized purely as systems of communication. In contemporary society, and perhaps as a result of technological developments and processes of globalization, communication is global; hence society today is a global society (Luhmann 1997). According to Luhmann a system is defined by a boundary between itself and its environment, and the boundary immunizes the system from the infinitely complex exterior. Because a system develops its own modes of operation communication within a system only selects a limited amount of information available from outside of the system. Hence, in this respect, any given system can be considered a zone of reduced complexity. Complexity is reduced because self-organizing systems emerge.

In terms of social systems Luhmann treats the various subsystems within society as themselves constituting individual, relatively isolated, autopoietic systems. Each distinct subsystem operates according to its own logic, but organizationally, each is similar insofar as communication is the sole mechanism of exchange in all systems. Equally, within any society certain subsystems will fulfill functions that contribute to "society" as a whole, but this is not a managed, or directed, process but happens more or less by chance, without an overarching vision of society. Again, according to Luhmann, each subsystem works strictly according to its very own logic and has no understanding of the way other systems operate; for example, the political system is about power and control; the economy is all about money. If Luhmann were correct it would imply the possibility of one theory accurately describing the logics of each subsystem. All that would be required would be one overarching theory of communication (the sole mechanism of social exchange) and a theory of communication relevant to each domain or subsystem, in which case theoretical pluralism is not required, or at least not at the level of individual disciplines.

Luhmann's theory is problematic on two interrelated grounds, both related to his treatment of the human individual. In Luhmann's theory human beings are neither part of society nor of any specific subsystem. Obviously, any social system consisting of communication requires humans as a necessary channel for communication to occur. But according to Luhmann, humans are not integral to the system itself, but rather constitute an environmental resource that the system draws on in order to maintain itself. Humans are the medium through which communication takes place, but they are not themselves communicators. Luhmann supposedly once claimed he was not interested in people. The ethical and normative consequences of this position have led a welter of criticism directed at Luhmann (Habermas 1987). But Luhmann's theory is both logically and empirically problematic without these moral objections.

First, in treating humans as mere communication ciphers, Luhmann replicates some of the worst excesses of systems theory. The "third wave of social systems theory," as R. Keith Sawyer (2005, 10–26) calls it, explicitly attempted to introduce CT into system thinking without embracing this strict antihumanism. Indeed, the aim of CT is to show how complex systems emerge out of the interactions of their units. Reducing the units to communication and treating the system as organizationally closed might help reduce the levels of complexity, but it does not seem a realistic strategy for any social science to follow. In many respects Luhmann's theory follows a path well trodden by many theories of social practice. Various forms of systems theory have ignored the individual and attempted to specify the formal characteristics of systems in the hope of reducing the complexity and contingency associated with individual behavior. Modern systems theory, however, sees complexity in the system itself. Human individuals are not only parts of one coherent system—such as the political system—but are parts of many systems at the same point in time; the units are part of the complexity. Hence political actors are also economic actors, and vice versa. Treating the two systems as wholly distinct fails to recognize the connections between them. Interestingly, this point indicates that the theorization of complex systems does not just imply theoretical pluralism at the disciplinary level, but that interdisciplinary research is also required.

The discipline which has most depended upon treating social systems as closed is economics; although approaches to political science that have been colonized by methodologies imported from economics adopt a similar view. Given the subject matter of economics, it is difficult to explain why it became so reliant on a methodology that assumes a closed system. Yet there is no doubt that such a commitment to closure exists (Lawson 1997; Rothheim 1998). Part of the answer might be some perceived link between mathematical models and science. The advocates of this approach clearly view themselves as taking a logical, more scientific, approach that is superior to the alternatives.

Early economic theory did not depend on the assumption of closure. Classical economic thinkers, such as David Hume and Adam Smith, embraced a relatively open system view. Hume believed that legal institutions demonstrated emergent properties and brought about "spontaneous order" through the independent actions of individuals (Hume 1986). This idea is replicated in theoretically varied attempts to explain the emergence of markets and other economic institutions (Hayek 1982; Olson 2000). In addition, Adam Smith dealt with the complex interactions of individual motives and related these to external factors (Smith 1984). It is difficult to view the "invisible hand" as anything other than an emergent property that comes about through the self-organizing principles of the system. Both Hume and Smith imagined an economic system open to external influences and subject to change. The idea that the economic system is open, complex, and displays emergent characteristics contrasts starkly with the assumptions underpinning the restrictive methodology of contemporary economics.

Another important property of complex systems is that they exhibit properties not expressible in terms of the constituent parts, and they have a propensity for novelty. This is the issue of emergence. There are three core ideas that underpin the notion of emergence. First is the idea of "supervenience"; this means that the emergent properties will no longer exist if the lower level is removed. Second, emergent properties are not aggregates; that is, they are not just the predictable results of the summation of unit properties, and they produce novelty into systems. Third, to be considered emergent, new entities, processes and so on should be causally effective; emergent properties are not epiphenomenal (either illusions or descriptive simplifications only). This means that the higher-level properties should have causal effects on the lower-level ones.

Emergence is often depicted as a process in which macroprocesses and properties "emerge" from micro processes and properties, that is, the properties of the whole emerge from the properties of its parts. These new entities have novel properties in relation to the properties of the constituent parts. In particular, it is not only that the emergent level has its own laws and modes of operation but rather, that it can interact, and causally impact upon, the parts from which it emerged—a process known as downward causation.

The concept of emergence is a central thread uniting many nonreductive approaches to social science. In this respect Durkheim was a key figure, and emergence was a major component of his theoretical and empirical work (Sawyer 2005, 100–24). Durkheim argued that the combined interaction of individuals gives rise to a new emergent entity called society and that this entity could only be understood on its own terms and not in terms of psychology, or even worse, human nature. For Emile Durkheim (1964, 98–103), "society is not a mere sum of individuals," and if it were, "sociological laws can only be a corollary of the more general laws of psychology; the ultimate explanation of collective life will consist in showing how it emanates from human nature in general." In the context of IR theory Durkheim was certainly vindicated when Morgenthau produced just such a theory of international politics. The emergentist reaction to Morgenthau came from the structural realism of Kenneth Waltz (1979).

Although not explicitly employing emergence as a central category it is clear that Waltz was keen to develop the notion of an international system structure that has the potential to causally influence the behaviour of its constituent units. His damning critique of "reductionism" begins with the specification of an international "system" composed of a "structure" and "interacting units" (Waltz 1979, 79). Noting that "the same causes sometimes lead to different effects, and the same effects sometimes follow from different causes," he concludes that "reductionist explanations of international politics are insufficient" (Waltz 1979, 37). In rejecting reductionism Waltz (1979, 39) argued that "outcomes are affected not only by the properties and interconnections of variables but also by the way in which they are organized." According to Waltz the structure of the international political system possesses causal properties which produce effects, "shaping and shoving" the behavior of the units in predictable ways.

All structural theories of international politics rely on emergence, even if they do not explicitly refer to this process. Although Wendt's structuralism idealism disagrees with Waltz about how to define structure, he treats his "cultures of anarchy" in emergentist terms, arguing that they have a logic that operates independent of the beliefs of any given individual (Wendt 1999). Wallerstein's systemic perspective likewise treats the relationship of dependency as an emergent property of the system as a whole, which can only be explained at the level of the system and not at all in terms of the behavior of the individual units (Wallerstein 1976; 1979). Emergence has important implications for how we theorize. It requires that we approach theoretical problems from the standpoint that simple relationships between any two phenomena or elements cannot, in aggregation, provide adequate explanations of the behavior of real world phenomena. Consequently, emergence encourages a multilevel mapping of processes and interrelationships, which despite the increased level of complexity, improves the standard of analysis.

Related to the concept of emergence is nonlinearity. Nonlinear systems are systems whose dynamics are not expressible as a sum of the behaviors of its parts. Most physical systems are inherently nonlinear; examples of linear physical systems are rare. The behavior of nonlinear systems is not subject to the principle of superposition. According to this principle it is possible to analyze the behavior of linear physical systems by considering the behavior of each component of the system separately and then summing up the separate results to find the total result. If this principle were to hold in social systems it would imply that such systems did not display emergent properties and that reductionism was a valid strategy. In nonlinear systems small changes in any part of the system, or in the system environment, can produce large changes throughout the system. It is this idea that underpins notions of chaos and "butterfly effects" (Lewin 2001; Gribbin 2004).

Taken together emergence and nonlinearity imply a complex view of causal processes. Any system displaying these two properties will not be susceptible to analysis predicated on the attempt to explain outcomes on the basis of a summation of its parts. Nonlinear systems that possess emergent properties are fundamentally incompatible with a scientific method that examines phenomena through the isolation of elements into dependent and independent variables. CT maintains that this approach is incapable of capturing the flux of causation in concrete situations.

Social systems, although complex, are not chaotic or disordered. As such, they can be understood as a form of organized complexity. The question is, How does this organization occur? The answer highlights another key property of complex social systems, and this is their propensity to *self-organize*. Self-organization can be defined as the spontaneous creation of a coherent pattern out of local interactions. As such self-organizing systems can be characterized as bottom-up systems. The organization that emerges in such systems comes about through the interactions of a mass of individual elements rather than the following of a plan or the influence of a single intelligent executive branch or architect. In open systems the dynamics of self-organization can be affected through an internal change in the system or through changes in the environment. Although many systems are self-organizing, they do not all display the same kind of characteristics or internal structure. Equally, although all social systems begin as self-organizing systems, over time they may develop mechanisms that attempt to exercise some control and direction over the system. Good examples here are the political system and the economic system. An economic system is self-organizing insofar as it changes its internal behavioral patterns and structure in response to a large number of factors (money supply, rate of growth, political context, resource availability etc.). Individual responses to these factors vary across actors with no single actor possessing complete knowledge of the complexity of the overall situation. Nonetheless, even though individual action only takes place within a limited understanding of its place in outcomes, order does emerge at the system level.

However, evolved social systems do exhibit some control mechanisms that attempt to steer the direction of the system as a whole. Governments, political elites, intellectuals, spiritual leaders, and business leaders all attempt to exercise control on the system through the implementation of policies on the basis of some understanding of perceived outcomes. The effects of these interventions, however, are only predictable in the short term since the spontaneous adjustment of the system involves the complex interaction of too many factors, many of which cannot be controlled at all. The fact that social systems do attempt to react, whether steered or not, in specific ways to changes within the system or the environment, however, does mean that they can be considered as complex adaptive systems (Holland 1995).

Complex adaptive systems contain parts which possess memories and have a series of detailed responses to the same, as well as different, contexts/scenarios. They often have the ability to learn from their mistakes and generate new responses to familiar and novel contexts. Feedback is an integral part of this process, since in their attempts to deal with changes in the system or the system environment, agents feed new processes into the system. Feedback is essentially a series of mechanisms that provide a connection between the output of a system and its input, in other words a causality loop. Feedback can be negative (tending to stabilize the system—order) or positive (leading to instability—chaos). The possibility of exercising some control in complex systems through feedback mechanisms is nicely captured in contemporary debates surrounding systems that can be considered teleological. Although contentious, discussion surrounding teleology in CT has concentrated on the distinction between a system displaying self-organizing principles, or one displaying "directedness," or purpose by design; evolution for example (Bar-Yam 1997). Because social systems do, however chaotically, consciously attempt to adapt to change through both planning and feedback they cannot be considered as purely self-organizing. Social systems display both self-organizing properties and organized properties, which probably makes it even harder to theorize them.

The idea of organized complexity and self-organization has been articulated in IR by Waltz (1979, 12). For Waltz (1979, 88), the organizing principle of the international states system is "decentralized and anarchic." Nonetheless, despite being "decentralized and anarchic," patterns of seemingly organized behavior nevertheless emerge, which he argues "derive from the structural constraints of the system" (Waltz 1979, 92). Drawing on microeconomic theory Waltz also alludes to the ability of social systems to self-organize: "order is spontaneously formed from the self-interested acts and interactions of the individual units" (Waltz 1979, 89). Hence, "[o]rder may prevail without an orderer; adjustments may be made without an adjuster; tasks may be allocated without an allocator" (Waltz 1986, 67). In the final analysis, however, Waltz's theory disregards these valuable insights in the hope of producing epistemological order through ignoring the more difficult aspects of complex systems in the hope of producing a parsimonious theory of international politics. In effect, he fails to heed his own warning that "[o]ne must choose an approach that is appropriate to the subject matter" (Waltz 1979, 13).

Integrative Pluralism and Institutional Structure

Given the properties possessed by complex social systems, what are the limitations on theorizing them? Even in a relatively simple complex open system there may well be multiple emergent levels and potentially hundreds of interacting feedback loops. Even if we had accurate knowledge of how many levels and an appreciation of all their properties this would still provide us with little understanding of how that system will behave. Causality is such systems is both networked and summative, making it very difficult, if not impossible, to untangle the contribution of individual causal mechanisms, or combinations of them, in explaining specific outcomes. In complex open systems often the only way to determine what is happening, and why, is to sit back and watch the process unfold.

The idea of sitting back and watching, however, is the empiricist fallacy; in order to watch we are going to have to have some idea of what it is we are looking for, and we cannot look for everything at once. Reducing complexity is one of the functions of theory. "Theory," as Waltz (1979, 8) puts it, "isolates one realm from all others in order to deal with it intellectually." In building representations of open systems, we are forced to leave things out. All theories, insofar as they attempt to isolate and identify the key components and patterns of interaction between elements, achieve their aims through abstraction. The process of abstraction is necessarily an attempt to reduce complexity (Sayer 1992). The level of abstraction possible while still permitting a theory to be "realistic" is always questionable. The extent to which abstraction is justified in modeling any system begins with an inherently subjective judgment but will eventually require validation by the wider scientific community. The pursuit of realistic theories will require lesser degrees of abstraction but produce more meaningful but very specific outcomes. Those keen to identify general laws may therefore resort to a greater degree of abstraction in the attempt. Waltz adopts just this strategy; he hopes to explain a lot of behavior by a limited number of variables.

The distinction between open and closed systems becomes important here. Newton, for example, developed a set of equations that could be applied to the real world, by assuming a closed system. He produced a model that represented a determinate system that was amenable to solution by calculus. Newton's system is a closed system because the equations rely on the fact that "no outside [effects] are to be considered" (Van Gigch 1974, 40). In many respects Newton managed to successfully develop an approach to scientific investigation that was to dominate the natural sciences because the systems he studied were susceptible to such an abstraction. However, despite its success in this domain this particular form of abstraction is not universally applicable. As van Gigch states, "[w]e can only optimize closed systems as models in which all assumptions and boundary conditions are known. Real-life situations are open systems, the portions of which can, at best, be partially optimized" (Van Gigch 1974, 34). Closed-system approaches are typical of the physical sciences, where relationships between variables can be isolated in experiments in order to reveal causal "regularities" in their connections. Denied this opportunity, the biological and social sciences need to oriente their abstractions in a way that reflects the complex nature of their subject matter. Relationships analyzed in the social sciences are more difficult to isolate in any coherent and meaningful way since they are more complex, interrelated, and dynamic. In abstracting a complex system certain properties are necessarily lost.

This implies that we should embrace a pluralist view of theory since each theory may, in its own limited way, capture something important of the object under study. The suggestion that there are multiple valid representations of the same complex system is not new or particularly revolutionary. Different representations capture different aspects of the system's behavior. The commitment to theoretical pluralism is an acceptance of the fact that there are multiple mechanisms at play in social outcomes. Because theories are abstractions, no theory can specify all the potential mechanisms that might produce outcomes. Equally, even if we had complete knowledge of all potential mechanisms it would still not be possible to specify their interplay in concrete situations. As John Collier puts it, "[e]ven if we can specify precisely what it is to be an X, it may well not be possible to specify what X's properties are without considering its relations to other things. This implies a sort of holism of a system and everything with which it interacts" (Collier 2004).

In this situation the importance of context becomes crucial. Each approach in the patchwork will be valid only for a certain range of contexts, so matching theory to context becomes fundamental. However, a feature of complex systems is that context recognition is not a trivial exercise. Contexts that appear similar may actually be quite different, so the process of matching theory to context is problematic at best. Furthermore, complex systems evolve (in a qualitative sense), so fundamentally novel contexts emerge requiring novel theoretical developments.

Sandra Mitchell suggests that one way to think about this is to view theory as an abstract characterization of mechanisms to be deployed in explanations. Theory, of necessity, can only partially describe a limited part of any complex system, yet events in a complex system evolve through the complex interactions of many causal components. "[A]t the theoretical level, pluralism is sanctioned. At the concrete explanatory level, on the other hand, integration is required. However complex and however many contributing causes participated, there is only one causal history that, in fact, has generated the phenomenon to be explained" (Mitchell 2003, 216). Accepting this view, however, requires a reconsideration of the claim that theory is about explaining the relationship between laws (Waltz 1979, 5). Laws, according to the view that dominates IR, are an "observed regular relationship between two phenomena" (Van Evera 1997, 8). Or they can be considered as "a regularity, or repeating pattern, that describes a causal relationship between two or more factors" (Dressler 2003, 390). This view of law is embedded in a Newtonian closed-system view of the world. However, laws in complex open systems do not operate in this way. And the process of theorizing does not depend on explaining relationships between laws, but rather on specifying the properties and potentials of mechanisms and processes. Most theory in IR already engages in this even if it is not explicitly acknowledged.

Waltz, for example, and despite his strong articulation of theory as an explanation of laws, provides an account that specifies the causal power of the structure of the international political system. Certainly, on the basis of this specification, he suggests that some relationships might be law-like, but these conclusions are only possible if the structure has the causal powers he has ascribed to it. Much the same can be said of Wendt's alternative theory of the structure of the system. Rejecting Waltz's overly materialist account of system structure, he suggests that we conceive of the structure in terms of competing cultural logics. He does not attempt to specify a relationship, or regular pattern, between these differing logics but rather articulates what effect they may have in shaping international outcomes. That is, he describes the causal power they are said to possess. On the basis of either theory it may well be that enough empirical research may one day demonstrate that there is a relationship between X structure and Y outcome. And if that were to happen we might be entitled to talk in terms of a law.

However, the complete absence of any such laws in international relations does not suggest the strategy is turning out to be a productive one. Moreover, the nature of complex systems provides an explanation of why such laws have yet to be discovered. Put simply, there aren't any. In which case, defining theory as the explanation of laws and defining laws as repeating patterns that describe a causal relationship between two or more factors seems doomed to fail. Empirical work, then, can be understood as the study of the interactions of theoretically grounded mechanisms in concrete explanatory problems. Such work will always be embedded within theory, but equally the results may actually lead to conclusions that contradict the theory. How is this possible? The answer to this question demonstrates both the possibility of integrative pluralism and how it is already implemented in practice.

All empirical work proceeds on the basis of some theory or other, but researchers are generally aware of other theories surrounding a given object domain. Obviously in the social sciences, it is not possible for any researcher to claim expertise in all theories. Nonetheless, the theoretical framework chosen for any given project will have been developed through a consideration of alternative views, even if these have only been identified in the process of constructing a literature review. As research proceeds through the design and implementation stages, the researcher, although pursuing the question through a chosen theoretical framework, nonetheless remains cognizant of the alternative views. Often disconfirming results of particular pieces of research are only recognized as being disconfirming because the researcher understands the results, not just as disproving the adopted theory, but lending support to another. In this sense integrated pluralism is at the heart of all research. The matching of theoretical positions to problems is not an arbitrary process but relies on the ability of the researcher, or research team, to make an informed decision about how to proceed. Equally, criticism of any piece of social research comes not only (or normally) from within one perspective but from theoretical competitors keen to demonstrate alternative views (Wight 1996). Hence integrative pluralism features at the beginning of every research project and at its end.

The fact of theoretical pluralism in the practice of research should not be taken to suggest that all theoretical positions are capable of being integrated in a straightforward manner. Some theories explicitly rule out a consideration of alternatives. But which ones can be integrated and which ones cannot requires a disciplinary conversation prepared to accept that integrative pluralism is at least a possibility. Current theoretical debate in the discipline does not seem conducive to this discussion. Theories seem to function as identity markers within a social system suffused by battles over resources and power. This should not surprise us. Academic disciplines, as social systems, are themselves complex, self-organizing systems, and as such, they possess all the properties detailed above. As a self-organizing system, however, we can at least recognize that we get the intellectual structure that we create (within the limits of already existing structures and environmental constraints), and this opens up the possibility of change, assuming of course we desire it. But change to what end? What institutional arrangements are more likely to facilitate tolerance, learning, and conversations? What are the conditions that might surround productive scholarly exchanges in the field? How might we restructure the field to increase levels of theoretical exchange? Answers to these questions can only be made on the basis of some theory that identifies some of the mechanisms that create an intellectual structure that produces little integrative pluralism.

According to Richard Whitley (2000), scientific disciplines can be understood as reputational organizations. In the sciences the primary mechanism for members to obtain a positive reputation, and hence an enhanced position in the hierarchy of the field, is to make contributions to the knowledge structure of their field. However, although all the sciences depend to some extent on reputation, the structural configuration varies across disciplines. Whitley identifies two mechanism that help explain the process of acquiring reputation: 1) degree of mutual dependency and 2) degree of task uncertainty.

The degree of mutual dependency refers to the process through which researchers in a discipline are dependent on each other to obtain a reputation. Disciplines that have an applied focus will be very open to their environment; hence reputational mutual dependency will be low, since the reputation of an individual researcher may be less dependent on colleagues than on external bodies. As one would expect in complex systems, differences in this dynamic can occur within systems. Hence political scientists in America have a tradition of interaction with political policy-making elites that those working in Britain do not. The political system in the United States constitutes a more open environment for political scientists than does the British political system. Of course, this is not a uniform process, and some political scientists in Britain do gain some reputational status from external involvement. In a discipline that produces little in the way of applied knowledge, the researchers have to rely on each other for obtaining their reputation. Hence, in such disciplines the process of gaining this recognition is much more dependent on the internal structure of the discipline.

The degree of task uncertainty is related to the uncertainty that surrounds any research when attempting to solve a specific problem. One of the claimed functions of science is to produce new knowledge. Yet, what counts as new knowledge depends, to a large extent, on the background knowledge of the field. If the background knowledge of the field is ordered, systematic, exact, and generalizable, then it increases the ease by which a new contribution can be assessed. Although an unlikely scenario, a good example of this might be a field that has one dominant paradigm. In such a field the background knowledge will be well structured, clear, and comprehensible to all working within the field; hence the task uncertainty of an individual researcher will be low.

Whitley also differentiates between technical and strategic task uncertainty. Technical task uncertainty refers to the degree of disciplinary inconsistency and variability in relation to the methods and procedures accepted to solve problems. In disciplines that are methodologically diverse, it will be difficult to interpret the relevance of test results; hence the degree of technical uncertainty is high. However, if a particular method has been universally accepted as the only legitimate method, the degree of technical task uncertainty is low. Task uncertainty also has a strategic/theoretical aspect. Researchers face uncertainty regarding which problems are important, and what the ultimate goals of their research are. In disciplines displaying a high degree of strategic/theoretical task uncertainty, researchers will be confronted with many different problems, and competing groups within the field will evaluate their relevance and importance differently. Whitley uses these two variables to identify seven structural configurations for scientific disciplines. The most important in terms of the social sciences are partitioned bureaucracy, the polycentric oligarchy, and the fragmented adhocracy.

IR, insofar as it can be considered a discipline, is a fragmented adhocracy. In disciplines of this type there is a high level of task uncertainty both in strategic and technical terms. The solution to both types of uncertainty is to align oneself with one particular approach. In fields of this type certain research methods can be more fashionable than others, but this may change over time because of the unstable overall situation. The fragmented nature of the field ensures that there is also low mutual dependence between researchers when the field is considered as a whole, which produces high levels of mutual dependency within particular research perspectives. Moreover, as Whitley (2000, 159) puts it, "[t]ypically, these fields are open to the general 'educated' public and have some difficulties in excluding 'amateurs' from competent contributions and from affecting competence standards. The political system is therefore pluralistic and fluid with dominant coalitions being formed by temporary and unstable controllers of resources and charismatic reputational leaders."

Fragmented adhocracies display intellectual variety and fluidity with no coherent configuration of clearly defined problem areas. In the absence of clearly demarcated problem areas in need of research, interaction between theoretical perspectives tends to operate on the metatheoretical level. Discussions surrounding ontology, epistemology, and the methodology of research replace the construction of new theories and research programs. To the outsider it is often difficult to identify what the participants do that makes them operate as a whole. There may be no strong coordinating mechanisms that systematically interrelate research results and strategies. No single group controls the discipline and is able to enforce norms of agreed research practices and general research strategies. There may be some interconnection across research groups, but specialization is a predominant feature. As a result, integration of research results into a general framework is not encouraged, and theoretical and empirical diversity is embraced for its own sake. Fragmented adhocracies function without coordination and central reputational control that results in diversity, specialization, and the lack of a theoretical center, or even a core problematique. The absence of such control allows room for more idiosyncratic research practices, since the individual researcher does not have to appeal to the wider research, or public, community for reputational gain. Interestingly, Whitley (2000, 168) argues that in fragmented adhocracies the only sustained controversy, over which the participants genuinely engage in debate, is that of theoretical diversity itself.

Conclusion

Most academic disciplines are in a constant state of flux. Nonetheless, it is possible for them to fall into one of two positions that lead to a state of equilibrium. Since equilibrium is death, disciplines approaching either of these two states need to take remedial action if they wish to survive. The first position arises when there is too much emphasis placed on the exploitation of an already existing research program and too little attention paid to innovative new approaches. In this state, the discipline focuses on short-term gains more than long-term prospects and consequently reduces the adaptability of the field to new situations. IR in the US might be said to be close to such a state. Complex systems rely on their ability to adapt to survive. Unpredicted crises and chaotic events in the environment of a discipline in this state can lead to crises within the organizational structure such that it is unable to adapt to the changing circumstances in a meaningful way. The end of the Cold War and September 11 might be two such examples.

The second position occurs when there is too much emphasis placed on the exploration of new theories in order to establish new research programs. This leads to a failure to exploit the potential of already existing research programs. Disciplines in this state pay too much attention to the long-term activities of exploration compared to short-term gains achieved through exploitation. IR outside of the United States might be legitimately described as existing in this state. Although it might be concluded that this leaves them well placed to deal with novel events and processes, this is not the case. In complex systems, prediction of novel patterns and new structural configurations is impossible, hence while the development of new theories and approaches might be invigorating, it could also turn out to be a waste of time. Moreover, a discipline in a state of enhanced fragmentation suffers particular problems since it may produce too many new theories at a too fast pace for the scientific community to evaluate them as well as inhibit attempts to integrate them into a reasonably coherent knowledge structure.

Understanding the dynamics of complex systems requires a broader understanding of the complexity that exists within them, and this can only be achieved through some sort of integrative pluralism. The preferred state for all disciplines is to find a balance between exploitation and exploration. There is a complex balance between theoretical unity and theoretical pluralism. Contrary to both the unification and the pluralist position, this chapter argues for a position of "integrated pluralism."

We need to be guided in our research practices by the fundamental properties that our systems embody, such as complexity, emergence, functionality, intentionality, and we hope, the capacity for symbolic communication. In such complex systems we are guided not just from the bottom up, but also from the top down. This is the most fundamental methodological principle of an organized complexity approach. Integrative pluralism is not an attempt to forge competing knowledge claims into one overarching position that that subsumes them all. It is not a form of theoretical synthesis (Kratochwil 2003), nor is it a middle ground that eclectically claims to take the best of various theories to forge them into a "grand theory of everything" (Wendt 2000). Integrative pluralism accepts and preserves the validity of a wide range of theoretical perspectives and embraces theoretical diversity as a means of providing more comprehensive and multidimensional accounts of complex phenomena. This should not be misunderstood as a suggestion that a summation of the various theoretical claims will produce a complete account. In the course engagement some theories may ultimately be rejected, and others may undergo substantial change and modification; hence it is not a form of relativism.

Engaging in integrative pluralism carries risks, and some theories may not survive. Which theories contribute to our overall stock of knowledge, and which fall by the wayside, however, is not an issue that can be resolved solely in the heat of metatheoretical debate. The ultimate test of integrative pluralism will be practice, but this is a practice that cannot even begin unless we have some sense of its problems, possibilities, and practicality. Because there are no precise solutions for complexly organized systems, there is no one method for their study. It isn't quite "anything goes," but we cannot tell what "goes" without trying it, and there are no rules we can specify in advance that might tell us either how to proceed or when we are achieving success. Integrative pluralism requires creativity and openness that is not necessarily encouraged in current disciplinary research training. The idea of theoretical pluralism is not new, and it is rare to find any theorist consistently arguing against it. Despite the consensus surrounding the need for pluralism, however, there are few, if any, clear attempts to put it into practice (Steinmetz 1993). This chapter has attempted, in its own limited way, to begin the conversation; it cannot end it.

Bibliography

Bar-Yam, Y. (1997). *Dynamics of complex systems: Studies in nonlinearity.* Boulder, CO: Westview.

Bhargava, R. (1993). *Individualism in social science: Forms and limits of methodology.* Oxford: Oxford University Press.

Campbell, D. (1998). *National deconstruction: Violence, identity, and justice in Bosnia.* Minneapolis: University of Minneapolis Press.

Chalmers, A. F. (1999). *What is this thing called science?* Buckingham: Open University Press.

Checkel, J. T. (1998). The constructivist turn in international relations theory. *World Politics* 50(3), 324–348.

Cilliers, P. (1998). Complexity and postmodernism: Understanding complex systems. London: Routledge.

Collier, J. (2004). Organized complexity: Properties, models and the limits of understanding. At Biennial Havana International Complexity Seminar.

Cudworth, E., and Hobden, S. (2011). Posthuman international relations: Complexity, ecologism and global politics. London: Zed Books.

Durkheim, E. (1964). *The rules of sociological method*. New York: Free Press.

Feyerabend, P. K. (1975). Against method: Outline of an anarchistic theory of knowledge. London: NLB.

Fuller, S. (2000). *Thomas Kuhn: A philosophical history for our times*. Chicago: University of Chicago Press.

Fuller, S. (2003). *Kuhn vs. Popper*. Cambridge: Icon.

Godfrey-Smith, P. (2003). Theory and reality: An introduction to the philosophy of science: Science and its conceptual foundations. Chicago: University of Chicago Press.

Green, D. P., and Shapiro, I. (1994). Pathologies of rational choice theory: A critique of applications in political science. New Haven, NJ: Yale University Press.

Gribbin, J. R. (2004). Deep simplicity: Chaos, complexity and the emergence of life. London: Allen Lane.

Habermas, J. (1987). *The philosophical discourse of modernity*. Cambridge, MA: MIT Press.

Hacking, I. (1983). Representing and intervening: Introductory topics in the philosophy of natural science. Cambridge: Cambridge University Press.

Hayek, F. A. (1982). *Law, legislation and liberty: A new statement of the liberal principles of justice and political economy*. London: Routledge.

Hume, D. (1985 [1777]). *Essays, moral, political, and literary*. Indianapolis, IN: Liberty Classic.

Hume, D. (1986 [1740]). *A treatise of human nature*. Harmondsworth: Penguin.

Jackson, P. T. (2011). *The conduct of inquiry in international relations: Philosophy of science and its implications for the study of world politics*. London: Routledge.

Jervis, R. (1997). *System effects: Complexity in political and social life*. Princeton, NJ: Princeton University Press.

Keohane, R. O., and Martin, L. (2003). Institutional theory as a research program. In C. Elman and F. M. Elman (Eds.), *Progress in international relations theory: Appraising the field*. Cambridge: MIT Press.

King, G., Keohane, R. O., and Verba, S. (1994). *Designing social inquiry: Scientific inference in qualitative research*. Princeton: Princeton University Press.

Koehler, W. (1981). Closed and open systems. In F. E. Emery (Ed.), *Systems thinking: Selected readings*. Harmondsworth: Penguin.

Kratochwil, F. (2003). The monologue of "science." *International Studies Review* 5(1): 124–128.

Kuhn, T. S. (1962). *The structure of scientific revolutions*. Chicago: University of Chicago Press.

Lake, D. A. (2011). Why "isms" are evil: Theory, epistemology, and academic sects as impediments to understanding and progress. *International Studies Quarterly* 55(2), 465–480.

Lapid, Y. (2003). Through dialogue to engaged pluralism: The unfinished business of the third debate. *International Studies Review,* 5(1), 128–131.

Lawson, T. (1997). *Economics and reality: Economics as social theory*. London: Routledge.

Leon. D. (2006). On the social science of international relations: Presuppositions, microfoundations, and the implications of emergence. *47th annual convention of the international studies association*. San Diego, USA.

Lewin, R. (2001). *Complexity: Life at the edge of chaos*. London: Phoenix.

Luhmann, N. (1995). *Social systems: Writing science*. Stanford, CA: Stanford University Press.

Luhmann, N. (1997). Globalization or world society: How to conceive of modern society? *International Review of Sociology*, 7(1), 67–80.

Maturana, H. R., and Varela, F. J. (1987). *The tree of knowledge: The biological roots of human understanding*. Boston. MA: Shambhala.

Mingers, J. (1995). *Self-producing systems: Implications and applications of autopoiesis*. London: Plenum Press.

Mitchell, S. D. (2003). *Biological complexity and integrative pluralism*. Cambridge: Cambridge University Press.

Moravcsik, A. (1997). Taking preferences seriously: A liberal theory of international politics. *International Organization,* 51(4), 513–553.

Morgenthau, H. (1973 [1948]). *Politics among nations: The struggle for power and peace*. New York: Knopf.

Olson, M. (2000). *Power and prosperity: Outgrowing communist and capitalist dictatorships*. New York: Basic Books.

Popper K. R. (1952). *The open society and its enemies*. London: Routledge.

Rosenau, J. N. (1990). *Turbulence in world politics*. Princeton: Princeton University Press.

Rothheim, R. J. (1998). On closed systems and the language of economic discourse. *Review of Social Economy* 56(3), 324–334.

Sawyer, R. K. (2005). *Social emergence: Societies as complex systems*. Cambridge: Cambridge University Press.

Sayer, A. (1992). *Method in social science: A realistic approach*. London: Routledge.

Schroedinger, E. (1944). *What is life? The physical aspect of the living cell*. Cambridge: Cambridge University Press.

Schweller, R. (2003). The progressiveness of neoclassical realism. In C. Elman and F. M. Elman (Eds.), *Progress in international relations theory*. Cambridge: MIT Press.

Sil, R., and Katzenstein, P. (2010). *Beyond paradigms: Analytic eclecticism in the study of world politics*. Basingstoke: Palgrave Macmillan.

Smith, S. (2003). Dialogue and reinforcement of orthodoxy in international relations. *International Studies Review*, 5(1), 141–143.

Snyder, J. L., and Jervis, R. (1993). *Coping with complexity in the international system*. Oxford: Westview Press.

Steinmetz, G. (1993). *Regulating the social: The welfare state and local politics in imperial Germany*. Princeton: Princeton University Press.

Van Evera, S. (1997). *Guide to methods for students of political science*. Ithaca, NY: Cornell University Press.

Van Gigch, J. P. (1974). *Applied general systems theory*. New York: Harper and Row.

Wallerstein, I. M. (1976). *The modern world system: Studies in social discontinuity*. New York: Academic Press.

Wallerstein, I. M. (1979). *The capitalist world-economy*. Cambridge: Cambridge University Press.

Waltz, K. N. (1979). *Theory of international politics*. Reading, MA: Addison-Wesley.

Waltz, K. N. (1986). Reflections on theory of international politics: A response to my critics. In R.O. Keohane (Ed.), *Neorealism and its critics*. New York: Columbia University Press.

Weinberg, S. (1992). *Dreams of a final theory*. London: Pantheon Books.

Wendt, A. (1999). *Social theory of international politics*. Cambridge: Cambridge University Press.

Wendt, A. (2000). On the via media: A response to the critics. *Review of International Studies* 26(1), 165–180.

Whitley, R. (2000). *The intellectual and social organization of the sciences*. Oxford: Oxford University Press.

Wight, C. (1996). Incommensurability and cross paradigm communication in international relations theory: What's the frequency Kenneth? *Millennium* 25(2), 291–319.

Chapter 3

Musings on Complexity, Policy, and Ideology

Christopher A. Ford

Complexity thinking (CT) has provided valuable insights in a number of fields. Its contributions have been most pronounced in the sciences, but there is also a significant and growing literature exploring the implications of CT in the social sciences. Precisely to the degree that one takes CT seriously as an important window upon the dynamics and phenomena of the natural world of chemical, biological, and physical processes, one must be willing seriously to consider its potential relevance in the human world of social interactions and cultural development.

As we shall see, there may be some important differences between these arenas, but at one level it would be startling if the insights of CT proved entirely inapplicable to interhuman interactions. After all, human affairs seem to be characterized by intricate positive and negative feedback loops, an acute sensitivity of outcomes to initial conditions, a concomitant resistance to linear predictability and susceptibility to rare but dramatic transformational effects, and a tendency to develop elaborate higher-order rules of interaction out of the raw material of comparatively simple unit-level behaviors. In these regards, the human world would indeed seem to have many of the characteristics of a complex adaptive system as understood by CT theorists. This has led social scientists to be increasingly interested in how the lens of CT can help them understand their subjects.

The emphasis of most work to date on CT in the "soft" world of social sciences and public policy, however, has for the most part been analytical, rather than normative or prescriptive. Yet if CT offers us lessons about the behavior of complex adaptive systems, and if it is indeed possible to conceive of human society as a complex adaptive *social* system (CASS), then CT may also have something valuable to teach public policy makers—whose job it is not simply to describe or understand their world but in fact also deliberately to *alter* its course in some fashion.

Yet this process of lesson learning is far from straightforward, for in some ways the shift from merely descriptive purposes to *manipulative* purposes—a term that I use here in a strictly neutral sense, and without the moral connotations that the word "manipulation" can sometimes imply, for it is a key purpose of public policy to bring about *change* in the human environment, and this requires the purposive manipulation of system inputs in order to achieve desired outcomes—is a more intellectually portentous one than the shift from the natural sciences to the interhuman realm. For policy makers, it is not enough to use CT as a way through which the world can be better understood. For them, the key questions are the degree to which CT-derived understandings can be used to improve leaders' ability deliberately to *change* the world in specific ways. How, for instance, can CT be used as a tool with which to improve the development of public policy alternatives and as a way of grappling with the challenges of incomplete information and unpredictability?

This chapter posits that policy makers can indeed learn from CT, but that it presents significant challenges to the very *idea* of public policy—challenges which must be overcome if CT is really to benefit public policy making—and the lessons it offers are by no means straightforward. If CT is to provide in any sense an "answer" to public policy problems, public policy makers must be able first to answer the vexing questions that complexity raises about the policy-making enterprise itself. If CT is right about the deep unpredictability of system outcomes in a complex adaptive system, for example, is it actually possible to talk intelligibly about public policy making at all? This is what I will term the "policy-maker's paradox": the conundrum presented by CT's suggestion that modest policy inputs *can* indeed bring about transformational change, but that such changes are deeply unpredictable and hence uncontrollable—making the very *idea* of policy making highly problematic.

I will argue in this chapter that CT offers valuable insights to the policy maker with regard to dealing with the problems of incomplete information and outcome unpredictability. Part of the answer to the challenges of the policy-maker's paradox lies in strategies of what one might call "perturbation management"—that is, the deliberate adoption of strategies and organizational forms through which leaders seek to equip themselves to cope with unforeseen events, either negative or positive. Scholars and analysts have focused with increasing interest upon these approaches in recent decades, though only quite imperfectly in the arena of public policy itself.

Such an emphasis upon perturbation management, however, is a reactive and largely negative vision, focused upon how best to armor the policy process against unplanned contingencies. Does CT offer us any hope of doing more? Does it offer any hope of salvaging a proactive and *affirmative* approach to public policy capable of surviving the subversive implications of the "policy-maker's paradox"? Perhaps. Herein, I attempt to go beyond the largely reactive agenda of unpredictability management in order to suggest—albeit in a necessarily speculative way—that applying CT insights in the realm of interhuman reactions is different from applying it in the natural sciences. This difference, I suggest, may provide leaders some ability to rescue policy making from utter unpredictability, thereby salvaging something of public policy's *positive* vision of purposive systemic change.

In particular, our answer may lie in the fact that the unit-level participants in a complex adaptive *social* system are *humans*, and not simply molecules in some autopoietic broth or lines of code in an agent-based software application. Because humans possess the ability, and indeed the tendency, to structure their behavior in important and at least partially predictable ways according to cognitive frameworks or memetic constructs that are themselves subject to deliberate alteration or influence—frameworks that are thereafter capable of more or less autonomous quasi-epidemiological propagation throughout any given human population—there may be some hope that the purposive manipulation of *ideational* inputs may provide a tool with which systemic outcomes may sometimes be influenced in broadly predictable ways.

To the extent that the articulation and manipulation of ideational frameworks provide a way of influencing events within a complex adaptive social system in ways that are at least *somewhat* predictable, therefore, CT may ultimately lead us back the ancient antimaterialist conclusion that *ideas* are among the things that matter most in the human world and that their development and advancement offers a remarkably powerful means by which to bring about change therein. The subversive implications of CT's lesson of deep, forward-looking outcome unknowability may present policy makers with special challenges, but it may yet be that policy making remains, for these reasons, possible after all—and that values, political ideology, cultural baggage, and memetic propagation should be issues of critical concern to complexity-informed leaders.

Attempts to Learn from Complexity Thinking

There is certainly no shortage today of efforts to bring CT to bear in understanding and better coping with various aspects of the world of interhuman relations. There exists, for instance, a sizeable literature seeking to apply complexity-related insights to organizational theory, particularly with regard to business structure and operations. Among other things, complexity-based organizational theory has suggested lessons for business organization and management—though not always ones that are easy to apply in practice.

In CT terms, for instance, the "fitness" of a complex system in its environment is a function of a sort of *managed tension*, of success in hovering at some indefinable (and perhaps shifting) "sweet spot" of dynamic balance between "tight" and "loose" organizational "coupling." According to Russ Marion (1999), for example, fit systems operate at the "edge of chaos . . . at a certain point between tightly coupled and loosely coupled." Their coupling is loose enough that they can dissipate much of the impact of unwelcome or dangerous perturbations, because each component can absorb and neutralize small pieces of perturbation "because of the nature of the relationships among units (*e.g.,* redundancy, overlap) and because the individual units have excess resources." At the same time, such organizations are tightly coupled enough that they are able to respond *adaptively* to change when this is needed—not least when so *directed* by organizational leadership. (If the coupling is *too* loose, a system can wind itself down into the organizational equivalent of heat death, a sort of dead stasis. If coupling is too tight, it can become dangerously rigid, unable to "resist unanticipated, potentially destructive perturbation" as disruptions cascade destructively through the system, shattering it).

A fit organization thus maintains itself at the point where its coupling is "sufficiently tight to allow the emergence of stable structures but sufficiently loose to allow flexibility and change." It is "coupled at the Edge of Chaos where it risks dramatic cascading damage but reaps the benefit of maximum fitness in taking that risk" (Marion 1999, 162, 167–69). Business executives and other leaders, one assumes, should thus seek to keep their organizations in this "sweet spot" of maximally adaptive middle-range coupling—though how this is to be done and where the optimal balance actually *is* would seem to be questions to which organizational theorists can provide no *a priori* answers. (By definition, the right balance point will shift with changing circumstances, and from one organization and institutional mission to the next. Here, perhaps, complexity-informed management is revealed to be more art than science.)

Charles Perrow and others have also done important complexity-infused work on the ways in which organizational failure can occur in complex systems, particularly where their shaping variables "follow different periodicity patterns and are highly coupled with each other." In this understanding, "crises are more the result of complex, tightly coupled relationships than the outcome of inadequate human actions" (Thiétart and Forgues 1995, 25). Such analysis has potential implications in a range of endeavors, including public policy making.

Scott Sagan, for example, has applied such insights to the peculiar public policy challenges of accident avoidance in nuclear weapons command-and-control (C^2) architectures. Taking Perrow's analysis as his conceptual starting point, Sagan has argued that the high interactive complexity and "tight" organizational "coupling" of modern U.S. and Russian nuclear C^2 systems make them highly accident prone regardless of the intentions of their leaders and operators and irrespective of the precautions such officials may take (Sagan 1991, 32–36, 39–46). (Some traditional approaches to reducing accident risks, he warns—such as increasing the use of redundant systems—may actually make things worse (Sagan 2004, 936–38).) From this foundation, Sagan has made a number of suggestions about how to reduce the dangers of accidents involving nuclear weapons (Ford 2010).

More broadly, Leon Fuerth has suggested that CT insights can also teach us something about the *methods* by which public policy decisions are reached. Borrowing the term from Horst Rittel and Melvin Webber, Fuerth describes a public policy world increasingly beset by "wicked problems"—that is, the challenges of managing situations characterized by resolutely nonlinear dynamics, complicated positive and negative feedback loops, and mind-bogglingly intricate interconnections among myriad variables. These, he says, are "a new order of . . . public policy issue[] that reflect[s] the axioms and postulates of complexity theory." (Cyber-security, he contends, is one such arena of "wicked" policy challenge, but hardly the only one.) Policy making in such an environment, Fuerth argues, requires a different approach than has usually been taken within governments. Such matters cannot be stovepiped as the responsibility of a single functional department or agency, he says, and instead may have to be addressed on a government-wide basis (Fuerth 2009, 560–61).

Others have suggested that we may perhaps also need different approaches to *who* it is who makes policy decisions, insofar as there may be no single human "skill set" that is "optimal" for leading a response to such challenges. Addressing "wicked" public policy challenges may therefore demand a variety of inputs and perspectives beyond that which normal functional specialization can provide. In this vision—which can amount, in some articulations, to an ideal of populating leadership ranks with a suitably "diverse" human capital stock (Lefkoff 2010)—theories of conceptual "requisite variety" (Heylighen 2001) should encourage decision makers to seek input from a broad collection of cognitive perspectives, thus helping keep available as large a repertoire of responsive actions as possible.

Other thinkers have sought to move beyond merely responding to "wicked problems" with more organizational centralization—which, somewhat disappointingly, seems to be all that Fuerth was really suggesting by urging the appointment of government-wide policy "czars" for such challenges—to undertake a more fundamental rethinking organizational decision-making precisely in order to avoid such centralization in the first place. Writing on military affairs, for instance, Thomas Czerwinski has urged *devolution* of decision making in order to "distribut[e] uncertainty"—that is, breaking tasks into smaller parts and establishing "forces capable of dealing with each of the parts separately on a semi-independent basis"—in order to enable organizations "to do the *complexity shuttle* better" by remaining in the sweet spot of adaptive survival between the suffocatingly brittle rigidity of Equilibrium and the ungovernable dissolution of Chaos (Czerwinski 1998, 95). Such explicitly CT-derived insights, in fact, lay behind the U.S. Marine Corps release in 1996 of a new doctrinal document on maneuver warfare, a publication that "explicitly rests on the complexity theory concepts" (Alberts 1997, xiii–xv).

In other multifarious efforts to apply CT to security affairs, attempts have been made to use "non-linear dynamical models" as a way to understand terrorist networks—and from this starting point perhaps devise strategies for *damaging* such networks (Vos Fellman 2011, 2, 6). Unsurprisingly, the seemingly nonlinear dynamics of the stock market have also been the subject of much study by economists and others who entertain hopes of better predicting or controlling it (McBurnett 1997, 193). Nevertheless, many scholars have worked hard to expand the subject areas in which "[c]haos has been confirmed by research" (McBurnett 1997, 193). Complexity-inspired work in the public-policy realm seems mostly to have remained descriptive and analytical (Hatt 2009, 314). It is no doubt true that our understanding of many complicated issues has been improved by complexity-based analyses. It has been said, for instance, to be of use in helping explain "the robustness of systems such as markets, cultures, and organizations like firms and political parties," while "[t]he notion of a search across a rugged landscape" can help us better understand "ideas like innovation and political platform formation" (Miller 2007, 215–16, 222, 225). That said, however, such understandings do not necessarily offer useful lessons for the policy maker.

It is not, of course, that descriptive studies have no policy implications. One might not have to look too far, for instance, to see policy implications in Alvin Saperstein's fascinating attempt to evaluate the stability of two-player versus three-player strategic balances by assessing the supposed *Lyapunov coefficient* of such relationships—that is, the measurement of "the rate at which initially neighboring configurations drift apart as the model system evolves." In the mathematics of complexity, a Lyapunov exponent is "linked to the amount of information available for prediction," (Kiel 1997), and a coefficient of less than zero implies predictability, because configurations starting close to each other will remain close over time. A positive coefficient, on the other hand, is "the signature of chaos or instability" (Saperstein 1997a, 152).

Saperstein's attempt to suggest lessons for real-world geopolitics in these terms is highly abstract and stylized, relying, as it does, upon the assumption of hypothesized "confidence" and "fear and loathing" coefficients for an international relationship, which are then assumed to be keyed to arms procurement decisions. Nevertheless, his conclusion that tripolar relationships have a positive Lyapunov coefficient—and are thus considerably more unpredictable and therefore unstable and dangerous than bipolar ones (Saperstein 1997a, 155)—is interesting, quite plausible, and could be seen as providing a sort of mathematical underpinning for the commonsense insight that the continued progress of nuclear weapons proliferation in adding "players" to the world of nuclear deterrence presents a grave threat to international peace and security. In policy terms, such conclusions should presumably reinforce our determination to enforce nonproliferation norms and encourage us to bear even greater burdens and accept greater risks in order to forestall a world in which the number of near-peer global nuclear "players" is greater than two. Saperstein has not, to my knowledge, attempted to tease out such specific policy lessons from these calculations. Nevertheless, it takes little imagination to see that it would likely be good policy to try to avoid high-Lyapunov situations in strategic affairs in which "[t]here is no way of knowing—even approximately—the outcome of any policy or action, and hence major fluctuations may result from minor perturbations . . . [creating the conditions] for crisis instability and war" (Saperstein 1999, 108).

Robert Jervis has also attempted to apply CT insights to the field of high-level policy making in the international arena. Though the examples he discusses are subtle and wide-ranging, however, he offers remarkably little that seems likely to be *useful* to most policy makers. His points are far from wrong, of course, for it is no doubt indeed important for leaders to be aware that they *do* operate within a complex system, that actions can have unanticipated effects, and that one would perhaps sometimes do well to approach goals indirectly and by multiple paths in order to reduce the risk of failure, adopting careful and cautious policies informed by the possibility of dangerous nonlinear consequences (Jervis 1997b, 258–66). The seeming thinness of such recommendations in a field accustomed to looking to deep thinkers for detailed policy guidance is probably not Jervis's fault, however, for as we will see below, CT makes the very *idea* of policy making notably problematic.

The Policy-Maker's Paradox

To my eye, one of the peculiar challenges of CT for the public policy maker— as opposed to, say, a biologist, computer scientist, chemist, mathematician, or even social scientist—is that the nonlinearity and unpredictability it posits as being fundamental characteristics of complex systems are profoundly subversive of how we have traditionally understood public policy making. Complex adaptive systems are highly sensitive to initial conditions, as well as potentially subject to a variety of both positive and negative feedback loops that act either to amplify or to dampen the effect of exogenous perturbations. As a result, although the development of such systems is not *random*, it nonetheless essentially *entirely* unpredictable over the long term.

This fundamental unpredictability introduces great challenges for the public policy maker, because it seems to explode the very idea that the complex adaptive social systems of the human world may be purposefully manipulated in order to bring about particular situational outcomes. What is public policy making about, after all, if not deliberately creating perturbations in the current state of affairs in order to produce a specific, desired situational outcome at some point in the future? If such affirmative, direction-focused change is one's objective, however, the complexity of global life would seem to present a paradox.

On the one hand, CT suggests that as a result of nonlinearity and positive feedback loops, even very small policy inputs do indeed have the potential to bring about transformative change in a complex adaptive social system. In a kind of policy-world analogue to Edward Lorenz's famous "butterfly effect," therefore, one might to this degree hope to change the world of tomorrow in important ways by the policies one chooses today—perhaps even through the use of very small policy inputs.

On the other hand, however, complex adaptive systems are often quite resilient, sometimes being able to absorb significant perturbations without undergoing system-transformative effects. Many inputs, in other words, will be successfully "swallowed" by the system without producing real change. But that's not the only problem. The extreme sensitivity of complex systems to initial conditions and the very potential for nonlinear feedback that makes it possible for small inputs to have dramatic effects also suggest that a policy maker will not be able to predict just *what* effects, if any, any particular intervention will have. Worse yet, we will not even be able to predict whether they will be "good" or "bad." While it may be true that even small actions today are theoretically capable of producing a transformed world tomorrow, in other words, most such inputs probably will not have any significant impact at all, and we can predict neither which ones *will* have a major effect *nor* whether this effect will be beneficial or catastrophic.

Through this prism, our world is thus characterized by a very deep unknowability, which imperils the factual predicate for public policy making. As has been said of complex systems more generally, their "sensitive dependence on initial conditions is profoundly disruptive of the ability to develop rational expectations, especially when any stochastic shocks are present" (Rosser 1997, 211), and indeed CT actually *denies* the possibility of long-term predictions (Harvey 1997, 309). If indeed in nonlinear systems results are not repeatable, and the same experiment may come out differently each time it is performed (Czerwinski 1998, 10), we face profound and essentially insoluble problems of outcome uncertainty. We should expect systems as complex as human society to be characterized by significant and irreducible uncertainties (Hatt 2009, 316), and since "[a]ny effort at long-term prediction in nonlinear systems is highly suspect" under the best of circumstances, it is surely all but "impossible to make long-term predictions concerning group interactions" in society (Kiel 1997, 6, 10).

CT scholars have long recognized that applying its insights to the understanding of human systems offers us, in Ilya Prigogine's words, "both hope and threat." It offers "hope, since even small fluctuations may grow and change the overall structure," but it also contains a sort of threat, "since in our universe the security of stable, permanent rules seems gone forever" (Prigogine 1984, 312–13). In Thad Brown's delightful description, if it is true that "[t]he purpose of theory is to make nature stand still when our backs are turned, [as] Einstein reportedly said," political scientists must confront the fact that "nature often laughs and dances around behind us" (Brown 1997, 136). In this sense, the complexity of global life seems quite unkind to theorists.

From a policy-maker's perspective, however, the problem is more insidious than just teaching us lessons in impermanence and insecurity or confounding our ability to articulate a clear explanatory model. Complexity is particularly subversive of policy making because of its implications for our ability to *control* the world around us. If the animating idea of public policy making is to apply effort and resources today in order to bring about a desired change in the future state of affairs, the complexity of global life seems to subvert its very core. If Michael McBurnett is right, for instance, that the opinion shifts associated with U.S. primary election campaigns have "a positive Lyapunov exponent" (McBurnett 1997, 193), perhaps the most important thing this demonstrates is that their outcomes really *cannot* be predicted.

This sort of conclusion is very problematic for the policy maker, as Alvin Saperstein has observed, because while "[t]he possibility of prediction implies the possibility of deliberate control," it follows that "[i]f prediction is not possible, there is no way of knowing the outcome of a given act or policy, which is synonymous with saying control doesn't exist" (Saperstein 1997a, 145–46). If there is no control, however, there can be no real policy making.

> The role of the policy maker, whether in a domestic or an inter-national system, is to *master* the system: to be able to take actions now which will lead to desirable events, or avoid undesirable events, in the future. Thus he/she must be able to *predict* the outcome of current activities: if I do A, A' will result; if I do B, B' will result, etc. (Saperstein 1997b, 103)

The *historian* might not mind overmuch if the system he studies exhib-its the characteristics of complexity, for as Robert Jervis has noted, that essentially backward-looking discipline is well suited to understanding and chronicling nonlinearity. ("[H]istory is about the changes produced by pre-vious thought and action as people and organizations confront each other through time" [Jervis 1997a, 60].) The policy maker, however, must perforce look forward and necessarily aspires to control outcomes. Yet it is precisely in this direction that CT suggests that our vision is inescapably impaired and our grasp all but completely crippled by outcome unpredictability. If there is no meaningful possibility of control, policy making is essentially impossible. This is the policy-maker's paradox presented by the complexity of global life.

James Rosenau has suggested that this problem of control could create problems for complexity more generally, by leading members of the policy community to reject CT out of frustration with its inability to speak to their needs. As he put it, "all the circumstances are in place for an eventual disillusionment with complexity theory," because despite the analytical value CT can provide, "there are severe limits to the extent to which such theory can generate concrete policies that lessen the uncertainties of a fragmented world." For Rosenau, the frustrations are likely to be most acute precisely to the degree that we look to complexity for guidance in the policy arena, for "it is when our panacean impulses turn us toward complexity theory for guidance in the framing of exact preductions that the policy payoffs are least likely to occur and our disillusionment is most likely to intensify" (Rosenau 1997, 74, 89).

As suggested above, however, I would submit that the problem is much more fundamental than simply that the policy world may come to reject CT. The deeper danger is that CT might demonstrate the fundamental irrelevance of the public policy enterprise as a whole. (If a complex world is indeed deeply unpredictable, and hence uncontrollable, why do we have policy makers in the first place?) This is indeed a challenge with which thoughtful would-be policy makers must struggle.

Responding to the Paradox

Planning for the Unplanned

One answer to the policy-maker's paradox might be that by sharpening their awareness of nonlinear unpredictability, complexity-infused thinking can encourage leaders to take approaches to policy making that *anticipate* the possibility of unforeseen outcomes. Complexity, that is, can teach decision makers to make postures, policies, and organizational forms as flexible and resilient as possible in order to maximize their ability to survive unexpected perturbations. This is only a partial answer to the paradox of course, for it addresses only the problem of unanticipated bumps along the road, rather than whether one can coherently plan one's journey at all. Nevertheless, the art of "perturbation management" provides at least some riposte to the challenges of unknowability.

In some sense, perturbation management long predates complexity theory, inasmuch as the famous Prussian military theorist Carl von Clausewitz, for instance, placed great emphasis upon the unpredictable impact of "friction" and the notorious "fog of war."

> The purpose of any theory of war for Clausewitz is to explore the entire range of possibilities, including counterfactuals in the sense that physicists understand them. It is not to generate a preconceived set of stable relationships, a checklist of laws valid upon any occasion, "since no prescriptive formulation universal enough to deserve the name of a law can be applied to the constant change and diversity of the phenomena of war." (Beyerchen 1997, 160)

On the basis of just such an understanding of the impact of friction—as suggested by Helmuth von Moltke of the Prussian general staff, perhaps best remembered today for his pithy but telling observation that no plan survives first contact with the enemy—much of modern Western military science has come to emphasize small unit autonomy and operational flexibility within broad guidance set by a higher-level commander's intentions (Schmitt 1997, 239–41). (Some modern writers, explicitly invoking CT, have advocated similar approaches for managing high-tech commercial enterprises [Maxfield 1997, 188].)

In the mid- and late twentieth century, the field of systems analysis also came to emphasize the kind of operational flexibility that would enable systems to survive and function in the face of unwelcome perturbations. The founder of the Washington, D.C., think tank Hudson Institute, for instance—the seminal nuclear strategist and futurologist Herman Kahn—preached the virtues for public policy making of what he called "a kind of planned muddling through." In this vision, it was the aim of policy research to "prevent[] the foreclosure of options that would make muddling through impossible, and enhance[] the consensus on basic directions and destinations that makes muddling through successful" (Kahn 2009, 164). As a result, he felt, "[s]ystems, programs[,] and policies should . . . be made as flexible as possible, and be designed to enable future decision-makers to 'muddle through'" (Kahn 2009, 182–83).

One way to do this, Kahn suggested, was to modify systems in order to "enable [them] to cope with 'off-design' situations," in the sense not only of "acquiring emergency capabilities for dealing with relatively less favorable—including improbable—contingencies than those expected" but also of being "able to take advantage of unexpected but more favorable situations if they arise" (Kahn 2009, 165). He also exhorted policy makers to approach their work with intellectual humility, alive to the inescapable possibility that their theories might be wrong. Advocating the "agnostic use of information and concepts," Kahn urged us to be

> genuinely agnostic about many of the themes we use; we simply do not know whether they are correct or not, or if they are, we are not sure of the extent of their validity. It is therefore important to hedge against these theories being right without relying on their being right. (Kahn 2009, 169)

We should, in other words, prepare not only our organizational forms and policy toolkits for "'off-design' situations," but indeed prepare our *minds* as well. In this light, an important criterion for evaluating policy alternatives is how any particular course of action would likely fare in the event that its animating assumptions turn out to be wrong.

Kahn's analysis was not explicitly built upon CT, but it is obviously quite alive to the challenges of nonlinear unpredictability and outcome unknowability, and thus provides one type of answer to the policy-maker's paradox. This is an answer that concedes that we *cannot* really predict or control the future, but which nonetheless aspires to limit the damage that might be caused by potentially destructive perturbations, and to make leaders as prepared as they can be to take advantage of unforseen opportunities.

And indeed, in recent decades there has been significant growth in organizational and management thinking designed to achieve these ends. Beginning with the work of Pierre Wack for Royal Dutch Shell in the 1970s, for example, businesses have been learning a great deal about the importance of scenario-based planning—a method of trying to cope with the unpredictable nonlinearity of one's operating environment that does not tie an organization's fate quite so dangerously to the linear assumptions of traditional trend-extrapolating strategic planning.

As popularized by Peter Schwartz and others, such scenario-based methods are not always articulated in terms of CT. Indeed, Schwartz goes so far as to suggest that scenario planning enables leaders to "*reduce* th[e] complexity . . . [and] unpredictability" of their future environment (Schwartz 1996, 15), which in CT terms is preposterous. In fact, as we have seen, scenario planning is aimed principally at preparing one to *handle* unforeseen events, by encouraging the development of institutional and psychological agility and the maintenance of a maximally broad repertoire of adaptive behaviors which can be drawn upon in unanticipated situations. (As indicated earlier, cyberneticists talk of a "law of requisite variety" pursuant to which the larger the variety of actions available to a control system is, the greater the range of perturbations will be that system can handle without failure. In effect, scenario planning is designed to help build just such variety. It is not, however, about making the future any more "certain" or "predictable" than before.)

As coping strategies in the face of uncertainty about one's future environment, such approaches do offer ways to help minimize hazards presented by the unpredictability that CT teaches us to expect in environments characterized by pervasive nonlinearity and extreme sensitivities to initial conditions. And indeed there is surely much that the public policy community can learn from such approaches, for with the exception of a relatively small number of components of the U.S. policy world—and here the

Pentagon's Office of Net Assessments comes to mind, headed as it has been
since 1973 by Herman Kahn's former colleague at the RAND Corporation,
Andrew Marshall—scenario-based planning seems to figure remarkably little
in America's civilian policy development. Nevertheless, since the domestic
and international political arenas probably *are* complex adaptive systems
(Mann 1997, 136)—and if indeed U.S. officials are today increasingly forced
to spend their time merely trying, as Leon Wieseltier once put it, to "catch
up with the contingencies" (Wieseltier 2009) of their environment—then
there is surely much to be said for trying more explicitly to plan not just
for a single hoped-for outcome but also against a broader landscape of possibilities, both positive and negative.

As we have seen, however, perturbation management is only a *partial*
answer to the policy-maker's paradox. Indeed, it must be admitted that it is
also only a reactive or negative vision, for it consigns public policy, traditionally an arena in which well-intentioned people aspire to change the world
for the good, to the unromantic and grimmer business of merely trying to
keep functioning under a hail of unexpected shocks. In Thomas Czerwinski's words, after all, CT teaches us to eschew "solving the problem" and to
focus instead, and more prosaically, upon how to "cope with the environment" (Czerwinski 1998, 57). As Professor Peter Senge of the Sloan School of
Management has also observed, the Complexity-wise systems analyst avoids
prediction, and remains content merely

> to perturb the model, trying out different variables in order
> to learn about the system's critical points and its homeostasis
> (resistance to change). The modeler is not seeking to control the
> complex system by quantifying it and mastering its causality.
> (Czerwinski 1998, 114)

Perturbation management, in other words, may be a critical skill, but it
does little to recue policy making from CT's subversion of control: it merely
aims to teach us to live a little more safely in an environment that *cannot*
be controlled. But is it possible to retain any more *positive* vision of policy
making? Can public policy makers yet hope to do anything more affirmative
and forward-looking than merely refining the reactive and largely negative
tools of perturbation management?

The Power of Ideas

One answer might be simply to respond in the negative. After losing money
in the collapse of the infamous South Sea Bubble investment scheme, after

all, Sir Isaac Newton allegedly observed in frustration, "I can calculate the motions of heavenly bodies, but not the madness of men." (Perturbation management might tell Newton that he shouldn't have invested all his money in any single place, but he might be right to despair of a theory that recommends any *particular* investment.) If the human world of complex adaptive social systems is indeed fundamentally nonpredictable and nonmanipulable in any kind of deliberate way, one might indeed be tempted to conclude that public policy making in the end is no more than a vain conceit—a sort of necessary joke we play on ourselves rather than admit our powerlessness and sink into an incoherent despair, or perhaps an outright fraud promulgated by those in positions of power in order to justify their existence.

To my eye, however, such despair seems premature, not least because we cannot be *entirely* sure that the lessons of CT translate directly or completely from the realm of mathematics and hard science into the world of human interactions. The conclusion of despair relies upon the assumption that complex adaptive *social* systems are in essentially all significant respects "the same" as complex adaptive systems more generally, and that the former are as deeply resistant to prediction and control as the latter. But is that actually true? If it turns out that the human world is in some meaningful way *different* from the systems studied with such success by Complexity scientists working in biology, physics, computer science, and other such fields, we might perhaps yet hope to find in this difference some basis for insulating the public policy project against the deeply subversive implications of CT's seemingly control-preclusive emphasis upon nonlinear unpredictability.

In this respect, I offer the speculative suggestion that all complex adaptive systems are *not*, as it were, created equal—and that there is something special about *social* systems that may allow us to salvage at least something of the affirmative project of public policy making. Specifically, as a tentative response to CT's seeming subversion of the policy-making paradigm, it may be possible—without too much traducing our emerging understanding of CT in social science applications—that *some* types of policy input seem more likely to have significant effects upon operational behavior and long-term systemic patterns in the human world than others. Some of these inputs may indeed also operate in ways that are less stubbornly "unpredictable" than CT might at first seem to indicate, thus permitting us to hope that enough of possibility for "control" exists for genuinely forward-looking public policy to remain possible.

The key point here is that human actors are *not* easily analogized to the constituent elements of most of the complex adaptive systems studied by CT scientists. We are not mere molecules, for instance, but sentient actors capable of thinking—and thus both of having some understanding of our environment and of acting on the basis of these understandings. And this may make a big difference.

Though CT scholars have long been intrigued by what their theories might teach us about social systems, they have also sometimes seemed uncomfortable with the implications of any attempt to translate things directly into the human realm. Some of them clearly seem to suspect that there is something wrong with assuming that systems of *human* actors are not meaningfully different from systems made up of other components. At least one has openly suggested, in fact, that human systems "cannot be totally assimilated to natural systems, where laws are immutable," because the structure of a *human* one is probably different as a result of "the action of actors inside and outside the organization" (Thiétart 1995, 22). In this vein, CT scholars have occasionally suggested that the very *humanity* of the unit-level components of a social system may to some extent make the lessons of Complexity *themselves* somewhat unpredictable. David Harvey and Michael Reed, for instance, have noted "the 'wild card' nature of human beings and their innovative abilities" as a sort of potential "exceptionality . . . in dissipative systems theory." This does not necessarily mean that Complexity *cannot* be used in the study of social systems, of course, but they stress that one must always be aware of this wild card and "recognize the indeterminate aspect of human nature" (Harvey 1997, 306).

There seems, in fact, to be some debate not just about whether CT insights offer any real "tangible solutions" to the problems studied in the social sciences, but also about whether CT can be applied there—*at all*—in anything more than a "metaphorical" fashion (Cooper 2003). Peter Stewart, for instance, questions the possibility of applying CT analytically in the social sciences. He suspects that adequate analysis of complex phenomena cannot really be done there at all (Hatt 2009, 319) because "[s]ocial processes and phenomena are far too complex for complexity theory to deal with, or profoundly elucidate," and "complexity theories do not provide a particularly effective metatheory of social processes" in the first place (Stewart 2001, 353). Harvey and Reid appear more optimistic, but even they seem to think that merely metaphorical or impressionistic analyses may sometimes be all that one can bring to bear on human problems. In fact, they suggest the greater use of what they call "iconological modeling"—a "heavily intuitive" approach "rooted in a *pictorial method*, in visual correspondences rather than in deductive reasoning," as well as conventional methods of social scientific data collection and analysis (Harvey 1997, 309–11).

It is important to keep such concerns in mind when evaluating Complexity's attempt to leap from the hard to the soft sciences. In fact, one might imagine there to be reason to believe that the policy-maker's paradox is not *quite* as debilitating as it might at first appear, precisely because this translation may be an incomplete one. If human interactions are indeed different from non-human interactions, this difference may provide a foundation for saving policy from the control-preclusive implications of deep unpredictability.

Just *how* different human interactions are from those of molecules in an autopoietic broth or the bundles of software code used in agent-based modeling is no doubt a question on which experts will disagree. It would certainly seem to be true, however, that complex adaptive *social* systems— that is, the subset of complex adaptive systems the unit-level constituents of which happen to be sentient humans—are capable of responding to a type of input that no other complex system seems to be: *ideational* ones. Inputs at the level of conceptual organizing frameworks, narratives that structure people's understandings and expectations of the world around them, seem to be important motivators for behavior in social systems and the political world. Moreover, in its response to specific ideational inputs, human behavior tends to display notable patterns and other regularities that are related to the substantive content of those inputs. If there is a critical locus for difference between complexity in the human and the non-human world, it may indeed lie along this axis.

The nature of humans as idea-seeking creatures, in other words, may limit the degree to which CT insights in the hard sciences can translate smoothly to the analysis of complex adaptive *social* systems. In this ideotropism, there may yet lie some hope for affirmative policy making. At the same time, however, it may be that CT provides useful tools for analyzing the idea systems around which humans tend to orient their behavior, with the result that we encounter a new paradox: our ideomotivational nature means that human behavior will not necessarily quite conform to one would expect from CT, yet CT can help us in understanding the very cognitive frameworks that *separate* us from nonhuman nonlinearity.

And indeed CT does seem to provide an interesting window upon the dynamics of our ideational world. As Robert Artigiani has noted, complex systems—including societies and idea-systems—have ways to police themselves in order to maintain a degree of stability as they dance at the "Edge of Chaos." This he conceives as helping give rise to the phenomenon of purpose or *telos* in a self-organized system, and he feel that the need for systemic self-maintenance in this regard "exerts top-down constraints on how members perceive and react to the world and . . . how the world responds to their actions" (Artigiani 2007). It is in this fashion that "values, ethics, and morals" can be seen as helping "reprogram" the behavior of individual humans in a system by mapping desired and undesired social states. Moral symbols stored in individual minds shape—though by no means rigidly determine—how individuals react in society (Artigiani 2007). This is how idea frameworks can serve as drivers for situational outcomes within complex adaptive social systems.

It may even be that many human systems *need* to organize themselves around relatively clear conceptual frameworks in order to achieve the sort of organizational "fitness" at the "Edge of Chaos" that CT would seem to require in order for a complex adaptive system to survive in a demanding environment. Political ideologies and other value systems, for instance, may serve most effectively as persistent policy guidance for human behavior within a system—providing "rules of thumb" about what outcomes or situations are desirable, what means of pursuing one's goals are acceptable, and other such matters—when they can be maintained at a level sufficiently detailed to be capable of application in most situations, yet sufficiently abstract to avoid systemic rigidity and an incapacity to cope with what Herman Kahn's "'off-design' situations." In this sense, they may function in ways analogous to "commander's intent" in modern, devolved, small-unit warfighting: providing actors with a framework around which to organize behavior and structure priorities as they engage in various improvisional strategies within the ambit of this overall direciton.

Importantly—especially if one is looking for some way to escape, or at least attenuate, the erosive impact of CT upon the very *possibility* of public policy—it must also be observed that ideational inputs and behavior-structuring conceptual systems clearly *can* be deliberately manipulated, for good or ill, by members of the policy-making community. If there are positive rather than merely reactive ways to escape the policy-maker's paradox, then, this seems a promising place to look. The deliberate shaping of *ideas* seems to offer us a chance to affect behavior within complex social systems in ways that are not utterly unpredictable, at least to the extent that such inputs may tend to exert recognizable patterning influences over time.

This insight is, on one level, simply common sense. The human unit-level components of a social system are capable of purposive action motivated not merely by biological needs and raw emotions but also by ideas and ideals. They care about, and change their behavior in response to, the thought structures that shape their interpretation of their environment. Participants in a complex adaptive *social* system, in other words, exhibit a tendency to *act* upon ideas they have come to possess. If these ways are not predictable in detail, then at least they may be quasi-predictable in the aggregate, for choices tend to be perhaps imperfectly but frequently *identifiably* related to the *substantive content* of the ideas that people have come to possess. One might thus suspect that interventions at the level of *idea-systems*—that is, policy inputs designed shape conceptual paradigms—offer at least *some* hope of allowing leaders purposefully to shape situational outcomes in a complex adaptive social system.

Policy Making as Memetic Engineering?

Is there some way more sharply to conceptualize this in terms that make sense through the lens of CT? In other words, is there some way to express the commonsense thought that *ideas matter*, that *some* ideas are stubbornly resistant to change, and yet that from time to time a new concept can catch on like wildfire, transforming the social environment around it? It seems to me that the answer to this question is "yes." Even though its lessons may not translate smoothly from the nonhuman to the human realms, I posit that CT can yet provide a way to help us understand idea systems, offering a window into the propagandist's ancient insight that the development, articulation, and manipulation of value systems can help leaders deliberately reshape the human world, for good or for ill.

One window into the potential power of ideational interventions might come through the concept of what complexity theorist Russ Marion, for one, has called *memetics*. This notion is based upon the idea—first articulated by Richard Dawkins in 1976 (Dawkins 2006), and subsequently picked up by E.O. Wilson (Wilson 1999) and others—that there may exist structured and semi-autonomous "genetic" units of culture that compete with each other for "reproductive" success within human minds. Memetics is a concept-based analogue to genetic evolutionary theory that builds upon Dawkins' neologism of the "meme," a conceptual unit of culture that shapes decisional behavior in conscious actors and which has a specific information content that can be transferred through mimicry, interaction, and teaching.

The academic community still seems to be struggling with precisely what to do with the notion of memetic development, though interesting work is apparently underway on such matters as what dynamics of natural selection are involved in how linguistic formulations compete for acceptance and evolve over time in human speech and writing ("How . . ." 2012). Nor has the security community been entirely idle either, for it has been reported that the U.S. Office of Naval Research recently signed a contract with a software firm to build a program to identify and characterize memes as they develop and propagate. (According to officials from the contractor in question, their approach analogizes "the spread of ideas" to "the spread of disease," using computerized natural language analysis of documentary sources to help intelligence analysts identify brewing social or political ideas, as well as specific populations likely to be particularly susceptible to them [Weinberger 2012, 41].)

Where all of this goes, and how productive such analytical approaches turn out to be, is of course presently unknown. Memetics, however, is a fascinating attempt to grapple in a scientific way with the ancient, and to some extent prescientific, insight that *ideas matter*. If indeed we are right to suspect that ideational influence operations represent as promising a way to achieve public policy-making goals as one could expect to have in an environment characterized by pervasive nonlinearity, memetics deserves more attention.

Memetics, of course, would make little sense as an approach to understanding systems that did not consist of conscious, willful human actors. But as a way of understanding complex adaptive *social* systems—which is precisely what we need to do if we are to bring any of Complexity with us as we make the leap from hard sciences to the human world—there are surely worse ways of conceptualizing the problem than to see systems as being potentially subject to transformative effects as a result of competitive and recombinative meme dynamics. And from this insight, if indeed it proves a valid one, it is but a short step to imagine policy making aspiring to *affect* the paradigmatic "memotypes" of the social system—that is, to deliberately alter the conceptual frameworks upon which human decisions are based as people evaluate their environment, determine what they wish to see happen, and apply themselves in myriad disaggregated ways to whatever tasks they perceive to be most immediately at hand.

A CT-informed approach to public policy making, therefore, might be supposed to require a twofold focus. First, acting upon the important insights into coping with nonlinearity that have been gaining traction in the private sector for years, public policy making would acknowledge its responsibility to help prepare the ship of state not just for what an extrapolation from current trends suggests may occur in the future, but also for *non*-anticipated perturbations. Such a "Black Swan" sensibility—to borrow from Nassim Nicholas Taleb's popularization (Taleb 2007)—would seek to maximize the system's ability to deal with sudden shocks, equipping it as well as possible for agility and responsiveness in taking advantage of whatever opportunities, and coping with whatever calamities, fortune may bring. As we have seen, this aspect of public policy—which I have called perturbation management—is less about determining *where* to lead the polity than simply about preparing it for resilience and flexibility in the face of the unforeseen.

Building upon the idea of purposive ideational input as a potentially system-transforming perturbation, however, the CT-informed policy maker may *also* need to devote time and attention to the realm of ideas as a source of general direction and behavior-shaping guidance for the sociopolitical system. Such attention would presumably involve, first and foremost, articulating and working to build support for a memetic framework that provides actors with a conceptual foundation and direction for their behavioral choices, not least by providing them with a coherent repertoire of policy-relevant "instincts" that will tend to structure actions in characteristic ways over time. It may also require working to *undermine* the legitimacy and perceived conceptual coherence of alternative, competing visions. One way or the other, however, the CT-informed policy maker must devote attention to shaping the world of ideas in the broadest and deepest sense. Precisely because of humans' tendency to use conceptual frameworks in organizing their behavior over time, a leader may by such means hope to influence complex adaptive social systems in ways that are at least *partly* foreseeable.

In this sense, the practical applications of public policy making tend to shade into public diplomacy, intellectual vision-brokering, or even propaganda. This is not really news to true statesmen, however, for the most accomplished practitioners have always understood their work to be as much art as science, and as much about persuasive alchemy as anything resembling an exercise in precision engineering by scientifically informed experts or policy "czars." (Niccolò Machiavelli, it should be remembered, once pronounced himself more awed by the founder of a religion than of a state [Machiavelli 2008, ch. 10].) It is nonetheless useful to recognize the ways in which CT seems to reinforce such ancient wisdom, lest we, in the hubris of our modern technocratic conceit, forget old-fashioned notions about the power of ideas. There is rich irony, of course, in having the *science* of complexity teach us that there may be sharp *limits* to the utility of "science" as a guide to decision making in the human world—even as it points us anew to the very old conclusion that *ideas* have special potency as a means of influencing our fellow man—but we should perhaps take our lessons where we can.

In Lieu of a Conclusion:
Some Thoughts on Ideology as Policy

If indeed the use of ideational influence provides the policy community with some hope of undertaking an affirmative public policy program notwithstanding the challenges presented by the complexity of global life— as I would submit that it does—we would be wise to study politico-conceptual history with special attention, in order to sensitize ourselves to the complicated relationships of reciprocal causality that cognitive frameworks have with their surrounding human environment. A CT-informed leader needs to be at home in the ebb and flow of subtle conceptual currents, for operations in this medium are critical to his chances of success. The history of ideas' development, propagation, and manipulation in the sociopolitical world, therefore, should be at least as important a focus of public policy research as any other.

One might perhaps imagine cognitive frameworks and sociopolitical ideologies as being complex adaptive meme systems that *themselves* function in some of the ways CT-derived organizational theories might expect. A "fit" cognitive framework, for instance, might be said to thrive "on the Edge of Chaos" by being tightly coupled enough that its conceptual elements provide, in a single "package," a coherent way for adherents to understand and cope with the principal challenges presented by their sociopolitical environment, yet without proving so rigid a doctrinaire that the schema crumbles upon encountering the first perturbation not foreseen by, or intelligible within, its frame of reference. Fit thought systems are loosely coupled enough that they can "explain" and accommodate a good deal of circumstantial caprice without suffering a catastrophic collapse of legitimacy or coherence, but they still manage to hang together in a form recognizable by their adherents, and third parties, as being the "same" framework over time.

Interestingly, the issue of ideational manipulation—and its potential importance—has not been overlooked in past approaches to policy development in the face of the complexity-driven challenges of nonlinear unpredictability. Along with his more well-known calls for making organizational systems more capable of dealing with "'off-design' situations," Herman Kahn also called, at various points, for the deliberate and systematic construction of a new "ideology" as a part of mankind's effort to shape (and improve) its future. Such an "ideology of development based on futurology," he felt, should not be a maladaptively rigid, all-encompassing framework, but it should at least provide people with a "valid vision of the future" that is "technically sound, psychologically relevant, and dramatically imaginative," and around which they can shape their responses to their environment. Kahn appears to have viewed the development of such an ideology not simply as a vague desideratum but as a very feasible public policy undertaking. The new framework, he felt, would need to be deliberately articulated by thinkers such as himself and would need thereafter to be propagated through "organized efforts to get people to accept or use the new vision of the future communicated to scholars, opinion leaders, and directly to the public" (Kahn 2009, 253, 256, 258).

Whatever one makes of Kahn's proposed "ideology of the future," it seems to flow from what we should now understand to be a reasonable insight. Because ideas matter in how humans organize responses to their environment, because some of these patterns of organization exist and propagate in recognizable conceptual "families" over time, and because such patterns impose a degree of regularity (or at least identifiable lineage) upon social systemic development, ideational manipulation may offer a way for leaders to shape the future notwithstanding CT's policy-subversive implications. If this is so, the study, development, and manipulation of the cognitive frameworks that help structure human actions in the social world—e.g., political ideologies—are perforce subjects of surpassing importance for public policy makers.

The political world offers many examples of how ideas shape decision making, how such concepts are sometimes purposefully manipulated, and how they can also come to acquire considerable power in shaping actors' behavior and acquiring a sort of cognitive "momentum" of their own. In such dynamics, particular thrusts and themes propagate themselves both laterally ("catching on" among greater numbers of people) and forward in time, maintaining a recognizable "family" resemblance even while changing in response to circumstances.

And such "families" can clearly prove seductive—compelling to the point of constituting both drivers and shapers of individual and collective behavior in social and political communities in ways that would probably not be considered outrageous by a traditional scholar of ideas, but which are too often ignored by those who prefer to see human affairs as being the result merely of "structural" economic interests, other relationships of raw power and instrumental choice, or reductionist biologies of biochemical or psychological determinism. Because memetic "families" are capable of exerting recognizable influences upon their hosts, however—and because political ideologies are clearly highly manipulable, for good or for ill, by political leaders—attention to them and their details is certainly important for those who would shape public affairs, as well as for those who would *counter* the efforts of others to do so. But there is more involved here merely than the existence of a tool whereby the cynical attempt to manipulate those more impressionable.

Idea systems are also, it would appear, capable of all but bewitching even some of the most thoughtfully self-aware political actors, sometimes even being "caught" by those who might originally have set out to manipulate or co-opt such frameworks with a cold opportunism. They can be tenacious shapers of behavior for masses and elites alike, with the result that policy choices can tend over time to exhibit patterns clearly traceable to the structuring and organizing principles of the conceptual framework.

More intriguingly, memetic frameworks can also be engines for public policy change in their own right. Idea systems can come to face internal contradictions or tensions as they struggle to reach a point of organizational "fitness" by accommodating exogenous reality *enough* to remain relevant and legitimate in the eyes of their adherents, yet without doing so in ways that forfeit their coherence and conceptual distinctiveness.

Memetic inheritance can be a powerful force, yet some of this power comes—as in the biological genetics from which the meme of memetics is itself derived—more from the ability to create a *lineage*, as it were, than from utter consistency. The "objective" of both genes and memes, one might say, is to propagate themselves through time, even though this often requires changes in form in response to selective pressures. Ideas have "momentum" that allows them to project their own characteristic patterns and themes forward through time, even in the face of considerable change, yet is precisely a meme's adaptive capacity for at least *some* change that conduces to its survival and propagation in a nonstatic environment.

Some such change, in fact, can occur precisely *because* of this conceptual inertia, for elements *within* an ideological system can come to exist in tension with each other, driving the system in new directions as meme adherents seek to resolve its contradictions or escape its paradoxes precisely because they *are* adherents. (Nonadherents, after all, would not trouble themselves to render such faithful service to the conceptual scheme.) And while ideological systems can sometimes absorb considerable perturbations, they can also reach the point at which the entire system disaggregates—thus permitting the crystallization of a new order around a *different* organizing concept.

If we conceive of a political ideology as a complex adaptive *memetic* system (CAMS), we can understand it as surviving—to the extent that it does, of course, for not all of them do—because it is ordered and structured in distinctive ways that make it attractive to its host population and as being "fit" for *continued* survival to the extent that it can evolve over time to remain attractive to its adherents as a conceptual organizing system in a changing world. This development can occur both as a result of deliberate choices by key actors and as a result of the memetic system's own internal dynamics and tensions.

This is consistent, for instance, with what organizational theorists informed by CT have seen in the phenomenon of entrepreneurship, which is envisioned as a form of structured and deliberate *instability* vital to the self-renewal and survival of an organization (or any other complex system) in new forms of order, but which must nonetheless be coupled with a degree of certainty and predictability so that it avoids the disorder of outright chaos (Thiétart and Forgues 1995, 24, 28). The perpetuation of memetic themes forward through time in progressive variations, each in some way different but nonetheless recognizable as part of the same conceptual "genealogy," recalls Robert Artigiani's point that in social systems operating on the edge of chaos, survival does not call for "stability" as much as "evolvability" (Artigiani 2007).

There could be any number of engines that drive the memotypical variation that results in such evolution. Conceptual frameworks can shape the behavior of policy-making actors by structuring how they define their policy ends and assess inputs from their decisional environment, but policy makers can also *deploy* specific memetic formulations in service of their policy ends. Purposeful and self-conscious ideological entrepreneurship by one or more conceptual manipulators, whether proactively (e.g., actually seeking to create a new policy-shaping discourse) or more reactively or defensively (e.g., in providing a rationalization for choices made on other grounds, or in supplying reasons to oppose the plans of others), can thus occur. Such entrepreneurship is in some sense akin to the sort of systemic change idealized by organizational theorists who seek to identify ways for corporate leaders deliberately to cultivate a degree of instability as a way of developing "a repertory of responses to environmental demand" (Thiétart and Forgues 1995, 23). Such instability makes systems "periapatetic in the sense that they constantly seek new organizational states" in their effort to survive over time in a changing environment (Harvey 1997, 303).

But this is not the only engine for change. In addition, as suggested above, a CAMS might in time be discovered to have its own internal contradictions. Artigiani suggests, in fact, that Gödel's theorem may indicate that internal contradictions of some sort are unavoidable for any system claiming to have theorems and axioms that are logically consistent (Artigiani 2007). This insight is worth building upon. In the language of formal mathematics, an axiomatic system is said to be *consistent* if the operation of its rules can never produce two mutually contradictory statements. Gödel tells us, however, that a consistent system will necessarily be *incomplete*, in that it will contain true propositions that cannot be reached by proceeding from the axioms according to the system's rules for deriving propositions. The price of being complete is apparently inconsistency; and the price of consistency is incompleteness.

If something as formalized as Gödel's theorem can be applied in the memetic realm, at least by analogy, it may be that every ideology will possess conceptual holes (incompleteness) or contradictions (inconsistency) with which its adherents will have to struggle at one point or another. This provides another source of memetic variation or divergence and a driving force for evolution over time—with perceived incompletness and/or inconsistency serving as points of contestation and catalysts for memetic evolution, at least where they do not precipitate outright memetic collapse. (Not entirely unlike biological ones, one should remember, memetic bloodlines can die out if they prove ill adapted to their environment.)

Whatever the mechanism, however, one might expect from CT that even though a CAMS evolves over time, it will often tend to exhibit characteristic "family" patterns and maintain distinctive conceptual themes. Artigiani and Gianfranco Poggi may be right that societies are most likely to evolve successfully when they are not tied inescapably to sets of transcedent, timeless ideological rules, because such inflexibility will likely prove maladaptive in the face of unexpected perturbations (Artigiani 2007). Nevertheless, survival on the "Edge of Chaos" does not reward *unlimited* flexibility. A degree of structure and consistency is also needed and must be maintained in some dynamic balance with a system's periapatetic search for environmentally adaptive phenotypical variations, which returns us to the koans of *order-within-disorder* and *disorder-within-order*.

In terms of CT, both stability *and* explosive instability are a kind of equilibrium. But the fitness of a complex system on the "Edge of Chaos" is not about equilibrium in the normal sense, but about managed tension—a sort of dance. Dissipative systems, it is said, are characterized by their ability to remain far from equilibrium, in a kind of

> dynamic tension between their ability to accumulate negentropy [negative entropy] and their need to transfer their positive entropy to the environment. If they can sustain this tension, then under proper circumstances they can achieve a state of *net negative entropy* and persist. (Harvey 1997, 303)

It is in the recurring patterns of a particular mode of sustaining this dynamic tension—a particular dance, if you will—that one may be able to see a conceptual "family resemblance" between a system's states in a time series.

This is complexity's order within disorder, for as its theorists tell us, dynamical systems seem to tend to organize themselves around what David Ruelle called "strange attractors." Behavior within an attractor's "space" can be highly unpredictable, but the system nonetheless tends to *return* to this space repeatedly. The attractor thus creates an "envelope" for permissible behavior, such that the system is able to absorb many perturbations without deviating fundamentally from a fundamental pattern (Thiétart and Forgues, 1995, 20–21, 26). From time to time a perturbation may come along that causes the entire system to undergo a transformation, jumping into the "space" of a *new* attractor that might be said to represent an alternative "family" of dynamical answers—a new paradigm that may itself be fairly stable over time—but complex systems are striking for the degree of consistency they tend to demonstrate over time.

This has important implications when applying CT insights to meme systems, for it is this consitency which enables us to speak of ideological intertia or momentum, to understand the possibility that memetic manipulation can have lasting effects in systems of social and political order, and to study sociopolitical behavior as it is shaped by complicated mechanisms of ideational entrepreneurship, environmental reactivity, and internal contradiction. It has long been understood that ideology is "a realm of contestation and negotiation, in which there is a constant busy traffic: meanings and values are stolen, transformed, appropriated across the frontiers of different classes and groups, surrendered, repossesed, reinflected" (Eagleton 1994, 187). CT provides a prism through which to express and help understand the development of such complicated conceptual relationships and their evolution over time.

Significantly, however, these ideas do not evolve entirely "on their own," for memes can have no existence or meaning without there also being the existence of *minds*. (The converse, by the way, may also be true.) These dynamics of contestation, appropriation, and transformation are what happens when minds interact with memes—that is, when people try to conform their behavior to what a memetic framework suggests is the "right" thing to do, to resolve tensions within and between value systems, and to *use* invocations or partial reformulations of cognitive frameworks as tools in their interactions with others. Such processes can clearly have a very real impact in shaping, and indeed helping to *constitute*, the social environment, and they are capable of doing so in ways that are not utterly unpredictable.

The concept of complex *memetic* systems may provide only an incomplete answer to the policy-maker's paradox that we see in CT's problematization of control, but this is something of an answer nonetheless. In general, it may be said of complex phenomena that within the "space" defined by a particular conceptual "attractor," behaviors are indeed unpredictable and hence uncontrollable. Except for the occasional case in which a perturbation causes the entire system to re-orient in a *different* "basin of attraction" around a successor attractor, however, behavior will tend to be fairly consistent and predictable—sometimes for considerable periods of time—in the sense that it will tend to keep its unpredictable cycles, most of the time, within a specified area of behavior space defined by a specific attractor.

In ideational terms, this is a way to understand the stability and quasi-predictability that can be provided by a political ideology or some other conceptual organizing scheme: such a framework serves as an attractor, defining the boundaries of what behavior is permissible, structuring actor preferences and priorities, and even helping determine what alternatives are conceivable in the first place. This stability is of indefinite duration, of course, for some perturbation could drive the system to reorient itself around a different attractor. Nevertheless, this dynamic offers a general degree of predictability as long as a particular attractor prevails—and with this degree of predictability, some possibility of control.

And this is perhaps our second answer to the policy-maker's paradox, for to the extent that one can shape the ideational attractors operative within a complex adaptive social system, one can influence behavioral outcomes therein in broadly consistent ways—at least for a while—by tying them to paths that are demanded or legitimated by the substantive content of those attractors. The memetic conception of CT-informed policy making, in other words, suggests that one might retain at least some hope of effecting purposeful systemic change by seeking to alter the concepts and conceptual interrelationships that constitute attractors around which orbit the ideological patterns that help shape unit-level operational behavior and thus drive concrete system outcomes. This conceptual model offers little hope of controlling system outcomes in detail, but it suggests the possibility of constraining them to some degree in the aggregate, at least for a while. Since human social environments are thus inherently ideocompetitive, policy makers should be keenly aware of the politically morphogenic properties of their memetic articulations; such conceptual framings, at least in part, are the stuff of which power and policy are made.

Even given all the difficulties of applying CT in the human realm, this may be a lesson that policy makers can learn beyond merely the hedging strategies of perturbation managemnt. If indeed CT reinforces the intuitive insight that an "ideology has its own law of motion" (Abercrombie 1994, 155)—and if such "laws" exercise a real influence upon outcomes that is predictable at least in the sense that memetic schemes tend to predispose specific *types* of behavior and relationship patterns—then the policy maker may have to become ideology's architect, engineer, attorney, and publicist. There is nothing particularly new in the observation that ideas matter, that leadership involves the invocation and manipulation of such cognitive frameworks, and that the use of such tools can produce powerful effects. It is fascinating, however, to have been led back around to such wisdom by the seemingly policy-preclusive teachings of CT.

Bibliography

Abercrombie, N., Hill, S., and Turner, R. S. (1994). In S. Žižek (Ed.), Determinacy and indeterminacy in the theory of ideology. Verso, London, 152.

Alberts, D., Thomas, J., and Czerwinski, T. (1997). Preface. In D. Alberts and T. Czerwinski (Eds.) *Complexity, global politics, and national security.* Washington, DC: National Defense University.

Artigiani, R. (2007). History, science and meaning. *Journal of Natural and Social Philosophy,* 3(1), 108–121.

Beech, M. F. (2004). Observing Al Qaeda through the lens of complexity theory: Recommendations for the national strategy to defeat terrorism. *Center for strategic leadership sudent issue paper,* vol. S04–01.

Beyerchen, A. D. (1997). Clausewitz, nonlinearity, and the importance of imagery. In D. Alberts and T. Czerwinski (Eds.), *Complexity, global politics, and national security.* Washington, DC: National Defense University, 153.

Brandoff, J, et al. (2008). Applying the methods and approaches of complex systems to counter-terrorism. *NECSI Summer School* manuscript.

Brown, T. A. (1997). Nonlinear politics. In L. D. Kiel and E. Elliott (Eds.), *Chaos theory in the social sciences* (119). Ann Arbor: University of Michigan Press.

Cooper, T., Musso, J. A., Oztas, N. (2003). The "new sciences" of self-organization: A model for implementation of governance reform. unpublished manuscript.

Czerwinski, T. (1998). Coping with the Bounds: Speculations on Nonlinearity. In *Military Affairs* (95), Washington, DC: National Defense University.

Dawkins, R. (2006). *The selfish gene (30th Anniversary Edition).* Oxford: Oxford University Press.

Eagleton, T. (1994). Ideology and its vicissitudes in western Marxism. In S. Žižek *Mapping Ideology* (179). London: Verso.

Ford, C.A. (2010). Playing for time on the edge of the apocalypse: Maximizing decision time for nuclear leaders. Washington, DC: Hudson Institute.

Fuchs, C. (2002). Social information and self-organisation. In Robert Trappi (Ed.), *Cybernetics and systems 2002* (225). Vienna: Austrian Society for Cybernetic Studies.

Fuerth, L. (2009). Cyberpower from the presidential perspective. In F. D. Kramer, S. H. Starr, and L. K. Wentz (Eds.), *Cyberpower and national security* (557). Waswhington, DC: National Defense University Press.

Harvey, D. L., and Reed, M. (1997). Social science as the study of complex systems. In L. D. Kiel and E. Elliott (Eds.), *Chaos theory in the social sciences* (295). Ann Arbor: University of Michigan Press.

Hatt, K. (2009). Considering complexity: Toward a strategy for non-linear analysis. *In Canadian Journal of Sociology*, 34(2), 313.

Heylighen, F., and Joslyn, C. (2001). The law of requisite variety, Principia Cybernetica Web, viewed August 31, 2001, <http://pespmc1.vub.ac.be/REQVAR.html>

How words evolve. (2012). *The Week* (April 3), 23.

Jervis, R. (1997a). Complex systems: The role of interactions In D. Alberts and T. Czerwinski (Eds.), *Complexity, global politics, and national security* (45). Washington, DC: National Defense University.

Jervis, R. (1997b). *System effects: Complexity in political and social life.* Princeton: Princeton University Press.

Kahn, H. (2009). *The essential Herman Kahn: In defense of thinking.* P. Dragos Aligica and K. R.Weinstein (Eds.). Lanham, MD: Lexington Books,

Kiel, L. D., and Elliott, E. (1997). Introduction, In L. D. Kiel and E. Elliott (Eds.), *Chaos theory in the social sciences: Foundations and applications* (6). Ann Arbor: University of Michigan Press.

Lefkoff, M. Personal communication to the author (February 2010).

Machiavelli, N. (2003). *Discourses on Livy*, J. C. Bonandella (Trans.). Oxford: Oxford University Press.

Mann, S.R. (1997). The Reaction to Chaos. In D. Alberts and T. Czerwinski (Eds.), *Complexity, global politics, and national security.* Washington, DC: National Defense University.135.

Marion, R. (1999). The edge of organization: Chaos and complexity theories of formal social systems. Thousand Oaks, CA: Sage Publications.

Maxfield, R. (1997). Complexity and organization management In D. Alberts and T. Czerwinski (Eds.), *Complexity, global politics, and national security* (171). Washington, DC: National Defense University.

McBurnett, M. (1997). Complexity in the Evolution of Public Opinion. In L. D. Kiel and E. Elliott (Eds.), *Chaos theory in the social sciences* (165). Ann Arbor: University of Michigan Press.

Miller, J. H., and Page, S. E. (2007). Complex adaptive systems: An introduction to computational models of social life. Princeton: Princeton University Press.

Prigogine, I., and Stengers, I. (1984). *Order out of chaos: Man's new dialogue with nature*, New York: Bantam Books.

Rosenau, J. (1997). Many damn things simultaneously: Complexity theory and world affairs In D. Alberts and T. Czerwinski (Eds.), *Complexity, global politics, and national security* (73). Washington, DC: National Defense University.

Rosser, J. B. (1997). Chaos theory and rationality in economics. In L. D. Kiel and E. Elliott (Eds.), *Chaos theory in the social sciences* (199). Ann Arbor: University of Michigan Press.

Sagan, S. D. (1991). *The limits of safety: Organizations, accidents, and nuclear weapons.* Princeton: Princeton University Press.

Sagan, S. D. (2004). The problem of redundancy problem: Why more nuclear security forces may produce less nuclear security. *Risk Analysis,* 24(4), 935.

Sagarin, R. (2012). Sink or swim. *Wired* (April), 21.

Saperstein, A. (1997a). The prediction of unpredictability: Applications of the new paradigm of chaos in dynamical systems to the old problem of the stability of a system of hostile nations. In L. D. Kiel and E. Elliott (Eds.), *Chaos theory in the social sciences* (139). Ann Arbor: University of Michigan Press.

Saperstein, A. (1997b). Complexity, chaos, and national security policy: Metaphors or tools? In D. Alberts and T. Czerwinski (Eds.) *Complexity, global politics, and national security* (101). Washington, DC: National Defense University.

Saperstein, A. (1999). *Dynamic modeling of the onset of war*. Singapore: World Scientific Publishing.

Schmitt, G. (2009). Thinking Big. *Weekly Standard* (September 7), 36.

Schmitt, J. F. (1997). Command and (out of) control: The military implications of complexity theory In D. Alberts and T. Czerwinski (Eds.), *Complexity, global politics, and national security*. Washington, DC: National Defense University. 219.

Schwartz, P. (1996). *The art of the long view*. New York: Doubleday.

Stewart, P. (2001). Complexity theories, social theory and the question of social complexity. *Philosophy of Social Sciences*, 31(3), 323.

Taleb, N. N. (2007). *The black swan: The impact of the highly improbable* New York: Random House.

Thiétart, R. A., and Forgues, B. (1995). Chaos theory and organization. *Organization Science*, 6(1), 19.

Vos Fellman, P. (2011). The complexity of terrorist networks. *International Journal of Networking and Virtual Organization*, 8(1), 2.

Weinberger, S. (2012). Mining the masses. *Defense Technology International* (March), 40.

Wieseltier, L. (2009). The well-wishers. *New Republic* (May 20), 48.

Wilson, E. O. (1999). *Consilience: The unity of knowledge*. New York: Vintage Books.

Chapter 4

Harnessing the Knowledge of the Masses

Citizen Sensor Networks, Violence, and Public Safety in Mugunga

Erika Frydenlund and David C. Earnest

Complex problems in international relations—environmental change; natural disasters and humanitarian relief; influenza outbreaks; civil violence—traditionally have overwhelmed the ability of decision makers to collect and manage the large-scale, real-time data necessary for effective governance. Yet the microelectronic and communications revolution of the last 40 years has provided new and unprecedented information resources for decision makers. By harnessing the power of mobile devices that either automatically sense or manually receive data from areas of concern, experts and decision makers can quickly analyze large amounts of information about a problem to identify workable solutions. Such "citizen sensor networks" (CSNs) are massively parallel, decentralized, and often highly adaptive to changing social conditions. Broadly defined, a sensor network is "a network of devices, denoted as nodes, which can sense the environment and communicate the information gathered from the monitored field . . . The nodes can be stationary or moving. They can be aware of their location or not. They can be homogeneous or not" (Buratti et al. 2009, 68–71). Citizen sensor networks—in which humans use mobile communications technologies to gather and distribute data—harness the power of complex adaptive systems to provide collective goods to a community, often with little or no assistance from traditional state authorities. A complex adaptive system is "a system in which large networks of components with no central control and simple rules of operation give rise to complex collective behavior, sophisticated information processing, and adaptation via learning or evolution" (Mitchell, 2009, 13). Human sensors contributing information collectively form loose, massively parallel networks that process and filter data and learn and adapt to the changing environment around them. Because mobile technologies are ubiquitous even in developing countries, CSNs are a global phenomenon, offering low-cost participatory solutions to the challenges of weak or failed states.

Practical applications for sensor networks are nearly unlimited in scope, ranging from passive weather-monitoring devices to dynamic social media applications such as Twitter and Facebook. As Michael Goodchild (2007, 25–26) stated, "Indeed, one might think of humanity as a large collection of intelligent, mobile sensors, equipped with abilities to interpret and integrate that range from the rudimentary in the case of young children to the highly developed skills of field scientists." As mobile technology becomes available in even the remotest parts of the world, scientists seek to tap the collective knowledge and intelligence of billions of humans globally through data input on mobile devices.

In this chapter, we discuss the possibility of using sensor networks in refugee camps to facilitate community-based self-policing in situations where formal security forces are inadequate to manage public safety concerns. Security in refugee camps has obvious policy and humanitarian significance, but we are interested foremost in how actors in complex systems may use networks to manage competition for resources. Such strategizing among actors not only characterizes violent social conflicts like insurgencies but also may occur when individuals compete for scarce relief supplies. For this reason, we are interested in the interaction of actor learning and sensor networks. Hypothesizing that CSNs are less effective in coevolutionary complex adaptive systems, we use an agent-based model of Mugunga III, a UN-run refugee camp in the Democratic Republic of Congo (DRC). This model demonstrates the challenges that arise when one group is attempting to "game" or adapt to the sensor network.

The chapter begins with an overview of CSNs and then describes conditions in refugee camps that could benefit from participatory public safety efforts. We present an agent-based model in which refugees use mobile phones to identify sites of violence and adapt daily routines to avoid them. Briefly, our results show that CSNs can indeed improve collective welfare in situations characterized by violence and competition for resources. However, not all sensor networks are alike: the network structure is important. The benefits, furthermore, decay over time as actors learn and adapt to this new element of their social environment. While sensor networks offer some advantages, then, they do not provide a permanent solution to the problems of violence due to scarce resources.

Background: Citizen Sensor Networks

A subset of the literature on sensor networks focuses on humans as sensors. Participatory, human-in-the-loop, or citizen sensing involves individuals collecting data, often through ubiquitous portable devices like smartphones and laptops (Boulos et al. 2011; Goodchild 2007). Remarking that sharing information is human nature, Boulos and colleagues (2011, 24) claim that "the real power and uniqueness of crowdsourcing lies in the active participation of intelligent humans in a task assigned to them . . . Social media and crowdsourcing . . . enable us to share and support more . . . with many more people and much more quickly." Individuals contribute observations to CSNs embedded with time and location information that situates them among other reports, thus providing multiple perspectives on a single event (Sheth 2009). As researchers on collecting crowd-sourced information from Twitter noted, "Perhaps, the most interesting phenomenon about such citizen generated data is that it acts as a lens into the social perception of an event in any region, at any point in time" (Nagarajan, et al. 2009).

The way actors use crowd-sourced information can challenge as well as complement the authority of the nation-state. The participatory nature of CSNs imbues actors with agency to observe, evaluate, and ultimately affect change in the world in which they live. Globalization has drastically changed modern society, heightened by technological advancements resulting in "knowledge formation and power over knowledge [moving] out of the control of the nation state" (Carnoy and Castells 2001, 9). Though speaking mainly of economic globalization, Carnoy and Castells (2001, 11) go on to state that "globalization has eroded the nation state's monopoly of scientific knowledge and its ability to use that knowledge to reproduce class power, even as the nature of class power relations itself moves away from nation state control." Inherent in the nature of CSNs is a "disembedding" of information-based power from traditional, statist government structures into polycentric spheres such as civil society groups (Scholte 2005, 185–223). In *Consequences of Modernity*, Giddens (1990, 21) defines the term "disembedding" as "the 'lifting out' of social relations from local contexts of interaction and their restructuring across indefinite spans of time and space." While he theorized specifically about modern society relinquishing certain localized systems to the "time-space distanciation" features of a globalized world (Giddens 1990, 21), here it describes removing the power of knowledge creation and access out of the hands of an elite few and into the hands of a participatory citizenship through communication tools.

This has profound implications for the conventional study of international relations. Decentralized, loosely networked, massively parallel participatory

networks epitomize Rosenau's (2003) concept of "fragmegration" in a globalized world. By this term, he intended to suggest "the pervasive interaction
between fragmenting and integrating dynamics unfolding at every level of
community" (Rosenau 2003, 11). Describing the many factors of globalization
that lead to feelings of fragmentation, Scholte (2005, 280) notes that

> contemporary globalization and the growth of supraterritoriality
> have unsettled previously familiar terrains of production, gover-
> nance, identity and knowledge. The new geography has in many
> ways disturbed previous, relatively clear, and largely unquestioned
> social bearings in terms of territorialist economy, statist gover-
> nance, nationalist identity, and rationalist knowledge. The resultant
> intensified sense of a loss of ties and groundedness has arguably
> contributed to a general environment of human insecurity.

CSNs embody integrating forces that reconstruct human connections and
perhaps even restore a sense of "ties and groundedness." Participating in
this form of data input constitutes a collective action—often by exception-
ally large groups of individuals—motivated by peer pressure to provide and
improve a collective good (Olson 1971), namely, human security.

According to Axelrod's (1984) four conditions for ensuring cooperation
among individuals, participatory sensor networks provide fertile ground for
fostering collective action to provide public goods. First, by publishing citizen inputs in publicly accessible sites, the resulting durability of the public
good (Axelrod 1984, 126–32) allows users to access consolidated information
as required in the future. For example, by publishing citizen-reported crime
hotspots, individuals can access maps highlighting dangerous areas to avoid.
Second, long-term payoffs improve (Axelrod 1984, 133–34) as more sensor
data is collected. In the previous example, as more information is collected,
maps become more thorough and useful, thus convincing users of its efficacy and encouraging more contribution (Wikipedia is also an example of
this). Even though admittedly some individuals will "cheat" the system by
using the collective knowledge without contributing, the positive feedback
dynamics of attracting new users more than offset the costs of free riders.
Third, Axelrod (1984, 134) notes, "an excellent way to promote cooperation
in a society is to teach people to care about the welfare of others." Citizen
networks allow individuals to "care about each other" even through self-
serving acts of contributing data to ensure their own access, for example, to
more informative violence hotspot maps. Finally, Axelrod (1984, 139) suggests that "the ability to recognize the other player from past interactions,
and to remember the relevant features of those interactions, is necessary

to sustain cooperation." While this feature is not inherently part of citizen networks, Kramer, Costello, and Griffith (2009, 220) found, in their model on citizen event reporting in hostile environments, a system of rating participants' reputation for providing correct reports increases the efficacy and provision of the public good in question. Such reputation mechanisms are essential for building cooperation when face-to-face interaction and other trust mechanisms are unavailable (Milgrom et al. 2006). In these ways, CSNs enable collective action.

It is no surprise, then, that around the world today CSNs abound. Ushahidi, a nonprofit company that develops free, open-source visualization software for citizen sensor-based data, stands out as a leader in the field of utilizing technology for grassroots social change (Ushahidi 2012). Originally responding to civil unrest in Kenya, Ushahidi's visualization tools have been utilized by many nonprofit organizations to track events like Egypt's first democratic elections to ongoing gender-based violence. Among the many individuals and organizations to use Ushahidi's platform, a Women's Media Center initiative led by Gloria Steinem is harnessing crowd-sourced information to get a real-time picture of sexualized violence in Syria beginning in 2012 (Women's Media Center 2012). With over 117 on-the-ground reports uploaded to Ushahidi's cloud-based platform, Crowdmap, Women's Media Center is using the data collected as a springboard for a public outcry against the Syrian government's human rights violations (Wolfe 2012). Survivors Connect, an organization that uses technology to fight against human trafficking globally, began a partnership with Ushahidi in 2009 to enable citizens in various project areas to report incidents of trafficking and gender-based violence (Rotich 2009). In its campaign to combat human trafficking for organ harvesting, Survivors Connect is collecting information from a global audience to begin systematic tracking of this illegal activity (Survivors Connect).

Already in implementation throughout many regions of the developing world, mHealth initiatives (or mobile-based/mobile-enhanced health information sharing) have proven effective in delivering or supplementing health services to dispersed and rural communities (mHealth Alliance, 2010; Dwivedi, Bali, Naguib, and Nassar, 2006; United Nations Foundation, Vodafone Foundation, and mHealth Alliance). This technology has a range of practical public health applications including health education, remote health status monitoring, prescription reminders, and biometric data collection through SMS text messaging. Rwanda, for example, has ambitiously initiated mHealth programs to reduce maternal and infant mortality rates as well as augment existing medical services to provide wider access to healthcare throughout the country and meet UN Millennium Development Goals (Rasmussen 2010).

Challenges with Crowd-Sourced Data

Citizen sensor data collection is not without its critics. One aid worker, Paul Currion, heavily criticized the concept of crowdsourcing to collect information in humanitarian emergencies. He notes that while Ushahidi successfully utilized crowd-sourced volunteers to manage and process data in the wake of the 2010 earthquake in Haiti, the data collected did not provide any new or useful information to aid workers on the ground. Based on his experiences, Currion believes that CSNs may be practical for cases where a request is made for a specific relief effort—like search and rescue—but add little value to the efforts of aid workers unless sensor data can be more reliably parsed and consolidated to reveal "the sort of detail that aid agencies need to procure and supply essential services to entire populations" (Currion 2010). Likewise, Refugees United, a Danish NGO helping refugees reunite with family members (Refugees United 2011), has concerns about the unintended harm of collecting personal information on a central database. While they advocate information sharing through their mobile device system, they warn all users that too much information may also allow the perpetrators from whom they fled to find them (Ulbricht 2010). In both cases, information collected from citizen sensors can be detrimental to the overall goal of the organization or relief effort. During natural disasters, a flood of information can distract aid workers from identifying the highest priority tasks. In a refugee crisis, too much information sharing may compromise physical security.

Beyond the challenge of providing software that can adequately parse and synthesize large volumes of citizen sensor input into meaningful output, many researchers and practitioners remain skeptical about the data collected from untrained populations. When relying on citizen sensor data, considerations include:

- Veracity: the input contains valid, relevant information and some that is invalid and irrelevant.

- Skew: information provision is swayed toward influential individuals with skills and access, marginalizing some voices.

- Personal bias: information provided by crowds is laced with opinion which may not be easily separated from fact. (Boulos et al. 2011, 8)

These challenges to citizen sensor data are not, however, insurmountable problems. Noting that, historically, scientific data collection has been largely conducted by amateurs with little or no formal training or advanced degrees, Goodchild (2007, 30) observes, "Nevertheless, it is clear from even the most cursory examination of some of these sources . . . that most contributors are well-meaning, and that the vast majority of the information they provide is of useful quality." Rather than abandon CSNs altogether based on challenges of data collection and analysis, Boulos and colleagues (2011) encourage future research to concentrate on ways to facilitate horizontal exchange of information between citizens instead of funneling data vertically to be consolidated before dissemination. Horizontal sharing of information between users facilitates data that are of higher quality, more complete, and timelier (Boulos et al. 2011, 24).

Crowdsourcing to Identify Violent Hotspots

To understand how CSNs may reduce violence, we consider the substantial and growing problem of crimes against refugees. Of the estimated 42.5 million people forcibly displaced globally in 2011, approximately 29.5 million fell under the care and protection of the United Nations High Commissioner for Refugees (UNHCR). The causes of this forced displacement vary from political, economic, or environmental events, but the persistent fact is that numbers of displaced persons are unreasonably high and continue to grow (UNHCR 2012a). Internally displaced persons (IDPs) and refugees flee insecurity in their places of origin to find safety in urban areas, spontaneous settlements, or camps established by host governments and nongovernmental organizations (NGOs). Nowhere are such problems more challenging than in the North Kivu region along the Rwanda-DRC border. While the DRC has begun to welcome some refugees back into its borders, more than 78,000 displaced persons occupied 31 IDP camps in the North Kivu region alone in 2011 (UNHCR 2012b).

Unfortunately, arriving at a temporary camp does not guarantee safety for forced migrants. The arduous journey facing those fleeing instability often includes a fracturing of community-based social networks, such as when parents become separated from children or family members die en route. This disruption of traditional social networks results both from the disorientation of flight and the tragedy of conflict and natural disasters (Martin 2004, 134–141; Segal and Mayadas 2005, 158). As multitudes of people congregate in densely populated temporary settlements, individuals may find themselves thrust into a situation of anonymity; and, where established community relations once may have provided a certain amount of security through accountability prior, anonymity of closely quartered neighbors in IDP camps brings insecurity with it (Martin 2004, 51). Additionally, the majority of refugees migrate into neighboring developing countries where host governments may be ill equipped to address special humanitarian needs, particularly security in refugee camps (Opaye 2005). Compounding this, fraudulent individuals, sometimes even perpetrators of the violence which caused the forced migration, often travel and intermingle with refugees, exploiting access to resources such as food, recruits to fill combatant ranks, relief supplies, and forced labor (Opaye 2005; Jacobsen 1999). Aid workers are encouraged by emergency management protocols to screen for combatants among the large, migrating populations (Jacobsen 1999); however, the sheer volume makes this task extremely challenging. For all these reasons, the security of refugees is a vexing problem.

Mobile Phones and Development

Mobile phones have become globally accessible as relatively cheap, reliable tools for communication. According to a 2010 UN news report, 1.6 of the 1.9 billion new mobile phone lines are in developing countries, with more than half of rural households having access to at least one mobile phone (UN News Centre 2010). These figures are promising for development strategies that empower vulnerable or dispersed populations through the use of mobile devices. During a 2010 research trip to Kiziba Refugee Camp in the Lake Kivu region of Rwanda, one of the authors observed extensive use of mobile phones. Residents charge phones at small, solar-powered stations along the camp's main walkways. They can purchase phone minutes at shops in the camp and access one of the many cellular towers located throughout even remote areas of Rwanda. In an environment with limited computer and landline access, these mobile devices provide a connection with the outside world that would otherwise not be possible.

Inspired by the success of mHealth technology and the increasing accessibility of mobile phones in developing countries, we hypothesize that IDP camp residents could use a CSN built around mobile phone technology to improve personal and community security—what we call "mSafety." For those areas with access to transmission towers, mobile communication technologies may provide a way to establish CSNs that provide a more direct flow of information from NGOs to camp residents (Barrow 2006). These virtual networks would provide a venue where refugees report acts of violence and gain awareness of known danger zones. Already, refugee camps have created such human sensor networks. Since 2007, the UNCHR and World Food Program have established initiatives to announce food distribution sites through text messages to displaced populations in urban areas (Pagonis 2007).

What we envision is not a conventional, reactive security force that responds to phone calls. Rather, we propose that CSNs could prevent violence by encouraging knowledge sharing in large communities. That is, networks would empower citizens to monitor threats by "naming and shaming" criminals and contributing to the collective good of human security. Mobile phone technology provides an inexpensive and practical method of pooling information in this way. Like the use of mobile phones to dispatch trained medical service providers, coordinated dispatching of security forces would augment CSNs for public safety. In the context of temporary settlements of forced migrants, the successful implementation of an "mSafety" strategy maximizes safety provision with limited security staff.

Mugunga III

Civil unrest leading to widespread violence within the DRC since the late 1990s has caused the forced migration of nearly half a million refugees scattered throughout the Great Lakes Region of Africa and over 1.7 million IDPs within the country's borders (UNHCR 2012b; 2012c; Central Intelligence Agency 2011). While stabilizing conditions in parts of the DRC have allowed for some voluntary repatriation, violence continues to plague the country and uproot its citizens (UNHCR 2011). Of course, each experience of forced migration is different, and temporary settlements evolve over time. Despite this, many camps share common features which we can draw upon to construct models. For the purposes of our study, we chose to focus on one particular UNHCR camp for which there exists public record of the camp's geographical layout. Mugunga III, located in the North Kivu region of the DRC, serves as a case study for the insecurity endured by forcibly displaced persons within NGO-supervised temporary settlements.

Established in 2008 to accommodate a rush of IDPs and violence in overcrowded camps, Mugunga III was built to house the most vulnerable of those remaining as troubled camps closed (Redmond 2009; van Bruaene et al. 2011, 30; Nthengwe and Shimo 2008). Able to accommodate up to 60,000 people, in 2010 it housed an estimated 4,625 IDPs in 1,210 homes (UNHCR and UNOPS, 2010). By 2011, reports of gender-based violence, particularly when women went to the nearby forest in search of firewood, had become prevalent among camp residents, prompting UNHCR to explore new assistance plans such as supplying fuel-efficient stoves. According to testimonials from within Mugunga III, women must take responsibility for collecting fuel in dangerous places because they may escape the perpetrators after being beaten and raped; for men, the trip would mean certain death (Schmitt 2011). In May 2012, 9,000 more IDPs were registered at Mugunga III in response to a surge in violence in eastern Congo (Kpandji and Bronee, 2012). Continued outbreaks in violence have reduced NGO workers' ability effectively to provide security within temporary settlements throughout the country (Mubalama 2011; UNHCR 2012b). While these conditions are particular to the Mugunga III IDP settlement, similar security issues threaten forced migrants in "safe" spaces throughout Africa and the world. For example, the Kakuma refugee camp in Kenya exceeded its capacity of 100,000 residents in 2012 causing NGOs to struggle to meet basic health needs and leading to security issues within the camp and between neighboring communities (Nyabera 2012).

The Model

Heterogeneity among agents' strategies allows the community in refugee camps to collectively learn and adjust to circumstances such as crime surges. As with the coevolutionary system of natural resource management, "it is diversity as a fundamental system property that provides the potential to enhance adaptability in terms of buffering and reorganizing after disturbance, crisis and change" (Rammel et al. 2007, 16). This stimulus for adaptation, however, can create dynamic equilibria as agent groups adjust to the strategies of each other. As with Kramer, Costello, and Griffith's (2009) model of citizen event reporting in hostile situations, some number of agents may be trying to "game" the system, thus requiring the other group to adjust its tactics. In the case of refugees reporting incidents of violence, as residents learn to avoid certain hotspots, perpetrators change positions to be less predictable. Thus, a coevolutionary system does not lend itself to a simple solution such as, "Always travel down the main route to visit latrine X," but rather is spatially and temporally contextualized. Despite the fact that this type of model will not result in one clear-cut solution for managing individual safety, it demonstrates how CSNs improve the adaptability of one group.

Because CSNs allow individuals to operate autonomously and pursue heterogeneous strategies, agent-based modeling (ABM) is a particularly useful method for testing our hypothesis. Researchers typically use ABMs to investigate research questions characterized by autonomous agents who learn, adapt, and interact repeatedly over time; systems with nonlinear cause-effect relationships; a large number of variables that exhibit interaction complexity; difficulties with gathering empirical data; and a scarcity of events (Lustick et al. 2004). Arguably, all five conditions characterize problems of personal security in IDP camps. In the absence of effective policing, displaced persons may rely on crowd-sourced information about violence to alter their routines and plans. Though refugee camp populations are diverse, our model focuses on three types of agents: refugees, insurgents, and security forces. While this limits the presence of other types of individuals—for example aid and health-care workers—it incorporates the actors who are relevant to effective CSNs.

To help contextualize the security situation, we used a map of Mugunga III IDP camp to locate facilities in the simulated settlement. The model represents the camp on a 360-by-290-unit grid and includes locations for roads, walkways, living quarters, water sources, bathing, latrines, refuse disposal, and security offices. No IDP camp is "typical": given the geographic, historical, economic, and political conditions in which such camps emerge, every IDP camp differs in the organization and location of infrastructure and other resources. Because our research interest is in sensor networks, however, we conclude that the Mugunga III layout offers a reasonable test of whether CSNs can improve personal security.

Agent Types and Objectives

The model's current form is an abstract representation of a particular kind of resource-stealing violence in forced displacement camps. Based upon numerous UN-generated reports detailing personal violence and loss of aid resources (Miles, 2013; MSF 2012; Schmitt 2011; UNHCR 2012a), as well as personal observations of a similar camp in Rwanda, the model generalizes this violence in a manner that admittedly depersonalizes the suffering of refugees. Nevertheless, by developing an abstract model of violence in camps, we provide an analytical tool to explore the possibilities of a cost-effective, potentially life-saving tool for humanitarian emergencies. Further research might use narrative data to understand refugees' experiences, situations, and priorities. Such stakeholder participation in the modeling process not only would allow for validation of the algorithms (Bousquet et al., 1999) but also would provide some voice to those who frequently face violence in IDP camps.

The model differentiates agent types by assigning each a different objective. Refugee agents collect resources by navigating established pathways to distribution sites. When a refugee successfully reaches a destination, he adds one unit to his pool of resources. In our conception, this addition represents not only tangible resources (such as water or food) but also essential activities such as schooling or healthcare. Our code requires refugee agents to move on designated thoroughfares, only veering off main walkways to go home or visit security stations. This restriction is not only a realistic one (avoiding walking through houses), but also allows for novel agent strategies. Refugee agents, for example, may learn to crowd together to increase their personal security, whereas insurgent agents may identify "choke points" in the camp's roadways that allow them to steal resources.

By contrast, insurgent agents avoid main walkways. This feature reflects the covert nature of those infiltrating camps to steal resources. Instead of approaching a distribution site to collect a resource, for example, an insurgent may linger outside waiting to steal from multiple refugees. After a certain period of time, the insurgent will move on to a new resource site. These individuals seek to "game" the system by gathering aid resources from largely ungoverned, vulnerable groups of people whose fragmented social networks limit peer pressure or other collective actions that would minimize crime. Whereas refugee agents seek the route that maximizes resources, insurgents look for routes that allow for resource theft. If there are no security agents around, the insurgent takes resources from the refugee under two conditions. If insurgents outnumber refugees at a site, or if the refugees at the distribution site are all "female" and the ratio of refugees to insurgents is no more than 3:1, the refugees become targets of violence. The second scenario represents acts of gender-based violence to which even small groups of women in camp situations can become victims. Although refugees can only gather one additional resource at a distribution site, victims of violence lose two units of resource. This reflects both the emotional and/or physical tolls of violence as well as the loss of a resource. Because the net exchange of resources is −1, this rule creates a negative-sum game between refugees and insurgents. In the simulation, if a refugee has lost all of her resources, she then "dies" out of the simulation.

In this particular implementation, the resulting system is coevolutionary. In general, a coevolutionary system is one in which "dynamic interactions between two or more interdependent systems . . . account mutually for each other's development" (Rammel et al. 2007, 12). The general population of refugees tries to maintain physical and resource security by identifying and avoiding dangerous areas. Insurgents then adapt to changing daily routes in order to steal from refugees while they are vulnerable. The actions of both groups are characterized by nonlinear behavior in that one's next move is dependent on the other's previous move. In this way, the system does not exhibit a static equilibrium, but rather adapts and changes as each group evolves to improve its own well-being.

We model a third agent type, security forces, to allow for some deterrent effect. The model prevents insurgents from stealing resources from refugees when security agents are present. We conceptualize security agents as units of security forces large enough to deter minor threats. Unfortunately, as mentioned above, security is often under-resourced and understaffed. For simplicity, in the model's security forces wander the main section of the camp randomly attempting only to deter crime by being "visible" (nearby) to insurgent agents. All agents repeat their movement rules for 900 "ticks" in the model. We arbitrarily chose 900 ticks to simulate a 15-hour working day, where one tick is equivalent to one minute of time in the real Mugunga. For each simulation, we hold the number of refugees constant (100). Likewise, because we are interested in the effect of CSNs, the simulations also hold constant the number of insurgent agents (5) and security agents (5).

The Simulated Sensor Network

To test whether CSNs improve camp security, we endow each refugee with communication connections ("links") to a subset of refugee agents (neighbors). By varying the number of network neighbors for each refugee, we artificially create a system analogous to a mobile-phone-based sensor network. After experiencing or witnessing an act of violence, refugees alert others they pass, meant to represent a conversational exchange about where the event occurred, as well as those in their communication network. Refugees receiving this information then update their memories of danger zones and modify their routes to avoid areas of known violence. The model arbitrarily limits a refugee's memory to five incidents, so she may continue to avoid a site until it is "forgotten" and replaced by more recent information. When refugees cannot technologically share information about violent events, the model allows "word-of-mouth" information sharing based on geographical proximity.

We experimentally vary the number of network neighbors of refugee agents in the model; this is the out-degree k for each refugee agent, the number of directed links to other refugees. The baseline simulation had $k = 0$—that is, no neighbors. This allows us to measure agent performance in the absence of sensor networks. For the other five simulations, we varied the mean refugee out-degree from $k = 1$ to $k = 5$. As an average, some agents will have a higher or lower out-degree, but always at least one neighbor. Within each simulation, we held constant the network degree and structure. We speculate that higher-degree networks will provide more complete information to refugees about violence, which in turn will improve refugees' collection of resources.

Learning and Adaptation

The model allows for both individual- and community-level adaptation. At the community level, the model reinforces learning by replicating the best-performing refugee agents. New agents supplant those who run out of resources and are removed from the model (dead). These replacements either replicate the best performers in the system (highest number of resources) or receive randomly generated new strategies. This best-performer replacement mechanism allows for conservation of top-performing strategies, possibly representing real-world strategy sharing among refugees. Introducing a small percentage of randomly generated strategies encourages variation and evolution. Through these mechanisms of conservation and exploration, the group of agents develops strategies of community-wide surveillance and information sharing similar to "crowd-sourcing" to reduce the risks of personal violence.

To simulate individual-level learning, we use a genetic algorithm (GA) that allows refugees and insurgents to learn new strategies (Holland 1992; Mitchell 2009). Researchers have found that GAs efficiently locate high-performing solutions to social choice problems for which there are multiple equilibria over vast parameter spaces. For both refugee and insurgent agents, a "strategy" is simply a pathway through the camp. The algorithm uses three mechanisms to simulate learning about the optimal path. First, agents select, from an initial population of randomly generated strategies, those that yield the most resources. Second, agents will "cross over" or combine top-performing strategies (the biological metaphor is that two successful strategies create an "offspring" strategy combining elements from each parent, likely producing fitter strategies). Finally, actors "mutate" their strategies or in other words, randomly try something different with some low probability (in our algorithm, $p = .001$). Table 4.1 provides the pseudo code for the entire model.

Table 4.1. Pseudo code for the ABM.

Initialization
    Create refugee agents
        Endow with resources = 10
        Endow with a social network
        Endow with a list of destinations
        Endow with a "gender", half female, half male
    Create insurgent agents
        Endow with a list of destinations
    Create security agents

Execution
    Loop for 900 ticks
        Refugee agents move to their next safe destinations
            If at destination
                Receive +1 resource
                Set the next location on their lists as the destination
            If total resources < 0, die
        Insurgent agents move to their destinations
            If (a) refugees are present; (b) no security agents are present; and
            (c1) the number of local insurgents is greater than then number
            of local refugees or (c2) the number of female refugees is less than
            three times the number of local insurgents;
                Receive +1 resource
                Nearest refugee receives −2 resources
            Wait 20 ticks to see if other refugees arrive
            Set destination as the next location on their list
        Security agents
            Move randomly throughout camp
        Measure the system
    End Loop

Genetic Algorithm
    Initialization
        Endow refugee agents with a set of 30 strategies (list of destinations)
        Endow insurgent agents with a set of 30 strategies (list of destinations)
    Run Execution once for each of 30 strategies = one generation
    Loop for 70 generations
        At the end of each generation, refugees and insurgents create 30 new strategies:
            Pairwise select the best strategies measured by total points
            Cross selected strategies with $p = .75$
            Mutate each bit of the strategy with $p = .001$
    End Loop

Findings

To assess whether sensor networks improve the security of refugee agents, we repeated the simulation six times. Each simulation consisted of 30 strategies for 70 generations of the GA, or a total of 2,100 runs. We varied the average degree of the network from a baseline of $k = 0$ (no sensor networks) to $k = 5$. For each generation of each simulation, we measured the average "score" (resources) of refugee agents. We also measured the average score of insurgent agents and the total number of dead. Because we measured these parameters for 70 generations for each of six simulations, we have 420 observations. Table 4.2 reports the average scores and number of dead for the refugee and insurgent agents. It also reports t-tests and p-values for the means comparison tests by the average degree of the sensor network. The baseline simulation found that the average refugee score was 10.06, while the average insurgent score was 32.56. The disparity in averages for refugees and insurgents suggests, in the baseline simulation, insurgents enjoy a number of advantages. Refugees rely only on the "word-of-mouth" rule to learn about violence. By construction, the model allows insurgents to move more directly through the camp than refugees. When insurgents steal resources, furthermore, there is a negative net gain: an insurgent receives an increment of one unit to its resources, while a refugee loses two units for every act of violence. For all these reasons, in the absence of sensor networks refugee agents perform poorly relative to insurgent agents.

Do sensor networks improve refugee scores? Table 4.2 provides a somewhat surprising answer to this question. As the t-tests show, some networks produce significantly higher refugee scores, while others produce significantly *lower* scores. When $k = 1$—that is, every refugee has one out-neighbor—refugees score significantly lower than when they have no neighbors at all. At $k = 3$, however, refugees score significantly higher than the baseline simulation. This finding suggests that the effect of the average degree of the network is nonlinear; it initially reduces refugee performance before improving it. This nonlinear effect is evident, furthermore, at the higher average network degrees ($k = 4$ and $k = 5$), where once again the average refugee score is lower than baseline. These statistical findings suggest that in the simulated system, there is an optimum network degree at $k = 3$, before and after which refugee performance is significantly lower than when refugees have no network. Table 4.2 shows this as well with the fewest average dead at $k = 3$. One can see this nonlinear relationship in the waterfall plot in Figure 4.1, which presents in three dimensions the average refugee resources by generation for each network degree. The "sheet" for $k = 3$ is on average

Table 4.2. Experiment results: t-test comparisons of mean degree (k) to baseline simulation of no network (K = 0).

Degree (k)	n	Refugee Resources	t-test	Insurgent Resources	t-test	Number of Dead	t-test
0 (baseline)	70	10.06	—	32.59	—	17.32	—
1	70	9.75	7.73 ***	36.27	10.25 ***	19.44	12.89 ***
2	70	10.00	1.14	33.98	5.10 ***	18.14	5.35 ***
3	70	10.27	4.15 ***	33.28	2.40 *	16.81	2.99 **
4	70	9.75	7.54 ***	36.70	9.49 ***	19.70	11.26 ***
5	70	9.92	2.88 **	35.62	8.56 ***	18.29	5.26 ***

*$p < .05$
**$p < .01$
***$p < .001$

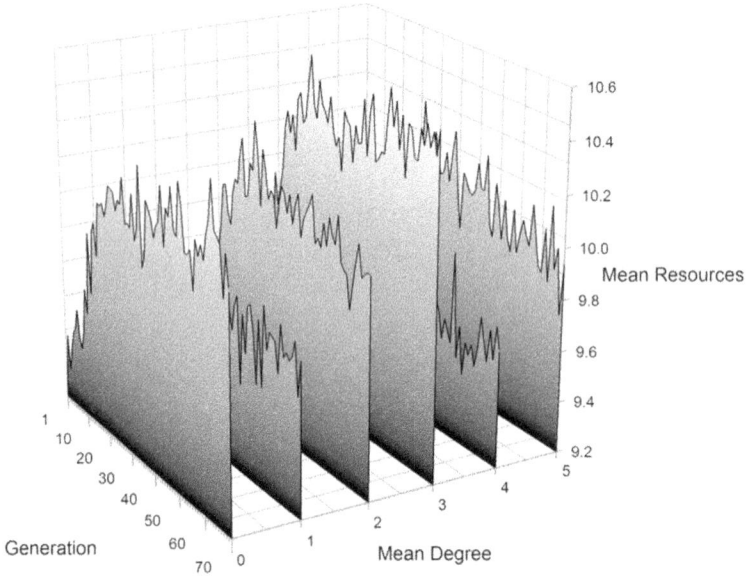

Figure 4.1. Waterfall plot of the average resources of refugee agents, by generation and average out-degree.

higher than the sheets at $k = 1$, 4, and 5. Interestingly, there is no significant difference in refugee scores between $k = 0$ and $k = 2$.

Why is $k = 3$ an optimum degree for the simulated sensor network? We offer a number of conjectures. The first answer may correspond with how agents adapt in the model. Because insurgents receive payoffs only from refugees, they depend in part on the efficiency with which refugees can gather resources. As the GA allows refugees to learn more efficient routes, this improves their resource collection *as well as* insurgents' opportunities for theft. This is typical of predation systems in which predators depend upon the efficiency of their prey. Table 4.2 provides some statistical support for our conjecture. For all five simulations with $k = 1$ through $k = 5$, insurgents score significantly higher than the baseline simulation with $k = 0$. In other words, every sensor network improves the welfare of insurgents. Yet the improvement was least when $k = 3$, the optimum degree for the refugees. Insurgents' improvement appears to be u-shaped, with the greatest improvements at $k = 1$ and $k = 4$, and the least but nonetheless significant improvement at $k = 3$. The waterfall plot in Figure 4.2 shows this u shape quite clearly, with the "shortest" sheet at $k = 3$.

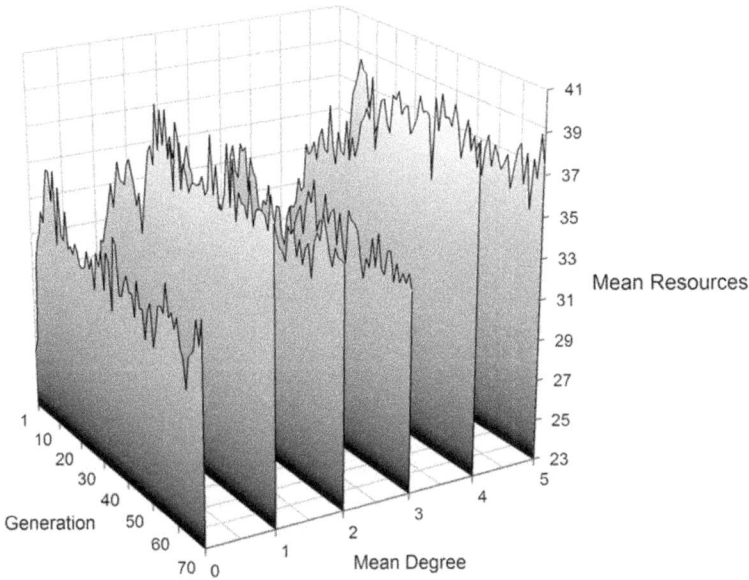

Figure 4.2. Waterfall plot of the average resources of insurgent agents, by generation and average out-degree.

This evidence suggests that, in coevolutionary systems, Pareto-improving opportunities may exist for all actors, not just those who use a sensor network. To illustrate this point, Figure 4.3 plots the average refugee and insurgent resources by generation, irrespective of network degree. The figure shows the important role agent-level learning plays in the efficacy of sensor networks. Early in each simulation, learning among agents allows refugees and insurgents to improve their welfare without harming the other. The ascending lines between generations 1 and 20 clearly show this Pareto improvement. Around the 20th generation, however, the opportunities for mutual gain decline. Once they have realized efficiency gains through learning, refugees and insurgents enter a zero-sum gain regime in which they seem to divide resources. As the plot shows, both refugee and insurgent agents vacillate between periods of improvement and decline in welfare. Both the absolute values of refugee and insurgent scores ($r = -.91$, $p < .001$) and the first differences in scores ($r = -.98$, $p < .001$) correlate negatively and significantly for the last 50 generations of all simulations ($n = 300$). This evidence is consistent with the interpretation that refugee and insurgent agents continuously strategize against each other. One possible explanation for this

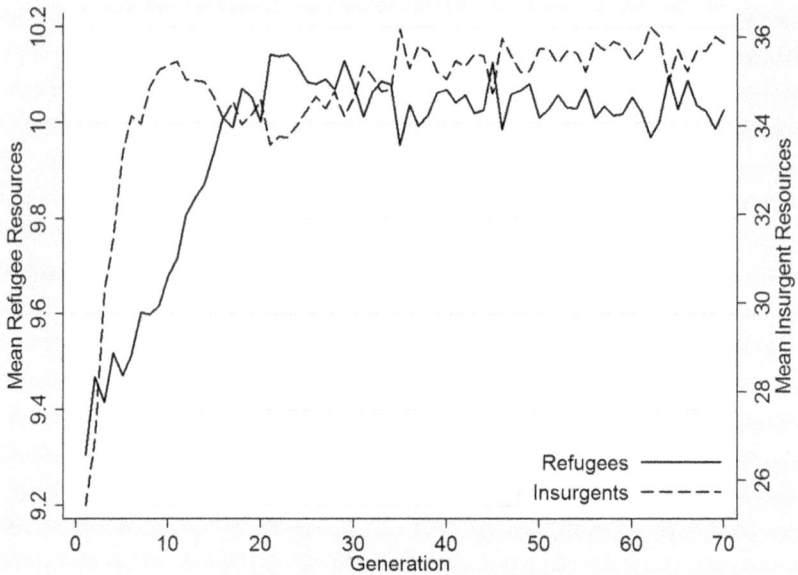

Figure 4.3. Mean scores of refugee and insurgent agents, by generation.

concerns how agents organize themselves in the space of the simulated camp. As refugees learn to avoid sites of violence, they congregate in new locations only to have insurgents discover them.

Given this evidence of learning among agents, we speculate that the efficacy of the simulated CSN may decline over time. That is, while CSNs may offer some initial advantages, it is possible that insurgents learn strategies that reduce welfare gains refugees receive from the network. To investigate this possibility, we conducted a polynomial regression on refugee scores that includes second-order estimators (i.e., squared terms) for both the degree of the sensor network and the generation of the GA. We also included an inter-action term between network degree and generation to investigate whether the effects of networks change as agents learn. Although these estimators have a high degree of colinearity, we nonetheless used robust standard errors to guard against finding effects when in fact none exist. Table 4.3 presents the results of this analysis. All estimators in the model are statistically sig-nificant at the .01 level or lower. Interestingly, for both the generation and degree parameters, the first-order estimators have positive signs, while the

Table 4.3. Estimated effects of degree and generation on refugee resources. Polynomial regression with robust standard errors.

					Number of obs. =	420
					F(5, 414) =	60.77
					Prob. > F =	0.0000
					R-squared =	0.3300
					Root MSE =	0.2603

Parameter	Estimated Coefficient	Robust Std. Err.	t	p > t	95% Confidence Interval	
Generation	0.033	0.002	13.430	< .001	0.028	0.037
Generation²	-3.4E-04	3.5E-05	-9.760	< .001	-4.1E-04	-2.7E-04
Degree	0.090	0.023	3.950	< .001	0.045	0.135
Degree²	-0.013	0.004	-2.970	.003	-0.021	-0.004
Degree × Generation	-0.001	3.0E-04	-3.480	.001	-0.002	-4.6E-04
Constant	9.348	0.039	239.380	< .001	9.271	9.424

second-order ones have negative signs. These estimates indicate that when controlling for agent learning, the degree of the sensor network has significantly positive effects on refugee scores, but this effect declines as the network degree grows. This suggests that, at some point, sensor networks obtain a sufficient size beyond which returns diminish. Likewise, the generation of the GA has positive but declining effects on refugee scores, indicating that learning has diminishing returns over time. Additionally, the network degree and generation interaction term is significant but negatively signed. This shows that although network degree has positive effects on refugee scores, the effect declines over GA generations. This is consistent with our speculation that in this model of coevolving actors, over the long term agent learning offsets the advantages that CSNs offer.

Of course, we recognize that our model of sensor networks is highly simplified. The analysis above focuses only on a single measure of network structure: the average out-degree of the agents in the CSN. Network theory has shown, however, that other attributes of a network may affect its performance. It may be that, in sensor networks, the average path length between actors (commonly known as "degrees of separation") is more important than out-degree. CSNs may benefit from forms that feature a few high-prestige actors with many in-degrees but a large number of low-degree actors (Wasserman and Faust 1994). Such scale-free networks tend to be robust to random disruptions, which may be particularly important if acts of violence remove actors from the CSN (Barabasi and Albert 1999). Among numerous other measures, researchers also have investigated the effect of clustering (i.e., networks in which subsets of actors tend to have a high density of ties) on network performance (Watts and Strogatz 1998). This brief discussion suggests that the structure of the network may be at least as important as simply considering its existence or the density of its connections. Future investigations into the effect of network structure might allow agents to learn to "rewire" the sensor network. This would provide insight into how sensor networks evolve over time in response to the learning and demands of actors.

These provisos notwithstanding, the statistical findings suggest that, as we hypothesized, CSNs can significantly improve social welfare. Yet in coevolutionary systems, actor learning may decrease the marginal benefits over time. In this respect, real-world CSNs may exhibit path-sensitive dynamics, particularly in systems characterized by actors playing against each other rather than against nature. Initially CSNs may provide Pareto-improving coordination among all actors in a system, but this may give way to distributive conflicts characterized by zero-sum or negative-sum gains. Independent of such coevolution, furthermore, actors may find that the benefits of sensor networks decline over time and that network growth provides diminishing returns to their welfare. This suggests that sensor networks may undergo natural cycles of growth and decay. For some social choice problems, CSNs may help, but they are not a panacea.

Conclusions

As adaptive, autonomous, and massively parallel organizations, CSNs facilitate provision of collective goods, from identifying priority tasks in emergency situations to improving the health and safety of citizens. Often, such beneficial networks emerge without the direct participation of the state, a form of governance without government. Thanks to the accessibility of many wireless mobile technologies, such networks cost relatively little to create and maintain. With large-scale participation and near real-time data sharing, CSNs hold the promise of transforming how states and citizens alike approach complex social problems.

Despite this promise, however, our findings suggest that there may be practical limits to CSN benefits. Catastrophic events create situations that game theorists call "games against nature," where environments are essentially static in the short run, feature dilemmas of coordination in which CSNs can help actors find numerous opportunities for Pareto-improving cooperation. Following the 2011 earthquake in Japan, relief efforts could focus on public services. Yet unlike natural disasters, many collective action problems feature actors whose strategies coevolve; rewards characterized by distributive conflicts; or both. Consider the example of social protests and police monitoring, such as in Tahrir Square in Cairo. Protestors and police may benefit from CSNs—to document violence as well as to learn about how crowds move. Yet protestors and police have few opportunities for cooperation and mutual gain, instead strategizing to out-smart the other. In this type of problem, the CSN paradoxically contributes to changes in behavior that ultimately undermine the effectiveness of shared information. The benefits of sensor networks, then, may decline over time. This may be one reason that most CSNs are issue-specific and temporary.

We speculate, furthermore, that researchers do not fully understand the structure and statistical properties of such networks nor how such properties affect the network's efficacy. Considerable barriers to gathering data on real-world networks exist. Participation in sensor networks is open to multitudes of people; is voluntary; and often is quite brief, perhaps as brief as a few minutes for some observers who share multimedia data. In this sense, the structure of real-world networks evolves rapidly and constantly, challenging researchers who wish to study its effect on performance. For this reason, agent-based social simulation is an invaluable complement to other empirical methods. No doubt the growing sophistication of simulation models will help us understand how such sensor networks harness the ability of citizens to provide for themselves when governments cannot.

Bibliography

Axelrod, R. (1984). *The evolution of cooperation.* New York: Basic Books.

Barabasi, A.-L., and Albert, R. (1999, October 15). Emergence of Scaling in Random Networks. *Science, 286*(5439), 509–512.

Barabasi, A.-L., and Bonabeau, E. (2003). Scale-free Networks. *Scientific American.*

Barrow, G. (2006, June 23). Mobile phone helps one Somali refugee send long-distance S)S. *UNHCR: News.*

Boulos, M. N., Resch, B., Crowley, D. N., Breslin, J. G., Sohn, G., Burtner, R., . . . Chuang, K.-Y. S. (2011). Crowdsourcing, citizen sensing and sensor web technologies for public and environmental health surveillance and crisis management: Trends, OGC standards and application examples. *International Journal of Health Geographics, 10*(67). doi:10.1186/1476–072X–10–67.

Bousquet, F., Barreteau, O., Le Page, C., Mullon, C., and Weber, J. (1999). An environmental modelling approach: the use of multi-agent simulations. *Advances in environmental and ecological modelling, 113,* 122.

Buratti, C., Conti, A., Dardani, D., and Verdone, R. (2009). An overview on wireless sensor networks technology and evolution. *Sensors, 9,* 6869–6896. doi:10.3390/s90906869.

Carnoy, M., and Castells, M. (2001). Globalization, the knowledge society, and the network state: Poulantzas at the millennium. *Global Networks,* 1–18. doi:10.1111/1471–0374.00002.

Central Intelligence Agency. (2011). *The world factbook.* Retrieved September 8, 2011, from Congo, Democratic Republic of the: https://www.cia.gov/library/publications/the-world-factbook/geos/cg.html.

Currion, P. (2010, October 20). *If all you have is a hammer—How useful is humanitarian crowdsourcing?* Retrieved from MobileActive.org: http://mobileactive.org/how-useful-humanitarian-crowdsourcing.

Dwivedi, A. N., Bali, R. K., Naguib, R. N., and Nassar, N. S. (2006). The efficacy of the m-health paradigm: Incorporating technological, organizational, and managerial perspectives. In R. S. Istepanian, S. Laxminarayan, and C. S. Pattichis, *M-Health: Emerging mobile health systems* (15–32). New York: Springer.

Giddens, A. (1990). *The Consequences of Modernity.* Stanford: Stanford University Press.

Goodchild, M. F. (2007). Citizens and voluntary sensors: Spatial data infrastructure in the world of Web 2.0. *International Journal of Spatial Data Infrastructures Research, 2*, 24–32.

Holland, J. H. (1992, July). Genetic algorithms. *Scientific American, 267*(1), 66–72.

Jacobsen, K. (1999). *A "safety-first" approach to physical protection in refugee camps.* Cambridge, MA: The Inter-University Committee on International Migration.

Kpandji, S., and Bronee, A. (2012, May 4). Almost 20,000 flee fresh fighting in eastern Congo's North Kivu Province. *UNHCR News Stories.* Retrieved from http://www.unhcr.org/cgi-bin/texis/vtx/search?page=searchanddocid=4fa3a79 79andquery=LRA.

Kramer, M. A., Costello, R., and Griffith, J. (2009). Investigating the force multiplier effect of citizen event reporting by social simulation. *Mind and Society, 8*(2), 209–221. doi:10.1007/s11299–009–0059–0.

Lustick, I. S., Miodownik, D., and Eidelson, R. J. (2004). Secessionism in multicultural states: Does sharing power prevent or encourage it? *American Political Science Review, 98*(2), 209–229.

Malik, S. (2011, June 20). *Microsoft unlimited potential blog.* Retrieved September 8, 2011, from Out of isolation: How technology is supporting refugees: http://blogs.technet.com/.

Martin, S. F. (2004). *Refugee women.* Lanham, Maryland: Lexington Books.

mHealth Alliance. (2010). *mHealth Alliance: Mobilizing innovation for global health.* Retrieved September 8, 2011, from Frequently Asked Questions: http://www.mhealthalliance.org/.

Milgrom, P. R., North, D. C., and Weingast, B. R. (2006, October 27). The role of institutions in the revival of trade: The law merchant, private judges, and the champagne fairs. *Economics and Politics, 2*(1), 1–23.

Mitchell, M. (2009). *Complexity: A guided tour.* Oxford: Oxford University Press.

Mubalama, P. (2011, March 9). State of Insecurity in Eastern DRC. *Radio Netherlands Worldwide: Africa.*

Nagarajan, M., Gomadam, K., Sheth, A., Ranabahu, A., Mutharaju, R., and Jadhav, A. (2009). Spatio-temporal-thematic analysis of citizen-sensor data: Challenges and experiences. *Tenth International Conference on Web Information Systems Engineering* (pp. 539–553). Retrieved from http://knoeisis.wright.edu/library/resource.php?id=00559.

Nthengwe, D., and Shimo, K. (2008, November 21). Tension mounts in two Congolese camps after woman shot dead. *UNHCR News Stories.* doi:http://www.unhcr.org/4926cc294.html.

Nyabera, E. (2012, August 6). Kenya: Kakuma Camp surpasses its 100,000 capacity. *All Africa.* Retrieved from http://allafrica.com/stories/201208070662.html.

Olson, M. (1971). *The logic of collective action: Public goods and the theory of groups.* Cambridge: Harvard University Press.

Opaye, C. (2005). *Refugee camp security in West Africa: An ECOWAS priority?* Accra, Ghana: Kofi Annan International Peacekeeping Training Centre.

Pagonis, J. (2007). *Syria: Food distribution to start for vulnerable Iraqi refugees*. Geneva: UNHCR.

Rammel, C., Stagl, S., and Wilfing, H. (2007). Managing complex adaptive systems: A co-evolutionary perspective on natural resource management. *Ecological Economics, 62*, 9–21.

Rasmussen, M. (2010). Celebrate Solutions: Training and Mobile Health Technology in Rwanda. *Women Deliever: News*, October 12.

Räty, T. D. (2010). Survey on contemporary remote surveillance systems for public safety. *IEEE Transactions on Systems, Man and Cybernetics: Part C—Applications and Reviews, 40*(5), 493–515. doi:10.1109/TSMCC.2010.2042446.

Redmond, R. (2009). *Situation in Democratice Republic of Congo*. Palais des Nations. Geneva: UNHCR.

Refugees United. (2011). *Harnessing the power of technology and self determination.* Retrieved September 8, 2011, from https://www.refunite.org/content/about-us.

Rosenau, J. N. (2003). *Distant proximities: Dynamics beyond globalization*. Princeton: Princeton University Press.

Rotich, J. (2009, November 17). Press release: Survivors Connect launches its Connection GeoMap Project. *Ushahidi.com*. Ushahidi.

Schmitt, C. (2011, March 16). Congolese victims of sexual violence call for help from the international community. *UNHCR News*.

Scholte, J. A. (2005). *Globalization: A critical introduction* (2 ed.). New York: Palgrave Macmillan.

Segal, U. A., and Mayadas, N. S. (2005). Assessment of issues facing immigrant and refugee families. *Child Welfare* (84.5), 563–583.

Sheth, A. (2009, July/August). Citizen sensing, social signals, and enriching human experience. *IEEE Internet Computing*, 80–85.

Survivors Connect. (n.d.). *About organ trafficking*. Retrieved from Organ Monitor: https://organmonitor.crowdmap.com/page/index/1.

Ulbricht, M. (2010, October 28). *Can you find me now? Refugees United goes mobile to help reunite refugees*. Retrieved from MobileActive.org: http://www.mobile-active.org/case-studies/refugees-united-goes-mobile.

UN News Centre. (2010, June 23). UN agency reports phenomenal mobile telephone expansion in developing world. *UN News Centre*. From http://www.un.org/apps/news/story.asp?NewsID=35114.

UNHCR and UNOPS. (2010). *Data Center for IDP: UNHCR DRC Portal*. Retrieved September 8, 2011, from Camp Interactive Statistics: Mugunga 3: http://www.dc4idp.org/htdocs/modules/camps/camps.php?nomcamp=50.

UNHCR (2011). *Central Africa and the Great Lakes*. Retrieved September 9, 2011, from 2011 Regional Operations Profile: http://www.unhcr.org/pages/49e45a6c6.html.

UNHCR (2006). Operational protection in camps and settlements: A reference guide of good practices in the protection of refugees and other persons of concern. Geneva Switzerland: UNHCR and The Ford Foundation.

UNHCR (2012a). *A year of crises: UNHCR global trends 2011.* Geneva, Switzerland: United Nations High Commissioner for Refugees.

UNHCR (2012b). *UNHCR global report 2011—Democratic Republic of Congo.* Geneva, Switzerland: United Naitons High Commissioner of Refugees.

UNHCR (2012c). *UNHCR D.R. Congo fact sheet.* Geneva: UNHCR. Retrieved August 30, 2012, from http://www.unhcr.org/4fab74189.html.

United Nations Foundation, Vodafone Foundation, and mHealth Alliance. (n.d.). *Health information as health care: The role of technology in unlocking data and wellness.* Geneva, Switzerland: UN Foundation.

Ushahidi. (2012). *Ushahidi one pager.* Retrieved August 28, 2012, from Ushahidi.com: http://ushahidi.com/uploads/docs/Ushahidi_1-Pager.pdf.

van Bruaene, M., Scheuermann, P., and Lukmanji, Z. (2011). *Evaluation of the NRC's Country Program in DR Congo (2007–2009).* Oslo, Norway: Norwegian Refugee Council.

Wasserman, S., and Faust, K. (1994). *Social network analysis: Methods and applicaitons.* New York: Cambridge University Press.

Watts, D. J., and Strogatz, S. H. (1998, June 4). Collective dynamics in "small-world" networks. *Nature, 393,* 440–442.

Wolfe, L. (2012, July 11). The ultimate assault: Charting Syria's use of rape to terrorize its people. *The Atlantic.* Retrieved August 28, 2012, from http://www.theatlantic.com/international/archive/2012/07/the-ultimate-assault-charting-syrias-use-of-rape-to-terrorize-its-people/259669/.

Women's Media Center. (2012). *Women under siege.* Retrieved August 28, 2012, from https://womenundersiegesyria.crowdmap.com/page/index/1.

Chapter 5

Ascertaining the Normative Implications of Complexity Thinking for Politics

Beyond Agent-Based Modeling

Mark Olssen

Introduction

Central to representing the world as a complex dynamical system is understanding it as pertaining to an interdisciplinary approach to nonlinear processes of change in both nature and society. Although complexity research takes its origins from its applications in physics, chemistry, mathematics, and the "hard" sciences, undergoing its formative development in the 1970s, during the last two decades it has exerted an effect on the social sciences as well. Today complexity research is generating what Stuart Kauffman (2008, Preface) calls a "quiet revolution" in both the physical and social sciences.

One of the earliest centers for complexity research was at Santa Fe, where researchers developed the first research program with application to politics based on agent-based modeling. Research by Holland (1995; 1998), Jervis (1997), Axelrod (1997; 2006a; 2006b), Axelrod and Cohen (1999), Cederman (1997; 2001; 2003), Cioffi-Revilla (2002), Epstein (2007), Epstein and Axtell (1996), Hoffmann and Riley (2002), Moss and Edmonds (2005), Resnick (1994), Poundstone (1985), and many others was in the forefront of advances in the science of agent-based modeling and simulation. In politics and international relations research there was a marked growth of simulation modeling-type approaches (Bhavnani 2006; Bremer and Mihalka 1977; Bremer 1987; Bennett and Alker 1977; Hollist 1978; Plous 1987; Sandole 1999; Stoll 1985, Taber and Timpone 1996a, 1996b; Tritzsch 1997 to name just some of the more obvious). As defined by Cederman (2003, 138), "[a] gent-based modelling is a computational methodology that allows scientists to create, analyze and experiment with, artificial worlds populated by agents that interact in non-trivial ways and that constitute their own environment." Cederman termed his approach as complex adaptive systems' (CAS) research, which constituted a variation on agent-based modelling, but within the broader tradition of agent-based research. It thus constitutes a programme that generates models that claim to represent reality in symbolic or numeric terms, where explanation and prediction are central aims.

I will argue in this chapter that what is distinctive about Complexity Thinking (CT) is largely missed by agent-based modeling approaches which confine research to a positivist-imitating style typical of the American environment in which it was developed. Its preoccupation with modeling, and the related concerns over prediction and validity, constitute the first set of major problems with the approach. These will be documented in the first part of this article. Of equal importance, to be explored in the second part of the article, the concern to emulate scientific standards has precluded any serious attention to politics in a normative sense, including a focus upon authority and institutionalization. Although recent debates within the agent-based modeling tradition, as well as the emergence of more empirically-minded 'evidence-directed' approaches (Alam, et al. 2007; Geller and Moss 2008; Bousquet, et al. 2009; Downing et al. 2000; Marks 2007) can be seen as efforts within the tradition to correct some of the problems I identify, such theoretical "soul-searching" only supports the thesis I offer and only goes a short way to remedy the problems to the extent that prediction is not a central issue. In addition, I argue that the agent-based modeling approach to the complexity of global life has not only been constrained by the positivist nature of the general social science research habitus, especially in the USA, but it has largely ignored the broader theoretical contributions to CT centering on the work of Gilles Deleuze, Niklas Luhmann, and others, within the European theatre of scholarship. It is because it has confined itself within a scientific approach based on modeling that it eschews any normative role for politics, institutionalization, or the role of the state more generally. Drawing more from the philosophical and systems contributions to complexity, and from writings in physics of the Belgium Nobel prize winner, Ilya Prigogine, CT, I will suggest, opens possibilities toward a rich new conception of "complexity-based" historical materialism. Such a conception, I will argue, moves beyond the classical conception of Marxist historical materialism, which schematizes and periodizes according to fixed stages, and which notoriously prioritizes the economy as both primary determining force and explanatory constant, in order to advance a radically nominalist and non-teleological historical conception based upon the principles of "contextual contingency," "time irreversibility," "non-reductionism," "self-organization," and "emergence" (concepts which will be discussed below). The strength of this approach in relation to politics is that it permits a normative emphasis on institutionalisation and authority, which the American tradition of agent-based modeling has signally failed to develop. To advance this thesis I will firstly outline and criticise agent-based modeling approaches to complexity more specifically, and then, in the latter part of this article, proceed to outline the implications of complexity for politics that such an approach misses.

Agent-Based Modeling

An Introduction to the Approach

Agent-based models aim to construct models of how social institutions and values arise from a consideration of the interactions between individuals, 'bottom-up,' (so to speak). As the science writer Philip Ball (2004, 441) notes, "agent-based modelling should make some of the greatest social and political questions of our time accessible to rational experiment, such as whether the globalization of the economy is likely to lead to greater cultural harmony or cultural conflict." A central pioneer of the approach was Robert Axelrod. For Axelrod (1997), building on the work of early exponents like Thomas Schelling and Herbert Simon, agent-based modeling is "a third way of doing science . . . which generates simulated data that can be analyzed inductively" (Axelrod 1997, 3–4). The approach became the core of what became known as the 'artificial societies' approach. As Axelrod states:

> Unlike typical induction, the simulated data come from a rigorously specified set of rules rather than direct measurement of the real world. Whereas the purpose of induction is to find patterns in data and that of deduction is to find consequences of assumptions, the purpose of agent-based modelling is to aid intuition. Agent-based modelling is a way of doing thought experiments. (3–4)

Axelrod's landscape theory, which was developed to predict alliances and aggregation patterns in political contexts, is a good example of the approach. As Axelrod (1997, 79) notes, the idea of "an abstract landscape has been widely used in the physical and natural sciences to characterize the dynamics of systems." Its first rigorous development was in reference to Hamiltonian systems, and "biologists have independently developed landscapes to characterize evolutionary movement in an abstract 'fitness landscape' of genes (1997, 79). In

Axelrod's hands, landscape modeling functions in the service of game theory. It "begins with sizes and pairwise propensities that are used to calculate the energy of each possible configuration" (1997, 79) in order to characterize "all possible configurations and the dynamics among them" (80). It is utilized "to make predictions about the dynamics of the system" (80) in relation to how actors will form alignments. Axelrod "retrospectively" conducts research to "predict" the alignment patterns of the Second World War in Europe. The question was, after the First World War, what caused the patterns of alliances? Axelrod fed key indicators into his computer model in order to predict the alliances. The information included such things as "the size of each country," "a national capabilities index," an "index of the degree of power held by each based on an index of military-industrial strength," and so on. In that it gave a picture of the historical landscape, it was very much as a map of the possibilities, where a statistical profile of "likelihoods" or "possibilities" documents a map of the terrain of the future. Axelrod also develops other models, based on computer simulation, to do with such variables as promoting cooperation (Axelrod 1984), norms creation, the setting of standards in commercial contexts (1997, Chap. 5), or the creation of new political actors (1997, Chap. 6). It is indisputable in one sense that agent-based modeling constitutes a powerful tool which enables the exploration of relationships that are neither analytically nor empirically tractable. Such an approach can reveal new qualitative dimensions of processes and thus enables the exploration of multiple possible histories via repeated computer simulations. It can do this through simulating interactions within a systems context characterized by non-linearity, emergence and interconnectness, in a way that permits the computer manipulation of variables in changed contexts.

The Limitations of Agent-Based Modeling

Although complexity ideas apart from agent-based modeling have been variously introduced into politics and international relations research (Bousquet and Curtis 2011; Bousquet and Geyer 2011; Geller 2011; Geyer and Pickering 2011; Hoffmann and Riley 2002; Harrison 2006a, 2006b; Harrison and Singer 2006; Jervis 1997; Kavalski, 2007; Lehmann 2011; Ma 2007; Rosenau 1990; 2003) outside of the modeling approach complexity-based research is relatively embryonic as a form of analysis. In their recent article, Bousquet and Curtis (2011), make the point that agent-based modeling has been to date "the only area to have generated a coherent and cumulative research agenda" (44), but also claim that such an approach should not "exhaust the potential of complexity thinking" (44). From their perspective, it is important to look for ways that complexity can "extend important debates within IR, and draw out many of the connections between IR and complexity that have remained either implicit or overlooked" (44). What is needed is a conception of complexity that "goes beyond its metaphorical and modeling applications" (44). What they fail to do is specify precisely where the acknowledged deficiencies of modeling approaches reside, and conversely, where the distinctive importance of complexity for politics is to be found. It is these dual lacunae that the main thrust of this article will seek to address.

In earlier work on complexity and world politics, David Earnest and James Rosenau (2006) maintain that agent-based modeling methodology fails on two counts. Firstly, it fails to achieve the status of a theory, maintaining only that of a general perspective or paradigm. This is to do with the fact that its methods are neither inductive nor deductive, but based on simulation modeling through computational and mathematical approaches. Second, they claim that "it is unclear . . . that empirical tests of computer-simulated processes can in fact test our hypotheses about actual dynamic systems" (Earnest and Rosenau 2006, 149). Hence, there is a lack of isomorphism between model and reality.

Although, since they wrote, various "evidence-directed" research has sought to engage such criticisms, their basic claim that agent-based modeling methods typically employ assumptions about human rationality and other simplifications about everyday decision-making which constitute foundations to the system, still constitutes a problem with respect to both the validity of models, as well their ability to predict. One central problem is that humans do not follow simple static decision rules. Given that model construction depends necessarily upon a trade-off between parsimony and reality, it is difficult to see in a theoretical sense how a model could contain dynamic response capabilities that enabled it to respond to or account for the complexities of the world. As decisions in the world depend on who we are, and as our identities for complexity theories, are *contingent assemblages* (to use a Deleuzean concept), shaped by dynamic events in the system, it would seem not possible, as Earnest and Rosenau (2006, 150) put it, "to capture the adaptive behaviour of agents through genetic algorithms." The writers they have in mind who do this include Holland (1995, 1998), Jervis (1997), Axelrod (1997, 2006a, 2006b), Axelrod and Cohen (1999) and Bhavnani (2006).

Whether it is strictly necessary, as Earnest and Rosenau claim, to reject complex adaptive systems research *in toto*, or whether simulation research based on "agency-level computational models" (Saunders-Newton 2006, 165) can not offer a "third leg" position (Marney and Tarbert 2000), yielding some useful knowledge, if nothing else, for different types of scenario planning, we do not need to dispute. Scenario forecasting is certainly useful, as is risk analysis generally, and the use of modeling can in these contexts be a useful form of analysis. We can concede also that agent-based modeling can enable the exploration of certain relationships and possibilities through simulation methods that are not tractable by other means. We can concede further that newer "evidence-directed" approaches (Geller and Moss 2008) and lively discussions about model validation (Marks 2007) are also constructive. Insofar as approaches to model building eschew the goals of prediction and generalisation, but confine their purpose to exploration or clarification, they escape some of the general criticisms being made. Agent-based modeling may, then, provide, as Axtell and Epstein (1994) maintain, a powerful computer technique for gauging the general lie of the land, exploring multiple possible scenarios, manipulating variables or altering environments. However, it is problematic as a predictive methodology, and will be of limited value concerning issues of validity consistent with the general epistemological constraints of modeling construction in terms of a necessary trade-off in terms of parsimony and reality. Although the literature reveals growing awareness of these limitations today, this criticism is particularly appropriate against the more traditional 'artificial societies' form of agent-based modelling as developed and inspired by Axelrod's research. This explains possibly, as Marks (2007, 281) notes, the relatively small uptake of the approach by many social scientists, including economists.

    In addition to this, in that such a methodology depends on ahistorical genetic algorithms and simulation, a pernicious form of foundationalism is introduced into systems thinking. Such genetic algorithms cannot emulate the processes of how human beings make decisions because the very process of making decisions will be affected by system inputs and dynamics. Neither can behaviour or future actions be predicted from such models since system perturbations are, in theory, unpredictable in open environments. This, at one level, is accepted by Axelrod (1997), who justifies simulation as a method on the grounds that the emergent properties of such models cannot be deduced. In that it employs simulation:

> it does not aim to provide an accurate representation of a particular empirical application. Instead, the goal of agent-based modeling is to enrich our understanding of fundamental processes that may appear in a variety of applications. This requires adhering to the KISS principle, which stands for the army slogan "keep it simple, stupid." (Axelrod 1997, 4–5)

The difficulty is that keeping it simple doesn't resolve the theoretical problems. Neither does making model building more complex by being more sensitive to empirical data in the construction of models. This is because what is crucial is not how accurate the model is in representing the past situation, but its theoretical inability, *once formed*, to ascertain dynamic events in either the present or the future. This is due to the complexity postulate of unpredictability and the general lack of isomorphism between model and reality with particular relation to dynamic events. The more recent 'evidence-driven' modelling tradition seems predicated upon the assumption that if models are empirically validated at the micro level they will exhibit macro validity as well, but this is not logically the case. Axelrod was at least aware that pursuing a more evidence-directed approach in relation to model construction and validity would not actually resolve the issues at stake.

The pivotal role of assumptions underpinning model formation is what must be appreciated here. By its very nature in providing predictions of the future, or even explaining real behaviour in the present, the technique trades on an elision between model and reality. In justifying his "landscape" modeling, Axelrod (1997, 88) claims that his theory "does very well in predicting the European alignment of the Second World War." His prediction is "accurate for all but one of the seventeen countries" (it was not clear why the Western alliance did not oppose the Soviet Union rather than Germany), even a single "error" or "discrepancy" of this type presents a potentially serious headache for policy planners relying on such a technique. It is the same situation for the other models Axelrod develops, or for those writing later in the tradition. As Ball (2004, 361) notes, it is not clear that it is any more useful as an approach than simple realist assumptions based on self-interest and suspicion. It is only as a form of 'retrospective prediction' that such a technique functions, for in an open system that predicts from the present to the future, there is an important sense in which it can not know where to look, or what to look for, and what is more or less significant. While a model can contain provision for unpredictability, we can only evaluate the effectiveness of such models ability to predict in hindsight. Only retrospectively can we decide on what the critical or spinodal point was, in order to conclude that between 1936 and 1939 "history seems to pass through a kind of spinodal point where the anti-Soviet alliance ceases to be viable" (Ball 2004, 366). Axelrod's landscape model, then, constitutes, as Ball (2004, 361) notes, citing Michael Oakeshott (1933, 128) a type of "counterfactual history" which claims to give us a picture of the historical landscape, but in fact provides *only a retrospective* "prediction" on history. It is noteworthy in this respect that Oakeshott opposed the method.

Furthermore, in what must appear as a positivist-style attempt to save a science of prediction in the face of complexity and non-linearity, there is a sense in which agent-based modeling as developed by Axelrod, alongside later proponents of the approach, functions generally as a form of *scientism*. In this sense, agent-based modeling can be seen as an attempt to reinstate a policy science of reliable prediction (a dominant concern of the American science community) *against* the main argument or insight of the complexity revolution: that prediction is theoretically not possible. While, of course, events maintain a normal order of regularity which we may come to rely upon, what cannot be excluded is the occurrence of surprise events. If complexity physics asserts anything through its emphasis on non-linearity and stochastic emergence it is this: that it is not possible to predict macrobehaviors or collective actions simply as a scaled-up version of individual behavior or microevents. Complexity by definition is not additive! Furthermore, even within the micro or macro, trajectories are not deterministic or linear. Given these points, as Ball (2004, 441) notes, there is an ever-present danger that "any particular agent-based model of a social phenomenon risks coming to conclusions that depend on the underlying assumptions of the model." Agent-based modeling depends on a prior specification of agent characteristics including genetic predispositions and static operational rules for engagement and interaction (as core features of the model). If simulation then proceeds in order to detect "properties that occur at the level of the whole society" (Ball 2004, 3) it thus contradicts the principle of non-additivity. In short, in that it seeks to generalise and predict, agent-based modeling seeks to ascertain what complexity declares impossible; *viz.* the impossibility of *scalable* measures of future or of macroorder behavior.

These criticisms are brought home forcefully by Thomas B. Pepinsky (2005) in his rigorous examination of the epistemological and ontological entailments of simulation modeling. Noting how simulation modeling aims to create "an artificial representation of a real world in order to manipulate and explore the properties of that system" (369), he notes how much knowledge and detailed information—concerning the "environment," the "agent," the "rules," and the "parameters"—any model constructor who attempts to model microinteractions for assessing macrooutcomes *must have*. Comparing politics and international relations to a small case study of aerodynamics of lift, he notes how politics is a much less certain arena where full knowledge permitting model construction is highly unlikely to prevail. It is dubious in his view whether all of the relevant rules and parameters that could possibly affect behaviour in real life can be captured in a simulation. He could, of course, have gone even further than this, for in open environments as theorized by CT there is first, an *epistemological* problem, in Donald Rumsfeld's sense, of knowing what one doesn't know, or even worse, of *not knowing what one doesn't know*. The model constructor can only construct using the awareness of the situation as it is presently understood. The issue extends, second, to the problem articulated by Alan Turing and Alphonso Church many years ago, of the logical inability of predicting in open environments on the basis of any specified algorithmic specifications. Both Turing and Church demonstrated in mathematics that decisions and events in the future were always in excess of the algorithm that was established to predict them, and could not be predicted on the basis of such an algorithm. Kurt Gödel's 'incompleteness theorem' demonstrated essentially the same thing. (see Hodges 2000, 493–545; Mitchell 2009, 60–70).

Marks (2007) recent robust discussion of validity and prediction issues (which highlights many of the issues I am raising), is certainly positive. However, the net effect is to limit the applicable scope of agent-based modeling as an approach. Furthermore, his discussion does not deal with an even more serious omission in agent-based modeling approaches to complexity that I will identify. This is the absence of any plausible consideration of a normative role for politics, authority or institutionalization. These are issues I will take up below.

Toward a Richer Conception of Complexity and Politics

Those advancing agent-based modeling approaches have taken their inspiration largely from theoretical developments occurring the Santa Fe Institute for the study of complex systems, in New Mexico, USA. I argue that what is required is an elevation of the more historical approach centering on Prigogine and the Brussels School, as well as the European social philosophers like Gilles Deleuze (1987; 1990; 1994) and Niklas Luhmann (1995). While Deleuze has developed a philosophical approach that is consistent with CT formulations, Luhmann has adapted systems theory in the same way. Modeling approaches have, to date, colonized much of the significance of complexity analysis, seeking to adapt CT insights in accord with game-theoretic approaches to a modified but otherwise resurrected predictive scientific model. The result has been that a great deal of the real significance of the complexity revolution has been obscured.

I will argue below that it is toward a new historical form of systems thinking constitutive of a nominalist historical materialism that complexity directs us. Although historical materialism has traditionally been associated with Marxism, the classical stereotype of the economy as a determining foundation, as well as a lack of attention to other forms of power differentials (racism, sexism, etc) renders Marxism as problematic as a vehicle for comprehending systems complexity. Although Louis Althusser advanced seminal insights in this regards, it is not within the scope of this paper to discuss these further, except to say that in my view, he failed to establish Marx himself as a complexity thinker. In the sense that complexity can be described as a form of historical materialism, then, it is as a specifically non-Marxist, nonfoundational systems approach, which, in the language of CT, is characterized by "self-organization," "time irreversibility," "contextual contingency," and "discursive mediation," concepts to be explained below. As such, it reconceptualizes what we mean by science, altering both our epistemological and ontological frameworks in relation to the way we understand and represent our world. The central importance for politics is that once the complexity of global life is more properly understood as this new form of systems thinking, it has implications for institutionalization, the role of the state, and for global politics, of a kind wholly missed by the agent-based modeling (mis)appropriation of the tradition.

If CT has a richer significance than that encapsulated in modeling approaches, in what does it reside? At its most general level, as Frederick Turner (1997, xii) points out, what complexity does is "place . . . within our grasp a set of very powerful tools—concepts to think with." Rather than focus on prediction via simulation modeling, what complexity enables is an approach that prioritizes axioms about indeterminacy; nonpredictability; uncertainty; emergence; self-organization; contingency and historicity; limited or partial knowledge; mutuality; and insufficiency or interdependency as basic postulates. What complexity physics has to offer politics is not new models that enable prediction but new tools and axioms concerned with how systems operate. It offers a way of understanding the role of structural factors in change, including nonpredictability and its consequences; the delayed, unintended, or indirect effects of actions; and the importance of "uncertainty," "noise," "accident," and "emotion." In introducing a systems perspective into knowledge generation and research it qualifies the stark individualism and reductionism of positivistic science as well as liberal philosophical approaches. When systems effects are considered, it elucidates how linear mechanical models frequently misrepresent the dynamics of events, preventing a genuine understanding of outcomes.

CT asserts, in short, that linear models of science cannot reveal the dynamics of complexity in systems. In addition, contextual contingency defeats the possibility of laws of behavior or development of being decisive. As with developments in fields such as thermodynamics, chemistry, biology, and across the sciences, CT has shifted understanding of science (and the world) in a way that also has application to the social sciences and politics. From continental philosophy, also, among writers like Foucault, Deleuze, and Luhmann, CT insights have assisted in resolving issues of determinism and indeterminism, structure and agency, nature and nurture, system and part, as they have calamitously played out in the philosophies of writers like Marx and Hegel in relation to determinism.

Complexity as a New Form of Historical Materialism

In a range of publications from 1980s to 2004, Ilya Prigogine has developed a complexity formulation relevant to both the physical and social sciences. In works such as *Order Out of Chaos* (1984), written with Irene Stengers, and *Exploring Complexity* (1989), written with Grégoire Nicolis, it is claimed that CT offers a bold new and more accurate conception of science and the universe. This new conceptualization is superseding standard models, including quantum mechanics and relativity, which came to prominence at the beginning of the twentieth century as "corrections to classical mechanics" (Nicolis and Prigogine 1989, 5). Prigogine criticizes Newtonian mechanics and quantum theory, which represented time as reversible, meaning that it was irrelevant to the adequacy of laws. If a film can represent motion running backwards in the same way as running forwards, then it is said in physics that time is reversible. The rotation of the hands of a clock is reversible, whereas tearing a piece of paper is irreversible. Prigogine does not deny time reversibility but wishes to add that in many domains, including life itself, time is irreversible. CT builds on and intensifies the "'temporal' turn" introduced by this "correction." Prigogine places central importance on time as real and irreversible. With Newton, say Prigogine and Stengers (1984), the universe is represented as closed and predictable. Its fundamental laws are deterministic and reversible. Temporality is held to be irrelevant to the truth and operation of the laws. As Prigogine and Stengers (1984, 11) say, "time . . . is reduced to a parameter, and future and past become equivalent."

The Challenge to the Principle of Ergodicity

If time is irreversible, the future never simply repeats the past. Prigogine's revolution in response to the classical and quantum paradigms in formal terms was to challenge the *principle of ergodicity* which resulted in Poincaré recurrence. Restated by Henri Poincaré, the theorem expresses the cyclic time of the Stoics to formulate recurrence in an isolated system. This was the principle which held, in conformity with the law of the conservation of energy, that system interactions in physics would eventually reproduce a state or states almost identical to earlier initial states of the system at some point in the future. The amount of time taken for repeatability is known as

'Poincaré cycle time.' It was based on such an approach that time reversibility had been defined as real, and time irreversibility was an illusion. Prigogine challenged the relevance and applicability of these assumptions to classical or quantum measurement. If systems are never isolated or independent from their surroundings, then in theory, even small perturbations or changes in the surroundings could influence the system functioning or trajectory. Even *very* small perturbations could cause *major* changes.

As physicist Alastair Rae (2009) notes, "The consequences of this way of thinking are profound," (113), for they replace assumptions of reversibility with irreversibility (114) and introduce notions of indeterminism into physics (113). Although quantum theory had introduced notions of indeterminacy, through the interaction with measurement, for Prigogine, such an indeterminism is more centrally associated with "strong mixing" in initial system interactions. 'Strong mixing' refers to the effect of influences or instabilities on a system, which are frequently chaotic, small or arbitrary. Another consequence explains how the individual subject can be both historically and socially constituted, yet unique. While each subject lacks an essence or substance (*ousia*), in Aristotle's sense, ontological uniqueness is constituted in terms of differential affects of environment in relation to the different locations in space and through the differential affects exacted as a consequence of time irreversibility.

Bifurcation and the Limitations of Prediction in Open Environments

CT also defeats the possibility of historical inevitability and forecasting. In introducing a systems perspective, Prigogine's innovation was to distinguish macroscopic from microscopic processes in explaining system behaviors, resulting in a different way of understanding order. Complex systems, in contrast to the classical mechanical and quantum models, are holistic in the sense that the whole is more than the sum of its parts, and where entities emerge from the interactions between part and part, and part(s) and whole. By defining order as a product of the system as a whole, as in a complex dynamical system, order or pattern associated with the macroscopic property of the entire system is not a property of the constituent elements of the system, yet can affect them through a variety of linear and nonlinear processes involving "feedback loops" or "endogeneity," "strong mixing," and "downward causation." Prigogine's contribution was to postulate that systems could also develop in states of nonequilibrium where, through a process of emergence, new features of the system develop in ways which are both practically and theoretically unpredictable.

When a system enters far-from-equilibrium conditions, its structure may be threatened, and a "critical condition," or what Prigogine and Stengers call a "bifurcation point," is entered. At the bifurcation point, system contingencies may operate to determine outcomes in a way not causally linked to previous linear path trajectories. Deleuze drew on writers like Prigogine in order to conceptualize indeterminacy at the level of philosophy. For Deleuze (1994), as Protevi (2006, 22) summarizes him, "a singularity in the [topological structure of the] manifold indicates a bifuricator." The trajectory is not therefore seen as determined in one particular pathway. Although this is *not* to claim an absence of antecedent causes, it is to say, says Prigogine (1997, 5), that "nothing in the macroscopic equations justifies the preferences for any one solution." Or, again, from *Exploring Complexity*, "[n]othing in the description of the experimental set up permits the observer to assign beforehand the state that will be chosen; only chance will decide, through the dynamics of fluctuations" (Nicolis and Prigogine 1989, 72). There is no way, even in theory, to tell what the future will be. Once the system "chooses," it "becomes an historical object in the sense that its subsequent evolution depends on its critical choice" (72). In this description, they say, "we have succeeded in formulating, in abstract terms, the remarkable interplay of chance and constraint" (73). As such, "bifurcation is the source of innovation and diversification, since it endows the system with new solutions" (74).

Figure 5.1 offers a schematic diagram of *bifurcation*. Nicolis and Prigogine (1989, 73) make the following comment about the model:

> A ball moves in a valley [a], which at a particular point λ_c becomes branched and leads to either of two valleys, branches b1 and b2 separated by a hill. Although it is too early for apologies and extrapolations . . . it is thought provoking to imagine for a moment that instead of the ball in Figure [1] we could have a dinosaur sitting there prior to the end of the Mesozoic era, or a group of our ancestors about to settle on either the ideographic or the symbolic mode of writing.

Although, due to system perturbations and fluctuations, it is impossible to precisely ascertain causes in advance, retrospectively, of course, we find the "cause" there in the events that lead up to an event, in the sense that we look backwards and point to plausible antecedent factors that contributed to its occurrence. While therefore not undetermined by prior causes, the dislocation of linear deterministic trajectories and the opening-up of alternative possible pathways that cannot be *preascertained* in open environ-

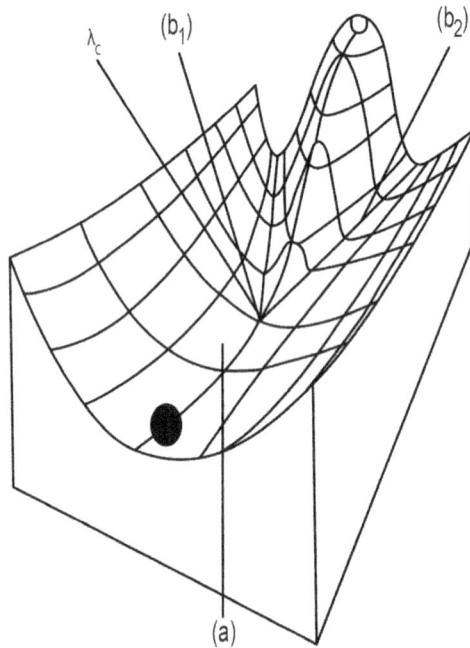

Figure 5.1. "Figure 31: Mechanical Illustration of the Phenomenon of Bifurcation" and "excerpted text" from the book *Exploring Complexity* by Gregoire Nicolis and Ilya Prigogine. Reprinted by permission of Henry Holt and Company, LLC. All Rights Reserved.

ments, is what Prigogine means by "chance." In thermodynamics, Nicolis and Prigogine give the examples of thermal convection, the evolution of the universe itself, as well as climate and all physical processes. They were also aware, however, that their conclusions extended across all open systems to the social and human sciences as well, embracing life, all biological organisms, and social and political processes, as an illustration of nonequilibrium developments. Indeed, all systems (1984, 9) contain "essential elements of randomness and irreversibility." In this context, the future is not simply *unknown*, but *unknowable*.

Self-organization, Emergence, Reduction and Contingency

For CT, there are no foundations or historical constants, such as self-interest, subject-centered reason, or economy, which guide politics. Therefore, predictability and political regulation are difficult, a fact that causes problems for agent-based modeling approaches of the "artificial societies" type that Axelrod developed. Two key ideas of CT which reinforce these views include *self-organization* and *emergence*. The idea of self-organization entails that systems are not organized or regulated by anything external to themselves, in the sense of a foundation or essential principle that is ahistorical. This is not to say, of course, that complex systems do not organize themselves by drawing on external resources, such as energy and information. Also, although laws apply, they operate as a consequence of the elements within a system, i.e., relationally, and are contingent and evolutionary. This also explains how systems generate new patterns of activity through dynamic interactions over time. Of relevance to both self-organization and emergence, complexity theorists also typically represent the world as stratified, characterized by levels or sub-systems, interconnected by interactions. Within complex systems, the interconnectedness of part and whole means that interactions of various sorts will define relations at various levels. Interactions characterize relations, both at the microscopic (organisms, cellular life) and macroscopic levels. Such interactions can be of qualitatively different types, both linear and non-linear, and "multi-referential" in Edgar Morin's sense. As he suggested, types of interactions that typify complex systems may be complementary or competitive, physical, biological, psycho-social, anthropological, economic, political, or so on. For Morin (1977/1992, 47):

> Interactions (1) suppose elements, beings or material objects capable of encountering each other; (2) suppose conditions of encounter, that is to say agitation, turbulence, contrary fluxes, etc.; (3) obey determinations/constraints inherent to the nature of elements, objects or beings in encounter; (4) become in certain conditions interrelations (associations, linkages, combinations communications, etc.) that is to say give birth to phenomena of organization.

In relation to the concept of *emergence*, within any system, the macrostructure and microstructure of parts interact, affecting each other, and permitting indefinite recombination, thus ensuring new entities and structures, resulting in novelty and change (Capra 1996). It is through interactions at different magnitudes, which push a system beyond a threshold, that ontological emergence takes place, and it is this that defeats the possibilities of reductionism. Kauffman (2008, Chap. 3–5) states that there is "quiet rebellion" within science as to the adherence to reductionism. He notes various Nobel Laureates, such as Philp W. Anderson (1972), Robert Laughlan (2005), and Leonard Susskind (2006) who argue for emergentism and against reduction to physical laws to explain life processes, or forms of social organization. Because relations and occurrences are contextual and contingent, it is not possible to predict macroproperties from a knowledge of the micro and vice versa. It also defeats the possibilities of universal laws as constituting a sufficient explanation for events—*context is all*. In this systems paradigm, the dynamic and non-linear assert themselves alongside the static and linear, and non-equilibrium and equilibrium operate as both temporary and intermittent.

Institutionalization and Complexity Management as the Basis of Normative Political Theory

If uncertainty and unpredictability are core complexity dimensions, then a strong normative role for political institutions would seem crucial. Yet, this is where agent-based modeling is most lacking. Extending their criticisms of the individualism of the approach, where political order is viewed as emerging solely from the interaction of agents, Earnest and Rosenau (2006) claim that it fails to be able to explain what is central to politics: *authority*. As they state:

> The pattern of authority in [agent-based modeling] is one of its distinctive features: it has none. Authority is perfectly decentralized; each agent decides and acts on the basis of internal rules that evolve in response to environmental feedback. This is the logical antithesis of social authority, in which the privileged agent makes allocative decisions for a group of other actors. (Earnest and Rosenau 2006, 153)

The fact that agent-based modeling eschews any model of collective authority not only facilitates its possible uptake by political researchers of a more libertarian bias but is also clearly inadequate given the anarchic implications of complexity for societies and global politics unless accompanied by a normative emphasis on institutionalization and regulation. The absence of attention to authority can be discerned, in part because, as it developed initially in the North American environment, both agent-based (AB) and complex adaptive systems (CAS) simulation modeling approaches tended to be ontologically reductive, seeing order as emerging purely through the interaction of self-interested individuals. As Pepinsky (2005) puts it, this treats individual interaction "as ontologically prior to emergent properties of the system under investigation" (379). Further, he notes that researchers who employ simulation share the supposition "that the topology of the environment will have no effect on the emergent phenomenon" (381). Such a reductionist tendency would be highly contentious within the broader confines of CT, which specifically emphasizes the effects of system on parts, as entailed in notions such as "downward causation." In the work of writers such as Stuart Kauffman (2008), and more specifically in the European complexity tradition, the strong emphasis on nonreductionism entails an approach that is more *systemic*, where part and whole mutually affect each other and where emergence is an outcome of the *system as a whole*. Such an approach has a different entailment for representations of authority and politics. In this and the final section, I will maintain that, contra agent-based modeling, any adequate theory of complexity and politics requires a normative conception of authority and its institutionalization, if we are to forestall the possible drift to anarchy and catastrophe.

There is an overwhelming abundance of research that now documents that when the complexity of the world is unregulated it results in entropy and disorder, resulting in "power-law," "non-scalable" distributions, productive of cumulatively unequal distributions in the social and economic world. 'Power-law' refers here to a statistical dynamic, but one which characterizes all areas of life—physical, biological, social, economic, political. Such power-law distributions were noted by Vilfredo Pareto in the last decade of the nineteenth century, with respect to wealth and authority. Here, unregulated contexts resulted in cumulative inequality, disadvantage, elitism, and *étatism*, based as they are upon inverse relationships between the numbers of people in the population and the amount of wealth or influence they hold. Power-law distributions are seen to be a function of what complexity researchers term *self-organized criticality* (SOC). They allow for extreme events and are indeed a pervasive feature of life and cancel out the significance of "average" behavior in Gaussian terms. As Ball (2004, 299) notes, "[s]elf-organised criticality is one of the few genuinely new discoveries to have been made in statistical physics over the past two decades, and it has proved an astonishingly fertile idea" (see Bak 1997, 191; Bak, Chen and Creutz 1989; Bak and Chen 1991; Buchanan 2000; Cederman 1997, 2003; Ball 2004, 297–300). Ball (p. 300) says it "seems to provide a powerful framework for understanding a wide range of phenomena." Linked to self-organized criticality, power-laws entail ideas of non-scalability or additivity, due to nonlinearity of relations between micro and macro order phenomena, as well as unpredictability, because change can occur due to minor actions, or actions from a distance (see Bak 1997, 191). According to Ball (p. 498) "[s]cale-free networks [which result in power-law distributions] are now starting to look like such a fundamental aspect of human culture that eyebrows are raised and questions asked when they do *not* appear." Not only does this apply to earthquakes, where "probability . . . diminishes as its size increases according to a power-law," but it also adequately characterizes many social or economic phenomena, *if unregulated through political action*, as well. This has especially occurred with regards to economic inequality during the era of neoliberal govermentality. According to Ball (p. 307), in the USA in 2006 some 40% of the wealth was now owned by 1% of the population. Wealth inequality thus conforms to a power-law distribution *unless regulated*, as does leadership and power. That power-law distributions emerge in social life, introducing potential disorder, also creates an *imperative of planning* was noted by Richardson (1960) and Zipf (1965).

Given CT's emphasis on unpredictability, uncertainty, and nonscalability, the role for politics is clearly an essential one of managing, containing, or even (in certain circumstances) permitting complexity. Because complexity gives us understandings about the unpredictable and interdependent nature of the world, politics and authority become the art, therefore, of complexity *management*. As Neil Harrison (2006c, 188) notes, politics in this sense becomes conceptualized as "the process by which the institutions governing collective behaviour are organised." More recently, a similar point has been reinforced by Ma (2007) who argues that theories of institutionalized politics are premised on CT formulations of the world. In this sense, from the point of view of politics, we must conceptualize authority as *normatively indispensable* to a complexity approach, because, as Harrison (2006c, 188) puts it, "authority operates through formal and informal institutions. Informal institutions, like cultural practices, are shared meanings and emerge from agent interactions mediated through prior states of such institutions." CT thus gives us a representation of the world which saves agency and choice as well as accident and error and which necessitates that it be managed.

Following from this, a number of additional but related insights regarding political management are generated by complexity. Because of uncertainty and the inability to predict accurately in open environments, politics can plausibly be represented inter alia as the art of managing the unexpected. This would suggest a positive role for the state, an argument which is strengthened by the fallibility of humans and the limitations of human reason in response to the complexity of environments. In that these are true, complexity mitigates against the individualism of the classical liberal tradition from Locke onwards, for individuals are conceptualized as insufficient and dependent upon other people and upon the systems and structures of social support. Such an approach has enormous implications for an ethics of action in world affairs, especially in regards to issues such as conscience, responsibility, and accountability in situations where prediction and control are elusive. My focus here, however, must be confined to the political and to the implications of complexity for authority in both national and global contexts. Because complexity places emphasis upon each individual's insufficiency in the face of a precarious and unpredictable environment, the normative implication for politics is *not* an antipathy to state and global structures, but rather an institutional-regulative approach to politics in general. Of possible assistance here is the approach described in the late nineteenth and early twentieth centuries by the welfare state liberals, from Mill to Keynes, including Green, Hobhouse, Hobson, Ritchie, and James Seth, which, as we face a precarious and uncertain future, might be profitably adapted, also, to new global contexts and conditions.

Such a politics also suggests a conception of social justice similar to that exemplified in the writings of David Hume. Hume can help us to understand how learning the arts of coordination can be understood. In part 2 of book 3 of the *Treatise on Human Nature*, Hume notes how justice is an "artificial virtue" (1978, 484). For Hume, justice is a coordinative virtue arising from insecurities about the possession of transferable goods. As Baier (1991, 228) notes, "Hume's justice-inventors know from prior experience that cooperation and mutual trust are both possible and advantageous." It constitutes for Hume a "will to cooperation, [which] by its very expression and replication, becomes the fact of cooperation."

Institutionalization, then, is a normative consequence of the complexity of global life where the future is precarious, dangerous, and uncertain. It is through institutions that complexity is managed and by which the present is channeled to the future. If coordination is the institutional requirement of life's *continuance,* that is, for survival and well-being, then democracy can be represented as a viable institutional mechanism for best enabling it. Indeed, contra agent-based modeling approaches, we can say that it is *because of complexity* that politics, institutionalization and democracy *become necessary.*

Toward Global Cooperation

If complexity *requires* institutionalization and an active state, the thesis can be extended to a consideration of Axelrod's (1984; 1997) thesis on cooperation. Formulated in terms of Axelrod's tit for tat model, currently the dominant approach to cooperation on offer, such an approach seeks to extend the assumptions of agent-based modeling in order to explain cooperation as resulting purely through the interactions between agents without any collective/institutional structures. This illustrates Earnest and Rosenau's point above, that agent-based modeling allows for no positive conception of political authority. I, too, will argue in this section, that Axelrod's tit for tat model is deficient, and argue for what I will call an objective ethic (OE) approach to cooperation. This is based on early-twentieth-century economists associated with the welfare state, as well as by recent work of my own (Olssen 2008; 2010). These works contend that the normative implication of CT supports institutionalization and a regulatory role for the state.

Axelrod's tit for tat strategy is premised on an iterated model of the prisoner's dilemma, where the prohibition on communication is overcome through repeated plays of the game. The original Prisoner's Dilemma accords to a Hobbesian-type pessimism whereby rational egoists will seek always to exploit each other. In the model, players do not (and cannot) communicate, the environment is inert, and only self-interest orientates behavior. In an iterated prisoner's dilemma game cooperation can evolve if the players can learn from their mistakes to consolidate relations of mutual trust. Axelrod invited people to submit possible strategies to his prisoner's dilemma in 1970, and Anatol Rapaport submitted the winning entry by suggesting that one begins by cooperating and then "echoes" one's "opponent's" moves. A great deal of store is placed, in the first instance, on cooperating. But, according to Ball (2004, 527), such a strategy would quickly fail, prompted by mistakes and misunderstandings, which would intensify in a capitalist market economy characterized by individualism and low-level paranoia as a generalized background habitus. Ball summarizes the critical literature concerned with Axelrod's theory asserting that "there is in fact no best way to play" (529) and noting that tit for tat is an "eye for an eye" rather than a "turn the other cheek" morality (529). As Ball extrapolates, if a mistake is made, then players "get locked into a cycle of mutual recrimination" (540–41). Ball notes that Axelrod agrees with the observation (541) that feuding societies, like Albania, the Middle East, or Northern Ireland are relatively common. Ball also refers to Stanley Kubrick's film *Dr Strangelove*, where through a succession of "errors," Armageddon ensues (541). By itself, "Tit For Tat does not guarantee a harmonious world" (541). What transpires in all of the criticisms and all of the revisions of Tit For Tat is that "nice" strategies do better than nasty ones.

It is not clear how Axelrod's tit for tat strategy, as a mechanism for cooperation, can work purely on the basis of interaction between agents, in the absence of authority or a positive-regulatory form of institutionalization. If I cooperate when you cooperate and defect when you defect, many have suggested that the world will very quickly be a "war of all against all." Axelrod's conception presumes a Nash-equilibrium where cooperation emerges purely through the interaction between agents and which presumes no supraindividual structures of authority as such. A set of strategies is a

Nash equilibrium if it constitutes the best set of responses in relation to all other strategies. 'Best' is defined as those strategies that succeed in market terms or, in other words, through the uncoordinated interaction of individuals. Such a theory would well suit those with a libertarian politics, as I observed above. While such game theoretic approaches are taken seriously by elite policy makers, it is difficult to see how such individualistic strategies could resolve the "tragedy of the commons" or promote cooperation in a global age. Many economists, including Keynes, Kalecki, and Hobson, disputed the equilibrium hypothesis. The 'tragedy of the commons' may well be exacerbated also by climate change, population growth, or the threat of nuclear terrorism, which would increase the requirement for authority.

This raises the question as to whether a game-theoretic approach based on self-interest is appropriate to explaining cooperation. The challenge I am interested in maintaining here is that "niceness," i.e., cooperation, cannot *theoretically* be explained as emerging simply through the interaction between agents! What is required for explanation is a positive theory of institutionalization, a positive role for the state, and an objective ethic at both state and global levels. And this is precisely what Axelrod, and agent-based modeling in general, has shown no interest in providing. Indeed, this criticism applies to the entire tradition of simulation modelling to date, including agent-based approaches, but also to closely related complex adaptive systems approaches.

If, in a complex world, we are to account for "niceness" and maximize the possibilities for cooperation in the absence of a theory of equilibrium as the basis of order, then (a) the creation of intermediary institutions, (b) an objective ethic (OE) based on a conception of justice and democracy, and (c) a system of punishment related to this which constrains and rewards defectors are necessary. An OE approach could explain the inclusion of "niceness," or "generosity," because it would be concerned first and foremost with the positive normative content of what enabled people to live and develop their lives into the future under conditions of dignity and mutual respect, with the best likelihood of success for all. Such an ethic of cooperation can be justified as *demanded* by complex systems analysis if the project of humanity is to survive in order to avert any tendencies to disorder and entropy. Such an OE could be adapted to Nowak and May's (1992; 1993) insights about the effects of space on cooperation, by adjusting the "rules" and "norms" according to the contingent circumstances of time and place. Two further concepts could augment this development: models of "Generous Tit For Tat" as developed by Nowak and Sigmund (1992) (in a critical response to Axelrod), and Fehr and Gächter's (2002) idea of "altruistic punishment" (where they note that the threat of punishment increases cooperation). Punishment, as they use the term, performs an adjunct societal function in keeping the project of humanity on track by appealing to each person and each community to exercise self-restraint. It is a *constructed* ethic for a complex world which permits life to continue into the future. Philosophically, it is based upon a theory of becoming. Politically, it depends on a theory of positive democratic state and global authority. It is the kind of normative politics demanded by complexity, but which agent-based modeling scientific approaches do not provide. For if the complexity revolution dictates anything it is that, more today than at any time previously, national and global institutions constitute preconditions for individual well-being, freedom, development, and survival.

Conclusion

In this chapter I have critiqued agent-based modeling as a pertinent approach to grasping the complexity of global life. There are several reasons for such critique. First, it has failed to appreciate or acknowledge the serious epistemological limitations of algorithmic modeling for either prediction or exploration for any purposes other than exploratory or heuristic intent. Second, as a consequence of its prior ontological focus on individual agents and their interactions, it fails to theorize systems adequately or to advocate and develop a necessary normative role for politics and institutions. Because it relies solely upon the interactions between agents, assuming equilibrium in nature, it fails to see how complexity requires a positive theory of state power and institutionalization as a "hedge" against anarchy, uneven development, or disorder. When extended, such a claim also undermines Axelrod's theory of cooperation.

Such omissions in turn suggest that agent-based simulation-modeling traditions have a philosophically naïve conception of complexity. To some extent I view this as a consequence of the fact that many of the early proponents were a part of the North American social science research environment, where a strong priority was given to positivistic norms and measurement quantification, as part of a reductionist scientific approach to understanding the world. While complexity was taken on board as a general social science approach, the general appropriation of the paradigm as developed by the likes of Axelrod and others lacked the philosophical coherence and rigor as it was developed by the early formulators of the approach, at Santa Fe by the likes of Kauffman, or in Europe by scientists such as Prigogine or philosophers such as Deleuze. Failure to understand the limitations of algorithmic modeling for prediction were only one aspect of this. To be so concerned with advocating a science of prediction, or with overcoming obstacles to prediction, given this was what CT announced as theoretically problematic, was yet another. Methods of prediction based on algorithmic models were developed and pursued, despite the important complexity insights of writers like Gödel, Turing, Church, and Wittgenstein, the significance of whose work is clearly not understood as complexity insights were appropriated for social science purposes. Although laws speak to important regularities, they cannot be certainties, and it is theoretically not possible to ascertain when a perturbation will derail a regular linear sequence of events. While such a postulate was theoretically applicable to all scientific prediction, in practice it is likely to apply more to the social as opposed to the physical sciences. And it is likely to be especially relevant to the messy worlds of politics and international relations.

Closely associated with modeling, we have noted other ontological shortcomings as well. In prioritizing agents and interactions, the simulation modelers' render structural features such as "system" and "environment" as ontologically secondary or derivative, failing to fully understand the entailments of non-reductionism, thereby marginalizing the importance of system affects, downward causation, part-whole interactions and coevolution. Under the influence of Axelrod, also, various "metaphysical" elements, already prominent in North American empirical social science disciplines, become secreted within the version of complexity articulated. Hence, ideas of "economic equilibrium," replete with metaphysical axioms concerning "self-interested egoism" (on which Axelrod's idea of equilibrium depends) become operative as the basis upon which cooperation occurs and become the mysterious largely unexplained "metaphysical" source by which interactions between agents can result in order. There is, then, within simulation modeling approaches an insufficiently rigorous understanding of the epistemological and ontological commitments that a coherent doctrine of complexity entails, especially with reference to the historically contingent character of systems and parts, as expressed through concepts such as coevolution, emergence, nonreductionism, downward causation, and the necessarily historically contingent interaction between system and parts. Agent-based modeling approaches have therefore retained metaphysical "deposits" of various sorts, failing to comprehend the full ontological significance of complexity, as given both scientific and philosophical coherence by writers like Prigogine and Deleuze.

This chapter also highlights, at a somewhat more general level, the importance of CT as a new and different *ontological* orientation to politics, international relations, and political theory. As such, it offers a new

162   Mark Olssen

conception of the world which leads us to a different understanding of the
possibilities and pitfalls for human collectivities as they seek to negotiate
and realize a future. Such a new ontology suggests an approach broadly
compatible with Heidegger's notion of *Abgrund,* or groundless ground. It is
in this sense "postmetaphysical" in that it seeks to self-consciously restrict
its formulations within the finitude of the phenomenal making no claims
about the noumenal character of the world *in-itself.* In abandoning the world
of the in-itself—concerning God, determinism, causality, soul, self-interested
egoism,and so on—one does not fall back into relativism and disorder, but
asserts postulates which make sense at the level of our shared sensations
and experiences oriented to a future geared to survival and well-being of life
itself in terms of a theory of becoming. In addition to rejecting all traditional
metaphysical foundations, by way of essences or substances, a complexity
approach reestablishes a holistic and nonreductionist approach to politics,
reconceptualizing agency and subjectivity within a broader theory of systems, structures, and historical change.

Bibliography

ibliAlam, S. J., Meyer, R., and Edmonds, B. (2007). Signatures in networks generat-
ed from agent-based social simulation models, *CPM Report 07–176,* Centre
for Policy Modelling, Manchester Metropolitan University Business School,
Manchester.
Anderson, P. W. (1972). More is different. *Science,* 177, 393.
Axelrod, R. (1984). *The evolution of cooperation.* New York: Basic Books.
Axelrod, R. (1997). *The complexity of cooperation: Agent-based models of competition
and collaboration.* Princeton: Princeton University Press.
Axelrod, R. (2006a). Simulation in the social sciences. In J-P Rennard (Ed.), *Hand-
book on research on nature-inspired computing for economics and management*
(90–100). Hershey, PA: Idea Group.
Axelrod, R. (2006b). Alternative uses of simulation. In Neil E. Harrison (Ed.), *Com-
plexity in world politics: Concepts and methods of a new paradigm* (137–142).
New York: State University of New York Press.
Axelrod, R., and Cohen, M. D. (1999). *Harnessing complexity: Organizational implica-
tions of a scientific frontier.* New York: The Free Press.
Axtell, R., and Epstein, J. (1994). Agent-based modelling: Understanding our cre-
ations. *Bulletin of the Santa Fe Institute,* 9 (Winter).
Baier, A. C. (1991). *A progress of sentiment: Reflections on Hume's treatise.* Cambridge,
MA: Harvard University Press.
Bak, P. (1996). *How nature works: The science of self-organized criticality.* New York:
Copernicus.

Bak, P., and Chen, K. (1991). Self-organized criticality. *Scientific American* 264, 46–53.

Bak, P., Chen, K., and Creutz, M. (1989). Self-organized criticality in the "game of life." *Nature* 342, 780–781.

Ball, P. (2004). *Critical mass: How one thing leads to another.* London: Random House.

Bennett, J. P., and Alker, H. R., Jr. (1977). When national security policies bred collective insecurity: The war of the Pacific in a world politics simulation. In Karl W. Deutch, Bruno Fritsch, Helio Jaguaribe, and Andrei Markovits (Eds.), *Problems in World Modelling: Political and Social Implications* (215–302). Cambridge: Ballinger.

Bhavnani, R. (2006). Agent-based models in the study of ethnic norms and violence. In Neil E. Harrison (Ed.), *Complexity in world politics: Concepts and methods of a new paradigm* (121–136). New York: SUNY Press.

Bouquet, A., and S. Curtis (2011). Beyond models and metaphors: Complexity theory, systems thinking and international relations. *Cambridge Review of International Affairs*, 24(1), 43–62.

Bouquet, A., and Geyer, R. (2011). Introduction: Complexity and international relations. *Cambridge Review of International Affairs*, 24(1) March, 1–3.

Bouquet, F., Barrette, O., Le Page, C., Mullion, C., and Weber, J. (1999). An environmental modelling approach: the use of multi-agent simulations, F. Belasco and A. Weill, eds. *Advances in Environmental and Ecological Modelling.* Elsevier.

Bremer, S. A. (1987). *The GLOBUS model: Computer simulations of worldwide political and economic developments.* Frankfurt: Campus/Westview.

Bremer, S. A. and Mihalka, M. (1977). Machiavelli in machina: Or politics among hexagons. In Karl W. Deutch, Bruno Fritsch, Helio Jaguaribe and Andrei Markovits (Eds.), *Problems in world modeling: Political and social implications* (303–337). Cambridge: Ballinger.

Buchanan, M. (2000). *Ubiquity.* London: Wiedenfeld and Nicholson.

Capra, F. (1996). *The web of life: A new synthesis of mind and matter.* London: Flamingo/HarperCollins Publishers.

Cederman, L-E. (1997). *Emergent actors in world politics: How states and nations develop and dissolve.* Princeton, NJ.: Princeton University Press.

Cederman, L-E. (2001). Modeling the democratic peace as a kantian selection process, *Journal of Conflict Resolution* 45(4), 470–502.

Cederman, L-E. (2003). Modeling the size of wars: From billiard balls to sandpiles, *American Political Science Review*, 97(1), 135–150.

Cioffi-Revilla, C. (2002). Invariance and universality in social agent-based simulations, *Proceedings of the National Academy of Sciences*, 99(3), 7314–7316.

Deleuze, G. (1987). *A thousand plateaus: Capitalism and schizophrenia.* Trans. Brian Massumi. Minneapolis: University of Minnesota Press.

Deleuze, G. (1990). *The logic of sense.* Trans. Mark Lester with Charles Stivale. New York: Columbia University Press.

Deleuze, G. (1994). *Difference and repetition.* Trans. Paul Patton, New York: Columbia University Press.

Downing, T. E., Moss,S., and Wostl, C. P. (2000). Understanding climate policy using participatory agent based social simulation, S. Moss and P. Davidson (Eds.), *Multi-Agent Based Social Simulation*. Berlin: Springer Verlag. Lecture Notes in Artificial Intelligence, v. 1979, 198–213.

Earnest, D. C., and Rosenau J. N. (2006). Signifying nothing? what complex systems theory can and cannot tell us about global politics. In Neil E. Harrison (Ed.), *Complexity in world politics: Concepts and methods of a new paradigm* (143–163). New York: SUNY Press.

Epstein, J. M., and Axtell, R. (1996). *Growing artificial societies: Social science from the bottom up.* Cambridge: MIT Press.

Epstein, J. M. (2007). Generative social science: Studies in agent-based computational models. Princeton: Princeton University Press.

Fehr, E., and Gächter, S. (2002). Altruistic punishment in humans, *Nature* 415, 137–140.

Geller, A. (2011). The use of complexity-based models in international relations: A technical overview and discussion of prospects and challenges, *Cambridge Review of International Affairs*, 24(1) March, 63–80.

Geller, A., and Moss, S. (2008). Growing qawm: An evidence-driven declarative model of Afghan power structures, *Advances in Complex Systems* 11(2), 321–335.

Geyer, R., and Pickering, S. (2011). Applying the tools of complexity to the international realm: From fitness landscapes to complexity cascades, *Cambridge Review of International Affairs*, 24(1) March, 5–26.

Harrison, N. E. (2006a). (Ed.) *Complexity in world politics: Concepts and methods of a new paradigm.* New York: State University of New York Press.

Harrison, N. E. (2006b). Thinking about the world we make. In Neil E. Harrison (Ed.) *Complexity in world politics: Concepts and methods of a new paradigm* (1–24). New York: SUNY Press.

Harrison, N. E. (2006c). Complex systems and the practice of world politics. In Neil E. Harrison (Ed.) *Complexity in world politics: Concepts and methods of a new paradigm* (183–195). New York: SUNY Press.

Harrison, N. E., and Singer, J. D. (2006). Complexity is more than systems theory. In Neil E. Harrison (Ed.) *Complexity in world politics: Concepts and methods of a new paradigm* (25–42). New York: State University of New York Press.

Hodges, A. (2000). Turing: A Natural Philosopher?. In Ray Monk and F. Raphael (Eds.) *The great philosophers: From Socrates to Turing* (493–541). London: Phoenix/Orion Books Ltd.

Hoffmann, M. J., and Riley, J., Jr. (2002). The science of political science: Linearity or complexity in designing social inquiry, *New Political Science*, 24(2), 303–320.

Holland, J. H. (1995). *Hidden Order: How adaptation builds complexity*, Reading, MA.: Perseus Books.

Holland, J. H. (1998). *Emergence: from chaos to order.* Cambridge, MA: Perseus Books.

Hollist, W. Ladd (Ed.) (1978). Exploring competitive arms processes: Amphlifications of mathematical modeling and computer simulation in arms policy analysis. New York: Marcel Dekker.

Hume, D. (1978). *A treatise on human nature.* 2nd Edition, P. H. Nidditch, ed., Oxford: Clarendon.

Jervis, R. (1997). System effects: Complexity in political and social life. Princeton: Princeton University Press.

Kavalski, E. (2007). The fifth debate and the emergence international relations theory: Notes on the application of complexity theory to the study of international life, *Cambridge Review of International Affairs,* 20(3), 435–454.

Kauffman, S. A. (2008). *Reinventing the sacred: A new view of science, reason and religion.* New York: Basic Books.

Laughlan, R. (2005). *A different universe: The universe from the bottom down.* New York: Basic Books.

Lehmann, K. (2011). Crisis foreign policy as a process of self-organisation, *Cambridge Review of International Affairs,* 24(1) March, 27–42.

Luhmann, N. (1995). *Social Systems.* Palo Alto, CA: Stanford University Press.

Ma,, S-Y. (2007). Political science at the edge of chaos? The paradigmatic implications of historical institutionalism, *International Political Science Review,* 28(1), 57–78.

Marks, R. E. (2007). Validating simulation models: A general framework and four applied examples, *Computational Economics* 30(3) (October), 265–290.

Marney, J. F., and Tarbert, F. E. (2000). Why do simulation? Towards a working epistemology for practitioners of the dark arts, *Journal of Artificial Societies and Social Simulation,* 3(4),

Mitchell, M. (2009). *Complexity: A guided tour.* Oxford: Oxford University Press.

Morin, E. (1977/1992). Method. *Towards a study of humankind. Vol. 1: The nature of nature.* New York: Peter Lang.

Moss, S., and Edmonds, B. (2005). Sociology and simulation: Statistical and quantitative cross-validation. *American Journal of Sociology,* 110(4), 1095–1131.

Nicolis, G., and Prigogine, I. (1989). *Exploring complexity.* New York: Freeman.

Nowak, M., and May, R. (1992). Evolutionary games and spatial chaos, *Nature,* 359, 826–829.

Nowak, M., and May, R. (1993). The spatial dilemmas of evolution, *International Journal of Bifurcation and Chaos,* 3, 35–78.

Nowak, M., and Sigmund, K. (1992). Tit for tat in heterogeneous populations, *Nature,* 355, 250–253.

Oakeshott, M. (1933). *Experience and its modes.* Cambridge: Cambridge University Press.

Olssen, M. (2008). *Toward a global thin community: Nietzsche, Foucault and the cosmopolitan commitment.* Boulder and London: Paradigm Publishers.

Olssen, M. (2010). *Liberalism, neoliberalism, social democracy: Thin communitarian perspectives on political philosophy and education.* New York: Routledge.

Pepinsky, T. B. (2005). From agents to outcomes: Simulation in international relations. *European Journal of International Relations,* 11(3): 367–394.

Plous, S. (1987). Perpetual illusions and military realities: Results from a computer-simulated arms race, *Journal of Conflict Resolution* 31(1): 5–33.

Poundstone, W. (1985). *The recursive universe: Cosmic complexity and the limits of scientific knowledge.* Chicago: Contemporary Books.

Prigogine, I. (1980). *From being to becoming.* San Francisco: W. H. Freeman and Company.

Prigogine, I., and Stengers, I. (1984). *Order out of chaos.* New York: Bantam.

Prigogine, I. (1997). *The End of Certainty: Time, chaos and the new laws of nature.* London: The Free Press.

Protevi, J. (2006). Deleuze, Guattari and Emergence, *Paragraph*, 29(2), 19–39.

Rae, A. (2009). *Quantum physics: Illusion or reality?* (Second, updated edition), Cambridge: Cambridge University Press.

Resnick, M. (1994). *Turtles, termites and traffic jams: Explorations in massively parallel microworlds.* Cambridge: MIT Press.

Richardson, L. F. (1960). *Statistics of deadly quarrels*, ed., Q Wright and C. C. Lienau. Boxwood Press: Pittsburgh.

Rosenau, J. (1990). *Turbulence in world politics: A theory of change and continuity.* London: Harvestor/Wheatsheaf.

Rosenau, J. (2003). *Distant proximities: Dynamics beyond globalization.* Princeton, NJ: Princeton University Press.

Saunders-Newton, D. (2006). When worlds collide: Reflections on the credible senses of agent-based models in international and global studies. In Neil E. Harrison (Ed.) *Complexity in world politics: Concepts and methods of a new paradigm* (165–182). New York: State University of New York Press.

Sandole, D. J. D. (1999). *Capturing the complexity of conflict: Dealing with violent ethnic conflicts of the post-cold war era.* New York: Pinter.

Stoll, R. J. (1985). Simulation government behaviour during disputes. In Michael Don Ward (Ed.), *Theories, models and simulations in international relations: Essays in honor of Harold Guetzko* (510–19). Boulder, CO: Westview Press.

Susskind, L. (2006). *The cosmic landscape: String theory and the illusion of intelligent design.* New York: Little Brown and Company.

Taber, C. S., and Timpone, R. J. (1996a). *Beyond simplicity: Focused realism and computational modeling.* Thousand Oaks, CA: Sage Publications.

Taber, C. S., and Timpone, R. J. (1996b). *Computaional modeling.* Thousand Oaks, CA: Sage.

Troitzsch, K. G. (1997). Social science simulation: Origins, prospects, purposes. In Rosaria Conte, Rainer Hegselmann, and Pietro Terna (Eds.), *Simulating social phenomena* (41–54). New York: Springer-Verlag.

Turner, F. (1997). Foreword: Chaos and social science. In R. A. Eve, S. Horsfall, and M. E. Lee (1997) *Chaos, complexity and sociology: Myths, models and theories.* Thousand Oaks and London: Sage Publications.

Zipf, G. K. (1965). *Human behavior and the principle of least effort.* New York: Hafner.

Part II

Complexity Thinking and Nonanthropocentric International Relations

Chapter 6

Complexifying International Relations for a Posthumanist World

Erika Cudworth and Stephen Hobden

This chapter argues for an approach to the study of international relations (IR) that is complex, post-Newtonian, and nonhuman centered. The combination of these three interrelated elements constitutes what we have called elsewhere posthuman international relations (Cudworth and Hobden 2011b). The starting point for our posthuman approach is an engagement with complexity thinking (CT). While there have been a variety of appropriations of complexity in the social sciences we advocate a "differentiated complexity" which sees the human world as complex, and while embedded in a multiplicity of nonhuman systems, containing distinctive features. CT, we argue, allows the development of a revitalized approach to thinking about systems—seeing systems as open, coconstituting, and overlapping. This allows the analysis of multiple, intersectionalized forms of social exclusion and hierarchy. Furthermore, CT implies a non-Newtonian approach—rejecting the mechanical models at the heart of much of social science. Finally the embedded character of human systems allows the development of a nonanthropocentic perspective. While the overwhelming focus of this chapter is the critique of established approaches in IR and an outline of our own perspective, we do begin to suggest the implications of our approach for reconstructing IR.

Complexity Thinking

As the various chapters in this book have indicated, CT provides us with a range of concepts and ideas that are usefully developed in the study of global life. We argue in this chapter that there is no one CT, yet all approaches include some common elements. For example, natural systems are understood to exist in a web of connections with other systems and to be internally differentiated. The term "emergent properties" is used to describe those specific qualities that emerge at a certain level of systemic complexity but that are not apparent at lower levels (Capra 1996, 34–35). This is a nonreductionist position in which phenomena cannot be reduced to the sum of their parts but gain their character from interaction. In the study of international relations this opens the possibilities to study multiple kinds and levels of institutions, processes, relations, and forms of exclusion while avoiding the pitfalls of reductionism.

A central contribution of the introduction of CT into the social sciences has been to revitalize the concept of "system." Systems in CT are multileveled, and complexity scientists often speak of systems as "nested," with larger scale systems enclosing myriad smaller scale systemic processes (Holling et al. 2002, 68–69). CT also sees systems as existing in the context of other systems and as interacting with them and often developing cross-system dependencies (Maturana and Varela 1980, 109). Systems have "autopoiesis" and are self-making, self-reproducing, self-defining or regulating. Rather than seeing systems as moving toward some kind of equilibrium, as the majority of social science models do, complex systems are viewed as potentially displaying the tendency to move both toward and away from equilibrium. Systems may exhibit negative feedback, which draws them back toward equilibrium, yet complex systems are also subject to positive (reinforcing) feedback, which takes them further from an equilibrium position. Furthermore "co-evolution" with other systems can lead to further destabilization.

These developments in systems thinking have sought to throw off some of the long-established criticisms of such approaches. Much of the theoretical legacy of the social sciences has been concerned with large-scale conceptualization and modeling, usually invoking some kind of conception of a system. In the path of Marx, for example, the capitalist system of relations has been seen as operating globally (Wallerstein 1979). The critique of systems theory in the social sciences has focused on an inability to account for the shifting nature of social life and its multiple differences, a rigid understanding of the relationship between parts and wholes, and a preoccupation with notions of balancing in the maintenance of equilibrium, or social order, as apparent in the functionalism of Talcott Parsons (1951; 1960). CT avoids such rigidity and stasis, understanding systems as simultaneously ordered yet disordered, stable yet unstable (Prigogine, 1980). Instabilities lead to new forms of order and disorder, and these are often (but not necessarily) of increasing complexity. Change and development depend on the systems history and various external conditions and cannot be predicted (Prigogine and Stengers 1984, 140). So, these kinds of understandings of complexity provoke a rethinking of notions of order, pattern, system, and change.

However, social scientists have made very different use of complexity insights. Four distinctive approaches can be identified (Cudworth and Hobden 2009). Some consider that CT can be used metaphorically (for example Urry 2003). Here, complexity provides a series of models which can be used as a means of describing social events. At the other end of the spectrum, "social physicists" perceive complexity as being an inherent quality of all matter (for example Capra 2002). In this view the social world is subject to the same forces as all other material entities. Two further approaches consider the presence of complex phenomena in both the human and nonhuman worlds, but acknowledge distinctive features of the human world. Herein, there are those who see complexity as a network (Watts 2004), or rather as a range of interlinking networks capable of understanding processes from localized minutiae to global events. Our favored approach, which we call "differentiated complexity" allows for analytical separation between social and natural systems and can account for the distinctive features of the social, while also allowing for inscribed complexity in both human and nonhuman systems. It also enables the possibility of analyzing the overlapping, interrelating and coconstituting qualities of social and natural systems, which has been described by Gunderson and Holling (2001) as "panarchy." CT allows us to consider both the embedding of "human" social relations within nonhuman systems and being constituted with those systems. This provides us with a "meta-theory"—as Luhmann (1995) would describe it—of complex systems. We consider this a necessary but not a sufficient approach to understanding international politics. Within this metatheoretical framework, we also need to flesh out an ontology that enables us to understand the particular kinds of complex systems of relations that constitute human social relations and our relations with the nonhuman life worlds. In doing this, we draw upon political ecologism and feminism.

CT is also a useful framework within which we can develop our understanding of human relations as socially intersectionalized. It enables us to think about the coconstituted qualities of systems of social relations, such as those based on class, gender, and ethnic hierarchy. Multiple complex inequalities are apparent in political relations, institutions, and processes from micro to macro levels. Relations of multiple inequalities have recently been addressed by the development of concepts and theories around "social intersectionality." This has mainly been associated with feminist work on the complicating effects of "race" for gender relations (Crenshaw 1991; McCall 2005; Phoenix and Pattynama 2006). Thus, we can understand social systems and nonhuman systems as coconstituted and also consider the intersected qualities of systems of social relations.

Furthermore, we can consider human social relations with "the environment" to be systemic and exploitative. By drawing on perspectives from political ecologism it is possible to consider the interplay between human domination of nature and our systemic domination of each other.

For many, environmental exploitation is the direct result of "intrahuman domination," and the exploitation of humans by other humans has been crucial to explaining the human exploitation of the natural environment (Bookchin 1990). Systemic analyses of capitalism have been deployed in suggesting that the nexus of environmental exploitation is the social organization of labor power in capitalist societies around the production of goods for the market (Dickens 1996). For others, contemporary developments in capitalist relations mean that "nature" becomes increasingly internal to the dynamics of capital accumulation (Castree 2001; Harvey 1996). Environmental difficulties have also been understood in terms of their embedding in the social relations of (post)colonial capital and gender (Anderson 2001; Cudworth 2005; Demeritt 2001). There is a social system of human domination, but we consider that this takes historically and geographically specific formations. Such domination is linked to multiplicitious intrahuman formations of domination. CT can help us to consider intermeshing multiple systems, because it allows for the existence of multiple and coconstituted systems. We conceive these systems as analytically distinct and also mutually constitutive. The domination of nonhuman nature is a system of exploitative relations that overlaps and interlinks with other systems of power and domination based on gender, capital, ethnic hierarchy, and so on, and we call this way of understanding the world "complex ecologism." The contribution of a complex ecology approach is the potential to analyze intersectionality and multiple power relations beyond the human.

Complex ecologism provides a politics and an analytics that takes account both of our imperative need to care for the biosphere and an understanding of the ways in which multiple and complex inequalities shape the securities of different populations. The environmental security approach has been preeminent in understanding "environmental issues" in IR and must be acknowledged for its prioritizing of global environmental problems and for mainstreaming this within the discipline. However, the way it has prioritized the state and seen the environment as something "out there" from which security can be provided has led to severe limitations as way of seeing human/nonhuman relations and theorizing international environmental politics. Complex ecologism stresses the embeddings of human systems within a panarchy and implies that the alleviation of environmental crises involves, not the provision of security, but rather a reorienting of human activity, which will reduce the risks for all systems within the biosphere. We consider this kind of theorizing to be "posthumanist."

International Relations

The notion of an international system has been central to the study of IR. The most famous and durable account has been that initiated by Kenneth Waltz (1979) in the form of structural realism. However many other writers have pointed to the value of a systems approach (such as Kaplan 1964). Likewise, Morgenthau, although he did not employ much in the way of recognizable systems nomenclature, did perceive international politics as being a self-regulating and equilibriating process. This operated through the balance of power (see Morgenthau 1960, 167). While structural realism may have provided a good account of international politics during the apparent stasis of the Cold War, the unexpected seems to have been the more typical feature of international politics since 1990.

Most accounts of system in IR have been based on a Newtonian model of physics which has been imported into the social sciences. Newton's study of gravity and force paved the way for many of the features of the contemporary world, such as industrialization. However, even Newton was aware that his theories did not explain everything, and through the nineteenth and early twentieth centuries shortcomings in the Newtonian worldview became apparent, especially with the advent of quantum mechanics. It wasn't so much that Newton was wrong—it's more that his laws only described a limited subset of physical reality (Wallerstein 2000, 30–31). The problem is that much of the social sciences are based on a mechanical and Newtonian view. For John Ruggie, theories of world politics are "reposed in deep Newtonian slumber" (cited in Harrison 2006, 6). In particular the world is seen as ordered, systems are seen as closed, and the same rules apply regardless of time or space. Post-Newtonian perspectives would dispute all of these ideas. The world may be ordered at times but is also subject to disorder, systems are open and subject to "time's arrow," what has occurred in the past will affect the present and future, and locality can matter.

The study of the social world, we would suggest, is also built on a humanocentric ontology that provides a poor and partial representation of international political structures and processes. The theoretical bedrock of all kinds of international political theory has been humanistic in its core assumptions of dualism (the human/nature dichotomy), the elevation of reason as a master category (and as constitutive of the political subject) and its understanding of political agency in rationalist and human-referential terms (see Plumwood 1993; 2002).

Complexity science undoes the notion that "matter" can be subjected to abstraction and prediction; rather, it suggests that the operation of natural systems is incredibly difficult to predict with any accuracy. The currently compelling evidence of ecological crisis, and the role of human social organization in contributing to it, suggests that our technologies may no longer enable an apparent "mastery" of the nonhuman world. While Latour (1993) may be right in arguing that we have never been properly modern—that this ideal has never been actualized—various more critical political ecologisms have suggested the narrow and unrepresentative nature of humanocentric modern political theory and the unsustainability of our systems of human relations (such as the capitalist free market economy, for example see Hutchinson et al 2002). Given this, then, the question posed for IR theory specifically is the extent to which it wishes to represent the constitution of the political world. Using complexity in understanding international politics provides a clear alternative to positivism as a basis for making claims about the "international system." However before we can start to map out the contours of posthuman international relations we need to clarify our perspective on posthumanism.

Posthumanism

The term "environment," as many critics have pointed out, is inadequate in that it reproduces a dualist understanding which sets the "human" apart from other species, natures, and entities and is grounded in the assumption that humans are not animals or are animals of a very special kind indeed. By simply incorporating "the environment" into the study of IR as an "issue" raising questions for security or governance, the separation of the "human" from other species, natures, and entities remains fixed, and the discipline continues to be anthropocentric. In order to move beyond anthropocentric IR, we need to build on a complex systems approach. We also require a more adequate comprehension of the ontological depth of the political world. To achieve this we need to be critically posthumanist.

Approaches to the study of international relations have been almost exclusively human centered and have ignored the vast variety of nonhuman populations of species and "things." As a result the discipline has failed to represent the ways in which human social and political life is neither exclusively social nor exclusively human. Rather political life is inextricably interconnected and coconstituted by relations with nonhuman beings and things (Braun and Whatmore 2010). The imperative of posthumanism is not just the desire to more accurately capture the complexity of the world; it also has a political incentive. Like Cary Wolfe, we would hope that posthumanist scholarship might contribute to "an increase in vigilance, responsibility and humility" that might accompany living in a world that is not understood "humanocentrically" (Wolfe, 2010, 47).

The historically situated and socially constituted understanding of the human and of the humanistic understanding of the human condition is a preoccupation of much of Foucault's work. The humanist rendering of the "human," he asserts, is largely dogma, owing much to pre-Enlightenment superstitions (Foucault 1984, 44). The category "human" is a social construct linked to formations of power. This insight is crucial in most definitions of the "posthuman." Katherine Hayles (1999), for example, considers that the notion of the "posthuman" indicates the extent to which narrow definitions of what it means to be human have lost credibility. Historically, however, our social world and our understandings of it have been defined and under-stood as "human centered" or anthropocentric, and as "exclusively human" (Midgely 1996, 105). The term "posthumanism" has entered academic and popular discourse as a descriptor for critical perspectives on our human centrism (see Badmington, 2004). Critics of exclusive humanism argue that we should approach the world from a "posthumanist" perspective and seek to understand more about the diversity of species and nonhuman beings with which our world is constituted (Gane and Haraway 2006, 140). The category "human" itself is a human invention, a social construct linked to formations of power that both set the "human" apart from other species and also constitute discourses of forms of intrahuman domination. Sets of historically situated discourses, be they religious or secular, reproduce the separation of man from matter—"the anthropological machine," as Giorgio Agamben describes it (Agamben 2004; Merchant 1980). The power relations and dominant social, economic, and political institutions of Western moder-nity have been constituted by and through constructions of social inequality, of class, race, and gender (Shiva, 1988). However, these social categories of difference and domination have also been cross-cut by prevailing ideas about "nature" and the separation of the human from it.

We need to be aware, however, that the term "posthumanism" is, in many ways, a contested one. It has operated as a somewhat inaccurate col-lective term for a range of discourses and philosophical claims about the constitution and construction of minds and bodies (both human and non-human) and of nature and artifice (see Miah 2007). First, we should make clear that we do not consider "transhumanism" to be a posthumanist position. Transhumanism is an ideology that emphasizes the possible good of a future in which humans are able to acquire "posthuman capacities" and extend their life and health spans, their capacities for happiness and their intellectual capabilities (Bostrom, 2003). While such positions use the terms "posthuman" and "posthumanist," we do not consider these to challenge human centrism. Rather, they represent a "hyperhumanism" through physical extension and disembodiment.

An understanding of "humanity" as a fundamentally socially and culturally constituted category and of humans as existent in webs of relations with other species has been foregrounded in the range of work within animal studies across the humanities and more latterly, some of the social sciences. From philosophy, literature, art history, and cultural studies, to sociology and politics, disciplines are delimited by human exclusivity. For Cary Wolfe (2010, 1), we need to develop modes of social and cultural inquiry that reject the classic humanist divisions of self and other, mind and body, society and nature, human and animal, organic and technological. What Wolfe and others emphasize is that it is not so much "the human" that is a difficulty, but the human-centric understanding of the human as the unique individual striving in the world, and not embodied and embedded in complex biotic lifeworlds.

There is a wide range of perspectives associated with the notion of the "posthuman." Common to them is a critique of humanism as a guiding normative framework for understanding the social/natural world, and all are preoccupied with the consequences of developments in technology, albeit they are often ambiguous on the desirability of biological interventions. As Wolfe (2008) suggests, posthuman work undertakes two related tasks. First, it challenges the ontological and ethical divide between humans and nonhumans that has been the philosophical linchpin of modernity. Second, it engages with the challenge of sharing this planet we inhabit with "nonhuman subjects," and of the coconstituted conditions of multiple species and biosphere.

Allowing space in political life and political analysis for nonhuman beings and things is radically transgressive for the tightly circumscribed discipline of politics and its smaller sibling, international relations. There is a profusion of complex materials, systems, and processes through and with which we humans live. We consider that a posthuman approach to politics involves the recasting of key debates around the subjects, actors, and objects of politics; the public/private divide in Western liberal societies; different levels of political activity and institutional arenas; and notions of change in political systems. What draws together different kinds of posthumanists is the idea of the politics of life, be it human or nonhuman. "We," the living, for example, are embedded in a carbon cycle that international politics seeks increasingly to regulate. Our embodied and embedded condition in a world of multiple species and systems which operate at multiple levels from domestic relations in the home to the regulation of the temperature of the planet raise deep problems for politics based on the fictive constructs of nation-states. Yet in the contemporary world, nation-states are multiplying, and many are strengthening.

The world of politics, national and international, is an artifice, just as Latour suggests. It cannot capture the cosmological reality of life on this planet, and attempts by institutions of human governance to regulate life, since the eighteenth century in particular, have remade a world in deeply problematic ways. Kuehls (1996) has argued that the space of ecopolitics must be beyond sovereign territory. Currently, it is not, and we are faced with the biopolitics of nation states and the international institutional system of states attempting to regulate life with such problematic consequences. The notion of bio-regionalism, developed in the 1970s, remains a pipedream; notions of 'environmental citizenship' poorly describe the identities of human citizens, and the speaking, human political subject remains a foundational discourse of 'the political.' We have not yet made much headway in developing theories, let alone politics, for *Homeland Earth* (Morin, 1999). In the second half of this chapter, we turn to a consideration of the impact of a complexity framework on the discipline of International Relations, and consider how an ontology of complex ecologism reveals both new and different subjects and processes of concern. In short, we set out what posthuman international relations might look like.

Contours of Posthuman International Relations

CT has opened up the possibilities of reenvisioning systems analysis. This suggests the possibility of conceiving of international politics as embedded within a range of human and nonhuman systems and the prospect of developing a nonhumancentric form of analysis. This would have serious implications in the development of a posthuman/non-Newtonian approach to thinking about international relations. Such an approach, we argue, has benefits to offer in thinking about global politics, and here we advance some reasons for adopting a posthuman analysis.

The Unpredictability of International Relations

Central to the development of rationalist theory in IR has been the claim that theories can be verified by their ability to make statements that can be confirmed by future events. However, these attempts to produce a predictive capacity in IR have been plagued by the uncooperative character of events. To a certain extent the discipline of IR has never recovered from the failure to predict the end of the Cold War. Through the 1970s and 1980s it was a shibboleth of the discipline that the bipolar system was stable and enduring. However the Soviet Union disappeared, virtually overnight. In the early 1990s there was much talk of Japan becoming the next global hegemon and very little discussion of the growing significance of China. The impact of the attacks of September 11, 2001, for some the defining international event of the current century, was not predicted. Significantly for the study of international relations, given their international impact, the attacks were carried out by a nonstate actor. These unexpected, and probably unpredictable, events suggest that an approach to studying IR is needed that has at its core a view of the world as unpredictable.

To be in the prediction business is not useful for IR, and we would argue, not possible. It may also be inherently harmful. Starting with a perspective that it is possible to predict future events, to foresee what the likely results of our actions will be, potentially gives policy makers a greater confidence about their actions than is warranted. Starting out from a perspective that the future is intrinsically unknowable, that in implementing policy decisions we need to allow for the unexpected, that greater caution is needed, and greater preparedness to respond to unexpected developments might lead to more effective decision making.

Rethinking Systems

IR, given its global scope, seems to imply the need for a way of thinking about world politics that can theorize the interactions among a range of units. We have already seen how systems thinking in the social sciences more broadly has run into difficulties. In IR, it has been plagued by a number of specific problems. We have noted how complexity approaches to thinking about systems draw on thinking from a number of disciplines in developing a much more dynamic account. In particular, the concept of the complex adaptive system provides a much more effective way of thinking about how systems develop and how they interact and coevolve with other systems. The focus in the analysis of complex adaptive systems is on change rather than the stasis of, for example, neorealism. Self-organizing systems will develop as a result of interactions at the unit level and are subject to change as the character of the units and their interactions change. Neither the character of the units or the outcome of their interactions is a "given." Complex adaptive systems also operate in an environment of other systems and adapt as these interactions develop. As systems come into contact with other systems, their character will change. Powerful actors may have the capacity to affect the fitness landscape in which other actors operate, forcing them to adapt to changing circumstances. Hence it is possible to interpret change from both within and outside of particular systems.

A Way Out of the Level-of-Analysis Problem

In David Singer's (1961, 77) initial formulation, the level-of-analysis problem was one where there were "manifold implications" to the choice of what level (system, unit) of analysis was chosen as the focus. IR could be studied at one of a number of levels of analysis, but the level chosen, and for Singer there always was a choice to be made, would introduce distortions. The problem was choosing the level of analysis that introduced the lowest level of distortion for a particular area of study. The level-of-analysis problem subsequently reappeared as the agent-structure debate, spawning its own enormous literature. Posthuman IR does not so much offer a solution to the level of analysis problem, but rather, it enables us to transcend it altogether.

This is because the perspective from a complex adaptive systems approach is somewhat different. The system level is emergent from the interactions of the units, and hence while perhaps a *different* level of analysis it is not a *distinct* level of analysis. It is different in that we can distinguish between system-level features and unit-level features. Indeed given that there are emergent features at the system level, an analysis simply of unit-level interactions will be incomplete. But it is not distinct as it is the interactions at the unit level that lead to system-level features. Hence to see system and units as separate is problematic. For Edgar Morin (2008, 85) the issue was that "not only is the part in the whole, but the whole is in the part." In order to understand the unit level we also need to understand the systemic level. International systems can be understood as a form of self-organization, emergent from the interactions of unit-level actors. These in turn are also systems with emergent features. In turn, systems take as their environment all other systems and will, if they are to persist, have to develop dependency on the exigencies of those relations.

Questions of Causality

The Newtonian basis of much IR theorizing has developed from a view of the world that perceives the possibility of determining the ultimate causes of particular events. A feature of this form of theorizing is the possibility of saying "if x then y" (all other things being equal). In a detailed discussion of causality in IR, Milja Kurki (2008) has argued that the discipline has had a very limited notion of what causality entails. Both sides of the "divided discipline" (in other words, positivists and postpositivists) have envisaged causality in Humean terms, whether they have supported causal analysis of that kind, or whether they have rejected it. Such a view has a limited view of causes that regards causal analysis as the study of regularities, which are observable, deterministic, and efficient (Kurki 2008, 6). This view of what constitutes a cause is closely linked to Newtonian approaches to physics, and as Kurki argues it will be of limited application to the study of the social world. However, as she argues, even those who reject causal analysis base their idea of what this constitutes on the Humean account of causality. In its place Kurki draws on philosophical realism to advocate the importance of "deep ontology" in "reclaiming causal analysis." By this she means seeing causes as "real non-conceptual 'naturally necessitating' ontological entities, structures, relations, conditions or forces that produce outcomes or processes" (Kurki 2008, 295).

CT theorists have a slightly different approach to thinking about causality. In the analysis of a complex world it becomes very difficult to talk about causes. As with the level of analysis/agent-structure debate, complexity theorizing suggests attempting to transcend these issues. Neil Harrison (2006) argues that there are four reasons why the Humean account of causation is not suited for the analysis of complex systems. First, it applies only to closed systems, whereas a keystone of complexity analysis is the analysis of open systems. He notes that "in an open system, a cause may have different effects at different times due to changed conditions. Therefore, it is not surprising that no general laws of world politics have been found" (Harrison 2006, 12). As David Harvey points out, "in nature's open milieu the constancy of causal sequences—the empiricist's guarantor of nature's 'iron-clad laws'—breaks down" (Harvey 2009, 25). Second, Humean causal analysis depends on very simple models, which may "dangerously oversimplify" complex events. Third, in complex analysis cause and effect may be nonlocal, a view that is rejected by both Hume and Newton. Finally, cause and effect can be simultaneous, again an idea that is rejected by Hume (also see Forrester 1971; Sterman 2002, 511).

The central issue is that in complex systems there is a "tangle of actions, interactions, and feedback" (Morin 2008, 84; Bertuglia and Vaio 2005, 282). This tangle is such that it is in practice not feasible to make sensible claims about causal processes. Complex systems are also subject to time's arrow, such that tracing causal processes, as many historians suggest, is an uncertain undertaking (Beaumont 2000, 178).

CT approaches therefore do not reject causality outright, but rather point to the phenomenal difficulties of ascertaining what those causes might be—given the characteristics of complex adaptive systems as nonlinear, sensitive to initial conditions and subject to action at a distance and simultaneity. As a form of analysis, then, CT suggests as an alternative the investigation of systems development, and in particular the forms of coevolution between systems. While it may not be possible to isolate causes in a traditional sense, or perhaps even in the wider sense promoted by Kurki, understanding how systems have developed as they have remains a fruitful line of study.

Overcoming Humancentrism

It is a "foundational myth" of IR that the discipline was founded in the wake of the First World War to study the causes of war and promote ways of avoiding conflict (Smith 2000, 376). War has remained at the center of the discipline, and for many scholars the prime form that such conflicts have taken is interstate war. While war, and the continued threat of the use of nuclear weapons remains a threat to global welfare, the occurrence of interstate war has declined (Gleditsch et al. 2002) (the 2003 invasion of Iraq being a notable exception), and other dangers have appeared. Potentially the most significant of these are environmental issues, in particular climate change. In our view, IR has a central role to play in the analysis of these issues: environmental questions are certainly transboundary and frequently global; and attempts to address environmental issues frequently involve international actors, whether states, international organizations, or nongovernmental organizations. IR as currently configured, however, has confronted considerable difficulties in addressing environmental matters. Posthuman international relations provides a way of rethinking global processes in order to tackle the issues that we confront.

We would argue for a posthuman approach because it provides a way of analyzing interactions among a range of systems and examines the ways in which those systems have coevolved. International systems are not independent of other systems but are better envisaged as embedded and interacting and coevolving with a range of other systems. Furthermore, international systems are embedded in a range of nonhuman and inanimate systems, and considering these as complex adaptive systems opens a mean of analyzing their interactions. Decentering the human, posthuman international relations stresses the contingent character of human existence and the embedded and overlapping character of human and nonhuman systems. Rather than seeing humans as the center of analysis, posthuman IR stresses that human activity depends on and affects the variety of other systems which comprise the globe. Hence posthuman IR provides a means of considering these interrelations, but it also stresses an ethic of shared dependence on the biosphere.

Implications of Posthuman International Relations

A CT-inflected posthumanism raises serious issues for how IR is approached and what the subjects and objects of its study are. The core element of our argument is that IR remains dominated by humancentric approaches. This places limits on what it is possible to say about international relations and on the ethical issues raised by human actions with regard to nonhuman nature.

A posthumanist approach to IR will certainly broaden the parameters of the discipline and offers an embarrassment of riches in response to the question of what we might be studying when we study IR. The nonhuman world becomes more than the stuff about which political actors, within more or less formal institutional contexts, make decisions and act upon. Rather, the nonhuman forms the landscape of decision making and human endeavor. Posthuman IR will be attuned to the possibilities of a fuller range of actors and constraints in any given context. We have argued that the impact of powerful relational human systems on the nonhuman lifeworld and on vulnerable groups of humans is deeply problematic and inherently unsustainable for many species, including our own. We have remade the conditions of life on this planet such that to speak of "the human" in an exclusive way is untenable, and our embedded condition in what is often referred to as the "environment" must undergird our efforts in international relations scholarship. Human institutions and social practices have effectively remade the world and our conditions of existence on this planet. Privileged groups of humans exercise considerable power over the lives of both human and nonhuman animals and intervene dramatically and often disastrously in nonhuman lifeworlds. This ontological claim has clear ethical implications for the ways in which human collectivities seek to act in and on the world.

A posthumanist approach implies that our world was ever more than human. Thus even the staple subject matter of international relations requires recasting, such as the nature of the military-industrial complex and the practice of war. A human soldier is a transhumanant, an uplifted human. Physical capacity of British troops for example, is enhanced by binoculars, gun sights, and amphetamines. The practice of conventional warfare has long been more than human with the use of dogs, camels, donkeys, horses, pigeons, sea lions, dolphins, and even bees as tools, weapons, and devices for the enhancement of human capability, and the mass killing of nonhuman animals and degradation of vegetation are strategically common. The language of virus (both organic and technic) and contagion infuses debates on security. Even the simple broadening of the subject matter to include nonhuman systems and their structures and agents will result in a more comprehensive disciplinary frame. We would hope, however, that more critical scholarship might grasp the nettle of a more than human emancipatory project. Herein the boundaries of ethics in global affairs are extended beyond both our current institutional forms of political endeavor and our species. Thus the ethical questions around engagement in and the practices of warfare involve transspecies considerations—for the lives of other animals, for the abilities of all kinds of nonhuman systems (from coastal and inland water ecologies to the planetary regulation of temperature) to resist shocks and strains, for example.

Our second point relates to issues of the analysis of change and the possibilities of intervention. Complex systems can present problems of analysis related to unpredictability, causality, and nonlinearity. A central feature of complex systems is the tendency for their characteristics to change suddenly and unexpectedly. This is not to say that patterns don't exist. Sequences of behavior and regularities can persist, but they are liable to sudden changes without warning (Baker 1993, 133). Likewise, interactions within complex systems are nonlinear—meaning that very small actions can create large outcomes, while very large actions can result in minimal change within systems. The implication of this is that very small actions can potentially have rather far-reaching effects. This means that the link between action and outcome is undeterminable. Complex systems operate in a "tangle of actions, interactions, and feedback," meaning that discussions of ultimate causality are somewhat closer to guesswork (Morin 2008, 84). As Morin (2008, 96) argues, "action escapes the will of the actor." Effective political intervention and policy making rests on recognition of the complexity that we confront. That we are embedded within a range of nonhuman systems and that our mutual existence is contingent on our actions should lead to a greater thoughtfulness in what we seek to achieve and how we seek to go about furthering those aims. A broader understanding of the potential range of actors and agents or structuring contingencies may aid the effectiveness of interventions designed. In addition, a less linear mode of policy making, monitoring, and evaluation may be of great help in responding to the unpredictable effects of intervention. An international politics that can address issues with an awareness of more than human interactions and entanglements potentially has much to contribute to an analysis of the problems inhabitants of planet earth confront.

Conclusion

Our purpose in this chapter has been to argue for an international politics beyond the human. CT both enables and implies such a position. Complexity approaches not only permit the theorizing of interhuman forms of exclusion; they also suggest the requirement to account for understandings of social, political, and economic relations as impacting beyond the human and as coconstituted by elements of nonhuman and human systems. We would argue that these theorizations should be *critically* posthuman in quality. In other words our analyses should start by acknowledging that the human condition is embedded in and constituted with relations with other nonhuman systems. A critically posthumanist analysis thus acknowledges forms of power and domination over nonhuman beings. This suggests the need for a radical reconsideration of the very concepts of politics to incorporate non-human systems.

In suggesting that there is a need for posthuman international relations we call for a discipline that does not prioritise the interests of one species, or indeed of particular sub groups of that species. CT does not offer any quick fixes for the problems that we confront but it does indicate why these problems are so difficult to resolve. It also indicates that our actions may result in very different outcomes from what we intended and suggests a broadened repertoire for potential intervention.

Bibliography

Agamben, G. (2004). *The open: Man and animal.* Trans. K. Attell. Stanford, CA: Stanford University Press.

Anderson, K. (2001). The nature of "race." In N. Castree and B. Braun (Eds.), *Social nature: Theory, practice, and politics* (64–83). Oxford: Blackwell. Oxford.

Badmington, N. (2004). *Alien chic: Posthumanism and the other within.* London: Routledge.

Baker, P. (1993). Chaos, order and sociological theory. *Sociological Inquiry*, 63(2).

Barry, A. (2001). *Political machines: Governing a technological society.* London: Anthone Press.

Bertuglia, C. S., and Vaio, F. (2005). *Nonlinearity, chaos and complexity: The dynamics of natural and social systems.* Oxford: Oxford University Press.

Bookchin, M. (1990). *The philosophy of social ecology.* Montréal: Black Rose Books.

Bostrom, N. (2003). Human genetic enhancement: A transhuman perspective. *Journal of Value Inquiry*, 37(4), 493–506.

Braun, B., and Whatmore, S. (2010). The stuff of politics: An introduction. In B. Braun and S. Whatmore (Eds.), *Political matter: Technoscience, democracy and public life* (ix–xl). Minneapolis: University of Minnesota Press.

Buzan, B., and Little, R. (2000). *International systems in world history: Remaking the study of international relations.* Oxford: Oxford University Press.

Buzan, B., and Little, R. (2001). Why international relations has failed as an intellectual project, and what to do about it. *Millennium*, 30(1), 19–39.

Capra, F. (1996). *The web of life: A new synthesis of mind and matter.* New York: HarperCollins.

Capra, F. (2002). *The hidden connections: A science for sustainable living.* London: HarperCollins.

Castree, N. (2001). Marxism, capitalism and the production of nature. In N. Castree and B. Braun (Eds.), *Social nature: Theory, practice and politics* (189–207). Oxford: Blackwell, Oxford.

Cudworth, E. (2005). *Developing ecofeminist theory: The complexity of difference.* Basingstoke: Palgrave.

Cudworth, E. and Hobden, S. (2009). More than a metaphor: Complexity in the social sciences. *Journal of Interdisciplinary Social Science*, 4(4), 59–70.

Cudworth, E., and Hobden, S. (2011a). Beyond environmental security: complex systems, multiple inequalities and environmental risks. *Environmental Politics*, 20(1), 42–59.

Cudworth, E., and Hobden, S. (2011b). *Posthuman international relations.* London: Zed.

Crenshaw, K. W. (1991). Mapping the margins: Intersectionality, identity politics and violence against women of color, *Stanford Law Review*, 43(6), 1241–99.

Dalby, S. (2009). *Security and environmental change.* Cambridge UK: Polity Press.

Demeritt, D. (2001). Being constructive about nature. In N. Castree and B. Braun (Eds.), *Social nature* (22–40). Oxford: Blackwell.

Dickens, P. (1996). *Reconstructing nature: Alienation, emancipation and the division of labour.* London: Routledge.

Dillon, M. (2000). Poststructuralism, complexity and poetics. *Theory Culture & Society*, 17(5), 1–26.

Dobson, A., and Bell, D. (2005). Introduction. *Environmental citizenship.* In A. Dobson and D. Bell (Eds.). Cambridge: MIT Press.

Forrester J. W. (1971). Counterintuitive behavior of social systems. *Technology Review*, 73(3), 52–68.

Foucault, M. (1971). *The order of things: Archaeology of the human sciences*. Pantheon, New York.

Foucault, M. (1984). Right of death and power over life. In P. Rabinow (Ed.), *The Foucault reader* (258–272). New York: Pantheon, New York.

Gane, N., and Haraway, D. (2006). When we have never been human, what is to be done? An interview with Donna Haraway. *Theory, Culture & Society*, 23(7–8), 135–158.

Gleditsch, N. P. (2002). Armed conflict 1946–2001: A new dataset. *Journal of Peace Research*, 39(5), 615–637.

Gleick, J. (1988). *Chaos: Making a new science*. London: Heinemann.

Gunderson, L. H., and Holling, C. S. (Eds.). (2002). *Panarchy: Understanding transformations in human and natural systems*. Washington, DC: Island Press.

Hables Gray, C. (2001). *Cyborg citizen: Politics in the posthuman age*. London: Routledge.

Harrison, N. E. (2006). Thinking about the world we make. In N.E. Harrison (Ed.), *Complexity in world politics: Concepts and methods of a new paradigm* (1–23). Albany: SUNY Press.

Harvey, D. (1996). *Justice, nature, and the geography of difference*. Oxford: Blackwell.

Harvey, D. (2009). Complexity and case. In D. Byrne and C. Ragin (Eds.), *The sage handbook of case-based methods*. London: Sage.

Hayles, K. (1990). *Chaos bound: Orderly disorder in contemporary literature and science*. Ithaca, NY: Cornell University Press.

Hayles, K. (Ed.). (1991). *Chaos and order: Complex dynamics in literature and science*. Chicago: University of Chicago Press.

Hayles, K. (1999). *How we became posthuman: Virtual bodies in cybernetics. literature and informatics*. Chicago: University of Chicago Press.

Holling, C. S. et al. (2002). Sustainability and panarchies. In L. H Gunderson and C. S. Holling (Eds.), *Panarchy: Understanding transformations in human and natural systems* (63–102). Washington, DC: Island Press.

Holsti, K. (1985). *The dividing discipline: Hegemony and diversity in international theory*. London: Allen and Unwin.

Hutchinson, F. et al. (2002). *The politics of money: Towards sustainability and economic democracy*. London: Pluto Press.

Kaplan, M. (1964). *System and process in international politics*. New York: John Wiley & Sons.

Kuehls, T. (1996). *Beyond sovereign territory: The space of ecopolitics*. Minneapolis: University of Minnesota Press.

Kurki, M. (2008). *Causation in international relations: Reclaiming causal analysis*. Cambridge: Cambridge University Press.

Latour, B. (1993). *We have never been modern*. Harvester Wheatsheaf, Hemel Hempstead.

Latour, B. (2005). *Reassembling the social: An introduction to actor-network theory.* Oxford: Oxford University Press.

Latour, B. (2009). A plea for earthly sciences. In J. Burnett et al (Eds.), *New social connections: Sociology's subjects and objects* (72–84). Basingstoke: Palgrave,

Lövbrand, E., and Stripple, J. (2006). The climate as a political space. *Review of International Studies,* 32(2), 217–235.

Lovelock, J. (2009). *The vanishing face of Gaia: A final warning.* London: Allen Lane.

Maturana, H., and Varela, F. J. (1980). *Autopoiesis and cognition: The realization of the living.* Dordrecht: Kulwer Academic.

McCall, L. (2005). The complexity of intersectionality, *Signs,* 30(3) 171–180.

Merchant, C. (1980). *The death of nature: Women, ecology and the scientific revolution.* San Francisco: Harper and Row.

Miah, A. (2007). A critical history of posthumanism. In B. Gordijn and R. Chadwick (Eds.), *Medical enhancement and posthumanity* (71–94). London: Routledge.

Midgely, M. (1996). *Utopias, dolphins and computers: Problems of philosophical plumbing.* London: Routledge.

Morgenthau, H. J. (1960). *Politics among nations: The struggle for power and peace,* 3rd edn, New York: Knopf.

Morin, E. (1999). *Homeland earth: A manifesto for the new millennium.* Cresskill, NJ: Hampton Press.

Morin, E. (2008). *On complexity.* Cresskill NJ: Hampton Press.

Naess, A. (1973). The shallow and the deep, long-range ecology movement: A summary. *Inquiry* 16(1–4), 95–100.

Parsons, T. (1951). *The social system.* London: Routledge and Kegan Paul.

Parsons, T. (1960). *Structure and process in modern societies.* Glencoe, IL: Free Press of Glencoe.

Phoenix, A., and Pattynama, P. (2006). Editorial: Intersectionality. *European Journal of Women's Studies,* 13(3), 187–192.

Plumwood, V. (1993). *Feminism and the mastery of nature.* London: Routledge.

Prigogine, I. (1980). *From being to becoming: Time and complexity in the physical sciences.* San Francisco: Freeman.

Prigogine, I., and Stengers, I. (1984). *Order out of chaos.* New York: Bantam.

Rosecrance, R., and Taw, J. (1990). Japan and the theory of international leadership. *World Politics,* 42(2), pp. 184–209.

Schmidt, B. (1998). *The political discourse of anarchy: A disciplinary history of international relations.* Albany: SUNY Press.

Shiva, V. (1988). *Staying alive: Women, ecology and development.* London: Zed Books.

Singer, J. D. (1961). The level-of-analysis problem in international relations. *World Politics,* 14(1), 77–92.

Smith, S. (1996). Positivism and beyond. In S. Smith *et al* (Eds.), *International theory: Positivism and beyond.* Cambridge: Cambridge University Press.

Smith, S. (2000). The discipline of international relations: Still an American social science. *British Journal of Politics and International Relations,* 2(3), 374–402.

Stengers, I. (2010). Including non-humans in political theory: Opening Pandora's box? In B. Braun and S.J. Whatmore (Eds.), *Political matter: Technoscience, democracy and public life*. Minneapolis: University of Minnesota Press.

Sterman, J. D. (2002). All models are wrong: Reflections on becoming a systems scientist. *System Dynamics Review*, 18(4), 501–531.

Urry, J. (2003). *Global complexity*. Polity, Cambridge, UK.

Wæver, O. (1996). The rise and fall of the inter-paradigm debate. In S. Smith *et al* (Eds.), *International theory: Positivism and beyond* (149–185). Cambridge: Cambridge University Press.

Wæver, O. (1998). The sociology of a not so international discipline: American and European developments in international relations. *International Organization*, 52(4), 687–727.

Wallerstein, I. (1979). *The capitalist world-economy*. Cambridge University Press.

Watts, D. J. (2004). *Small worlds: The dynamics of networks between order and randomness*. Princeton: Princeton University Press.

Wolfe, C. (2008). Flesh and finitude: Thinking animals in (post) humanist philosophy. *SubStance*, 37(3), 8–36.

Wolfe, C. (2010). *What is posthumanism?* Minneapolis: University of Minnesota Press.

Chapter 7

Prolegomena to Postanthropocentric International Relations

Biosphere and Technosphere in the Age of Global Complexity

Antoine Bousquet

Over the last decade, momentum has been building toward an official scientific recognition of a new geological era, one defined entirely by the presence of humans on earth: the anthropocene. The candidates for translation into the geological record are multiple, including pollen deposits left by centuries of intensive agriculture, large-scale deforestation, urbanization, a rate of species extinction that puts it among the five largest mass extinctions in the planet's history, and the global migration of plants and animals that would accompany significant climate change. While there is disagreement whether to date the onset of this new era at the advent of agriculture 10,000 years ago or to the much more recent Industrial Revolution, the increasing number of earth scientists in support of a revision of the geologic time scale all concur on one thing: the impact of human societies has been such that it will leave its own recognizable strata in the global geological record. Such a trace of human activity would be all the more remarkable given that it represents an infinitesimal sliver of time on a planet 4.5 billion years old whose geological eras are more commonly measured in millions of years (*The Economist* 2011).

In one sense, the discovery of the anthropocene could well be seen as the ultimate expression of the unparalleled success of the human species in the domination of its environment, inscribing its brief stay on the planet into the latter's very sedimentary stratification. And yet such a conquest and the undoubted riches it has bestowed, however unequally distributed, on humankind appear to have come alongside growing anxiety and self-doubt over the sustainability of such a dominion and the collective forms of human existence it supports. The early twenty-first century is pervaded by the increasingly widely held conviction that the current models of socio-economic development, reliant as they are on the depletion of nonrenewable resources and the overexploitation of the natural environment, are breeding environmental crises whose effects are already being felt and that in the fullness of time, if left unaddressed, may even threaten the continued existence of the human species. This sense of looming catastrophe, now supplemented by the most serious global economic crisis in eighty years, is for many the clarion call for a radical reinvention of our societies, the scale and thorniness of the task at hand more than equal to its urgency. While the present chapter cannot possibly hope to offer an immediate solution to such a momentous undertaking, it does propose to examine one of the related intellectual developments of our anthropocenic age, the full realization of which may well be proven to be an obligatory point of passage for any resolution of our present predicament.

Indeed, if it is to modern scientific rationality and its associated technological wonders that we can most clearly attribute the dramatic extension of humanity's powers over its environment in the past few hundred years, the accompanying cumulative effect of the discoveries and percolation of techno-science throughout social and cultural life has been to increasingly challenge our very conceptions of the "human." Writing in 1917, Sigmund Freud held that three major blows had been dealt by science to human narcissism, each of which had further decentered humanity from the exclusive position it deemed itself to occupy at the heart of the universe (Freud 1955). The first of these came with Copernicus's cosmological revolution that made earth only one planet revolving around the sun, itself a single star among the countless other such celestial bodies. Darwin would subsequently further undermine humanity's elevated view of itself by showing that it was an integral part of the animal kingdom and had evolved from mere bacteria over the course of millions of years. Freud modestly added himself to this illustrious list, claiming that his discovery of the unconscious and the powerful hold it exerted over conscious life had shown that even "the ego is not master in its own house." To these three narcissistic wounds can be added, it will be argued here, a fourth and perhaps final one that tries to place humanity within the full mesh of dependencies that have allowed its emergence, sustain its continued existence, and may permit its eventual overcoming.

There is no small irony in the fact that a scientific mind-set that originally grounded itself in a humanistic outlook which placed man at the center of the universe has progressively displaced him from this position of ontological primacy, revealing to us further every day that we are merely a particular manifestation of a wider material continuum in which we are deeply entangled. The central paradox at the heart of this development is that with each increase of our knowledge of the world and of our immanent relations to it, we are being made simultaneously a little less certain about what it is that we really are and more aware of what we may yet become. We are continuously being empowered to act upon the world in new and more far-reaching ways while at the very same time becoming conscious of the extent to which we are transitory concrescences of that very same world. It is with this paradox firmly in mind that we should apprehend the postanthropocentric turn that can presently be discerned within contemporary thought as it strives to shrug off its humanist shackles. While the humanism instilled by the Renaissance and prolonged by the Enlightenment undoubtedly served as a formidable vector of knowledge and emancipation, insofar as it remains wedded to fixed transcendent notions of the human it increasingly appears today as an obstacle to their furtherance. The recognition of "the embodiment and embeddedness of the human being in not just its biological but also its technological world" (Wolfe 2010, xv) thus comes with the hope of a better (self-)governance of the collectives thereby disclosed.

With regard to such a cognitive shift, it must be acknowledged that the discipline of international relations (IR) remains to date firmly anthropocentric in its outlook. While its traditional unit of analysis is not the human per se, the conception of the state deployed within it is resolutely anthropomorphic with the attribution of interests, identity, rationality, and unity of action entirely modeled on common notions of the sovereign individual (Wendt 2004). If IR's state-centrism has long been the object of critique, its underlying anthropocentrism has, however, remained largely unexamined. Yet at stake is much more than an abstruse metaphysical dispute. Caught between mounting environmental crises and disruptive technological acceleration, the international state-system's increasingly evident inability to devise effective solutions to a thickening complex of problems denotes as much a philosophical as a political impasse. A renewed understanding of the contemporary manifestations of global life and their attendant politics is urgently required, and as undoubtedly daunting as the task is, it is one that we can ill-afford to dispense with given the gravity of the challenges we are faced with.

A first step toward the necessary overhaul of the conceptual frameworks employed within IR entails a recognition of the fundamental decentering of the human that is currently being undergone within wider social and cultural thinking and has yet to be fully acknowledged within the discipline. This decentering is one being essentially enacted along two main axes that will be considered here in turn. The first of these axes is a biogeochemical one that locates humans within the wider natural ecosystems of which they are a part: the *biosphere*. The second is a technological axis that draws out the interactions and coevolutions of human societies and their technical objects that together constitute the *technosphere*. It is my contention that the emerging accounts of life in each of these spheres are consistent with a systems approach informed by the insights derived from complexity thinking (CT). With its understanding of system dynamics across the organic and inorganic domains and its embrace of the flux of being, CT provides an invaluable conceptual framework and methodological toolkit for grappling with the acute theoretical and practical challenges facing us in the nascent twenty-first century.

CT has by now been afforded some substantial attention in the field of IR as in the wider social sciences (Bousquet 2009; Bousquet and Curtis 2011; Harrison 2006; Kavalski 2007). Yet the full measure of the extent to which it participates in a postanthropocentric turn in thought remains to be taken. Erika Cudworth and Stephen Hobden (2011, 75) have recently made an important contribution to such a cognizance with their proposal of a complexity-derived "posthuman international relations" tasked with decentering the human and bringing to the fore the "complex interweave of numerous systems nested, intersected and embedded in each other, all undergoing processes of co-evolution and linked by innumerable feedback loops." While deserving of credit for advancing a postanthropocentric perspective in IR, their focus on "our co-constituted relations with other species and natural systems" needs to be supplemented by an analysis of those same relations that pertain between human societies and their technical objects (Cudworth and Hobden 2011, 110). Only then can the "complex ecology" of relations Cudworth and Hobden call for be fully realized.

A postanthropocentric reinvention of IR is obviously no small undertaking, and most of the work remains ahead of us. Consequently, I will have to satisfy myself in this chapter with outlining some of the fundamental theoretical and conceptual shifts that must underpin such a rearticulation of the study of global life, drawing upon research and scholarship that substantiate and assist this overhaul of our established categories and frames of analysis. Since it is in the investigation of ecosystems and biological evolution that complex systems thinking has most clearly blossomed to date, this survey will begin with the examination of the manner in which this inquiry is unsettling some of the most deep-seated notions of nature and humanity's place within it.

Biosphere and the Flux of Nature

Although the overarching case I wish to put forward is in favor of a fully rounded ecology of relations that encapsulates both biosphere and techno-sphere, it is undeniable that it is the study of the natural environment that has so far provided the richest accounts of the tight interconnection and coevolution of systems with their environment, that which Fritjof Capra has referred to as the "web of life" (Capra 1996). From the study of individual species within their immediate ecological niches and of the food webs link-ing various plants and animals to analyses of the relation of the physical environment and climate to living systems, ecology has shed considerable light upon the warp and weft of organic and inorganic elements that hold together the natural world through their continuous systemic interplay. The final logical extension of this ecological outlook is to be found in the Gaia hypothesis proposed by James Lovelock in which the entire planet earth is conceptualized as a single biogeochemical complex system whose self-regulation sustains life upon it (Lovelock 2000).

If a degree of uncertainty still surrounds the broadest predictions of the scale and effects of systemic environmental change due to the signifi-cant imponderables inherent to the modeling of the complex interactions involved, it is clear that contemporary political and philosophical thought can no longer seriously dispense with an ecological dimension. This is an assertion that will in itself hardly encounter any robust opposition today; such has been the mounting evidence of the severe impact of human soci-eties on their natural surroundings and the consequent growth in environ-mental awareness among wider populations and their leaders in the past few decades. Nevertheless, the sea-change that this marks in terms of the representation of the relation of humans to the natural world, at least in the Western world, cannot be understated. The modern injunction to make humans, in Descartes's words, "masters and possessors of nature" was an aspiration founded on the assumption of an inexhaustible cornucopia from which limitless wealth and power could be extracted through the application of reason. Across the very ideological fault line that divided the West for most of the twentieth century, proponents of liberal capitalism and advocates of state socialism were united by a shared belief in a boundless progress that could draw upon inexhaustible natural resources. This view, so ubiquitous only recently, is one that no longer can be credibly upheld.

Today, recognition of the vital intertwining of human life and the environment, and with it of the specter of extinction that haunts the species, has indeed become inescapable. Over and above a new set of political demands and policy prescriptions, we are in the presence of a longer term cognitive shift that is undercutting the anthropocentric worldview that has prevailed till now. From a presumed position of dominion over a nature we deemed to stand outside of, our notions of humanity are being redefined by the awareness of the mesh of symbiotic relations with the environment that are necessary to keep entropic processes at bay. The study of living systems is challenging the ontological unity customarily ascribed to the human body, giving rise to new material significations to conceptions of embodiment (Nicholson et al. 2004, 1268). *Anthropos* is increasingly being understood as a phenomenon emergent from a broader ontogenetic flux.

In a sense, contemporary thought is still coming to terms with the ramifications of the intellectual upheaval that Darwin's discovery of biological evolution heralded, in particular with regard to what it tells us about the plasticity of life and the absence of any overarching *telos* to its metamorphoses (Dupré 2012). Beyond the blow it deals to various literalist accounts of divine creation, Darwinism inherently breaks with any Aristotelian conception of essences in foregrounding the innate mutability of the genetic phylum ahead of the particular forms that punctuate it (DeLanda 2004, 46–48). And yet such essentialist understandings stubbornly endure, nowhere more evidently than in common conceptions of human exceptionalism and of its unique position at the apex of evolutionary history. Thus the long-standing belief in the cardinal status of humans as the pinnacle of divine creation finds itself reinscribed in widespread notions of a great evolutionary ladder of being leading from humble bacteria to primates and their quasiteleological culmination in *Homo sapiens* and its putative monopoly on language, culture, or tools.

Yet new discoveries are continuously challenging such views, situating humans within a much wider biological continuum and progressively hollowing out a previously unquestioned "humanity." Only recently, studies of the fossilized skeletal remains of "Ardi," a hominid specimen 4.4 million years old uncovered in Ethiopia in 1992, have led to a dramatic revision of prevailing assumptions about the evolutionary history of humans, namely, that the last common ancestor of modern apes and humans in their phylogenetic lineage would most likely resemble a chimpanzee. Indeed *Ardipithecus ramidus* took paleoanthropologists by surprise when it became clear that it was likely already bipedal and omnivorous, suggesting that such great ape traits as knuckle-walking and predominantly fructivorous diets are specialisms that evolved subsequent to the divergence from the last common ancestor (White et al 2009). Bipedalism, to which some have attributed the enlargement of the human cortex and the emergence of tools and language (Leroi-Gourhan 1993), can hence no longer serve as an unambiguous evolutionary marker of the emergence of humanity from animality.

The point here is not to deny that modern humans do display certain remarkable traits which, certainly with the extinction of all the other lines of the *Homo* genus around 30,000 years ago, find no match anywhere else in the natural world today. Rather it is to underline that scientific enquiry is incessantly pushing further back into the phylogenetic record the origin of such traits while revealing numerous affinities in the behavior of other species, from cognition and language to tool use (McPherson et al. 2010; Shumaker et al. 2011; Oller and Griebel 2008; Shaviro 2011). Attempting to identify a caesura that definitively marks out the passage from animality to humanity and to define a "human nature" have become increasingly futile exercises rooted in the mental vestiges of a pre-Darwinian universe. This blurring of the boundaries of the human undoubtedly presents momentous challenges to the established tradition of political theory, not least in terms of the identities and entitlements of rights-holders within it. The last few decades have indeed seen increasing calls for the extension of human rights to animals and even the biosphere, along with invocations of "speciesism" to denounce perceived discrimination against nonhuman beings (Singer 1975; Regan 1983). If such debates have been to date essentially confined to the domestic political sphere, it seems ineluctable that they will acquire global salience in the future in the manner that previous rights advocacy has done. Issues of environmental governance certainly already possess a marked transnational character and will only climb the international agenda as the dependence of societies upon the environment for sustainable economic prosperity and even survival becomes ever more evident.

Locating the emergence and persistence of humans within wider natural processes is however only half of the task before us in order to complete a postanthropocentric turn with regard to the biosphere. Indeed, it is just as necessary to divest ourselves of those persistent conceptions of nature that are unsupported by our present scientific understanding and prevent us from properly grappling with the concrete problems that we face. Thus, while it is necessary to recognize the very real impact of contemporary human societies on the environment, it is equally important to dispel widely held beliefs in an ecological fall from grace that would have seen humans sin against a benevolent and harmonious Mother Nature (an anthropocentric narrative if there ever was one!). As a notion that was in no small part propagated by early ecological thinking such as the Gaia theory but taps into much deeper cultural tropes, the idea of a "balance of nature" or ecological equilibrium to which the natural world tends and whose disruption is the sole work of humans must be entirely abandoned (Kircher 2009). There is no possible return to a putative ecological Eden, above all because there never has been one.

Although it is still a notion that retains currency among the wider public, scientific ecology has indeed by now decisively broken with the idea of a "balance of nature" in favor of that of a "flux of nature" (Stevens 1990; Ladle and Gillson 2009). Nature is found to be dynamic, proliferating, and inherently unstable. The population dynamics of species display highly sensitive nonlinear properties with minor changes in predator-prey relations or reproductive success liable to provoke wild fluctuations in population numbers that typically show no inherent tendency toward self-regulating equilibrium. External shocks such as short-term climatic variations are constantly disrupting ecosystems that are perpetually reconfiguring themselves. If it was previously held that "ecological systems were closed, self-regulating, possessed of single equilibrium points by deterministic dynamics, rarely disturbed naturally, and separate from humans," Pickett and Ostfeld (1995, 274–75) identify a new paradigm "that recognises ecological systems to be open, regulated by events outside of their boundaries, lacking or prevented from attaining a stable point equilibrium, affected by natural disturbance, and incorporating humans and their effects."

Indeed, not only is there no natural equilibrium for humans to disturb, but many of the ecosystems we take to have been only belatedly exposed to significant human influence have in fact long borne the imprint of the hand of man and even owe to it some of their rich biodiversity. Against those anthropological accounts that saw the environment as merely a constraint to which "primitive" peoples adapted, historical ecology has shown that human societies have shaped their environment since prehistoric times (Balée 1988). Among the oldest means of this human production of landscape is the practice of controlled burns. Dickinson thus tells us that over the course of millennia "aboriginal peoples burned the land deliberately, to flush small game and drive big game, to deny covert to dangerous animal predators, to clear the growth that might provide cover for enemy ambushes around their settlements and camps, to foster fresh shoots of vegetation that attract favored game, to keep woodlands clear of underbrush and easy to traverse, and to keep relatively unproductive woodlands from encroaching upon grasslands richer in usable resources" (Dickinson 2000). Alongside other indigenous activities such as water management and the systematic replacement of vegetation, we now know that these anthropogenic fires have played a major role in shaping supposedly "virgin" rainforests in Amazonia and Africa as well as creating and maintaining ecosystems such as savannah grasslands (Erickson 2008). There is also strong evidence that, in many cases, this resulted in increased rather than reduced biodiversity.

While there is no denying that the intensity and character of human activity on the planet presently threaten global biodiversity, the findings of historical ecology problematize conservation efforts in that they undermine any notions of a static past natural world unspoiled by humans to which one should strive to return. Indeed, many of the landscapes and ecosystems that are particularly prized today for either their beauty or the richness of their fauna and flora and are the object of particular protective measures owe these features in part to sustained human action. Furthermore, "conservation" is evidently in no sense a retreat of human influence on the environment but merely one of its modalities according to which the environment is consciously shaped on the basis of certain preferences as to that which must be preserved and guided by the existing understanding of ecological dynamics. Dickinson (2000, 494–95) sums up our present condition well:

> The popular concept of wilderness as pristine wildland free of any human influence is largely a psychocultural myth, springing more from an uplifting vision of the proverbial Eden than from any historical reality. For charting the future, we will have no substitute for understanding the dynamics of varied ecosystems and the rules of landscape evolution well enough to be able to gauge in advance the results of specific actions that we are able to control . . . The task for future human culture is to acquire the knowledge of environmental history and dynamics needed to choose the sorts of human impact that will lead to a posterity of our liking. Faith in a self-regulating and self-restorative nature, independent of humankind, cannot guide us into any environmental harbor where we would wish to moor.

The realization of the embeddedness of human societies within a wider ecological mesh does not therefore bring with it the comfort of a putative return to a harmonious and constant natural world. It does however better equip them with some of the necessary knowledge for the task of managing the flux of nature and establishing more sustainable relations to the environment.

Ultimately what is required of us is the overcoming of the entrenched dichotomies between nature and culture that prevent us from grasping the coevolutive systemic relationships that cut across such conceptual domains. For Bruno Latour, modernity was founded on the establishment and main-tenance of just such a rigid demarcation between the spheres of nature (the nonhuman) and culture (the human) but whose paradoxical effect has been the proliferation of hybrid entities that escape such exclusive categorization (Latour 1993). It has become increasingly vital that we escape the conceptual straitjacket that this partition has imposed on us, namely, the perennial and by now exhausted attempts to explain one domain in terms of the other, through either the naturalization of society or the social construction of nature. Breaking with such accounts while retaining the ability to think sys-temically requires a complex ecology of relations that draws on both wider philosophical reflection and conceptual tools informed by the nonlinear sci-ences. But such an approach also entails going beyond the conventional concern of ecological thinking with the natural environment and bringing into its ambit the technical beings that arise and evolve alongside humans in the domain we may refer to as the technosphere.

Technosphere and the Becoming of Technology

Our current environmental crisis is intimately bound up with the techno-logical development of human societies, and short of endorsing a deindus-trializing primitivism, any resolution of it will necessarily pass through the reorganization of our technical civilizations. It therefore seems incongruous to call for a complex ecologism that "understands the embedded situation of the human species in networks and scapes populated with non-humans" which would dispense with an engagement with the technical nonhumans we are so intimately bound up with (Cudworth and Hobden 2011, 125). Cudworth and Hobden's concern that the common uses of the concept of posthumanism "underplay the significance of the embodied condition of our species" through the commonly associated fixation with "virtual" technolo-gies and fantasies of bodily transcendence is quite legitimate (Cudworth and Hobden 2011, 141). Yet this causes them to miss that through the question of technology we are actually touching onto the very materiality of human soci-eties. After all, what is tool-use if not the predominant modality of human interaction with the environment? As Latour (2010, 59) points out, "we are sociotechnical animals and each human interaction is sociotechnical." *Contra* transhumanist dreams of disembodiment, a proper theoretical consideration of technology can thus bring into sharper focus human embeddedness in the world.

The central difficulty facing such a theory is an eschewal of the twin pitfalls of technological determinism and social constructivism that mar so many existing accounts of technology. Indeed, these two interpretative approaches are merely mirror effects of the same partition that Latour identified as constitutive of the modern compact. Technological determinism attributes to technology the power to shape a malleable social body while frequently leaving the origins and evolutions of technical objects entirely mysterious. Conversely, social constructivism sees in technology merely a screen for the projection of human intentions, desires, and interests, thereby denying technical objects any autonomy or specificity. In fact, technology is both less and more than what it is typically taken to be: less because it is not an external material agency that unilaterally transforms a passive social body, and more because it actually permeates every aspect of the social. The question of technology directs us toward the ubiquitous materiality of social relations, the very glue that holds human collectives together. On one level, the material objects and structures that populate the human world can be thought of as congealed social relations, not merely in the sense that they are the product of human labor but in that they frame and orient human actions, giving some endurance to social norms and conventions that would otherwise have to be endlessly reenacted (Latour 2005, 193–199). Yet it is necessary to simultaneously acknowledge the unintended effects of material objects and recognize that they possess their own causal powers and internal logics (DeLanda 1994; Kelly 2010).

One of the most fertile sources for thinking beyond conventional oppositions between technique and culture is the work of the French philosopher Gilbert Simondon (see De Boever et al. 2012). Unsatisfied with just such a partition, Simondon (1989) sought in his *Du Mode D'Existence des Objets Techniques* (On the Mode of Existence of Technical Objects) to grasp technical objects in themselves without either reducing them to mere appendages of human will or elevating them to prime movers imposing change on a passive social body. For one, Simondon refused to treat machines as stable entities of which one could elaborate a definite classification in terms of genera or species, since the technical object is to be understood as part of a continuous process of evolution through its relations to both its internal and external milieus. So while one can analyze a given technical object in its specificity or individuality, these characteristics are secondary concretions of the object's genesis. Simply put, the technical object is "a unit of becoming" (Simondon 1989, 20).

This becoming of the technical object is one that proceeds simultaneously with regard to the coevolutive relation of its internal elements to that
of the broader technological ensembles it is part of:

> The opposition between technique and culture will last until culture
> discovers that each machine is not an absolute entity, but only an
> individualized technical reality, open in two directions: that of the
> relation to its elements, and that of the inter-individual relations
> within the technical ensemble. The role assigned by culture to
> man towards the machine is inadequate to technical reality; it
> supposes that the machine is substantialized, materialized, and
> consequently devalued; in fact, the machine is less consistent and
> less substantial than supposed by culture; it is not in relation to
> man as a bloc but in the free plurality of its elements or in the
> open series of its possible relations with other machines within
> the technical ensemble. (Simondon 1989, 146)

In the first instance, the internal mode of operation of a technical object
is thus immediately determined by the way the various internal elements
composing it act upon each other, this set of relations generally gaining in
intimacy and synergetic efficiency as a particular technical object is indi-
viduated in the process of engineering or craftsmanship. Simondon provides
detailed examples of the way in which combustion engines and vacuum
tubes went through processes of "concretization" whereby these machines
moved from "abstract" designs in which each constitutive internal element
serves a single purpose in a linear causal chain towards "concrete" forms
of greater internal coherence in which their parts take on several functions
that mutually support the operation of one another and enter into multiple
relations of reciprocal causality. In the second instance, the technical object
is enmeshed in its external relations, whether it be through its immediate handling by human operators or its connection to wider technological
ensembles. In either case, the technical object is then put to a specific use
and incorporated into an encompassing scheme of operation:

> One cannot consider technical objects as absolute realities exist-
> ing by themselves, even after having been built. Their technicity
> is understood only through their integration in the activity of a
> human operator or the functioning of a technical ensemble [. . .]
> The technical object, because it is either a tool or the element
> of an ensemble, must be known through philosophical thought,

that is to say through a thought that possesses the intuition of the becoming of the modes of relation between man and the world. (Simondon 1989, 239)

If Simondon thus provides us with the philosophical basis for an ontogenetic account of technical objects, we are simultaneously impelled to reconceptualize the human accordingly. Following Wolfe, the human is here to be understood as "fundamentally a prosthetic creature that has coevolved with various forms of technicity and materiality, forms that are radically 'not-human' and yet have nevertheless made the human what it is" (Wolfe 2010, xxv). This particular point can be made perhaps most fittingly with regard to human cognition to which we conventionally attribute the capacity for tool-making. Through a loosening of its exclusive association with the brain, a new understanding of cognition can indeed be fashioned, together with an insight into the manner in which the forms of human intelligence have coevolved alongside the material objects that support them.

Andy Clark and David Chalmers (1998, 7) have strongly argued against using the "demarcations of skin and skull" to delineate the mind from the rest of the world, emphasizing "the active role of the environment in driving cognitive processes." They do not here simply mean that the mind responds to external cues in its environment but that cognition itself is something that is frequently distributed among different individuals and material artifacts, constituting cognitive systems that are best understood through the totality of the relations of their elements. Clark and Chalmers offer the example of Otto, a hypothetical sufferer of Alzheimer's disease, who uses a notebook as a support for all the useful information he cannot dependably rely on his brain to retain and retrieve. In what sense, they ask, is the functional role of Otto's notebook in his cognitive processes and actions in the world any different from neurologically inscribed memory? "If, as we confront some task, a part of the world functions as a process which, *were it done in the head*, we would have no hesitation in recognising as part of the cognitive process, then that part of the world *is* . . . part of the cognitive process" (Clark and Chalmers 1998, 8).

If one accordingly admits the principle that "a cognitive process is delimited by the functional relationships among the elements that participate in it, rather than by the spatial colocation of the elements," it becomes possible to examine cognition as a distributed system that breaches the human corporeal boundary (Hollans et al. 2000, 175). For Edwin Hutchins, such a system "includes objects, patterns, events and other living beings in the setting in which human (and non-human) cognition takes place" (Hutchins

2008, 2011). Cognition, in this view, is thus not only socially distributed but instantiated in physical objects such as pen and paper, a slide rule, an abacus, or any artifact that can act as a "material anchor" for conceptual representation or symbolic manipulation (Hutchins 2005). Such objects should not be considered here as simply external props for the brain's internal cognitive processes but as constitutive elements within a wider cognitive ecology. Hutchins further suggests that such material anchors may have in the past played an important role in the development of human cognitive faculties through their mental internalization, although ultimately the above insights render such terminology inherently problematic:

> Internalization has long connoted some thing moving across some boundary. Both elements of this definition are misleading. What moves is not a thing, and the boundary across which movement takes place is a line that, if drawn too firmly, obscures our understanding of the nature of human cognition. Within this larger unit of analysis, what used to look like internalization now appears as a gradual propagation of organized functional properties across a set of malleable media. (Hutchins 1995, 312)

With regard to cognition as to other domains of enquiry, preestablished categories of the biological and technical are thus increasingly found to be obstacles to a greater understanding of the organizational characteristics and functional properties of real-world systems. The growing evidence of the intertwined evolution of the constitutive elements of such systems only further supports Stiegler's claim that *anthropogenesis* is simultaneously *technogenesis* (Stiegler 1998). There is no doubt that technoscientific developments in the fields of genetic engineering and artificial intelligence and the new forms of synthetic life they seem to augur are a powerful spur to the radical interrogation of our most commonly accepted conceptions of the human. And yet, as the previous discussion has sought to establish, a postanthropocentric turn in thought does not hinge upon them, much as it may be necessary in order to effectively engage with them. An acknowledgment of the crucial role of technical objects to postanthropocentrism is therefore not premised on any longing for a gnostic transcendence of human corporeality through technology but simply on the necessary recognition that "we have always been post-human" (Hayles 1999, 291).

The picture that emerges here is one in which human beings and their societies occupy together with their technical objects a single technosphere in which sociotechnical ensembles coalesce and deploy themselves. If a recognition of the role of material objects appears today essential to an understanding of the processes of individual human cognition, it can hardly be any less indispensable to our comprehension of the various collectives that inhabit our world, whether they be scientific laboratories, factories, financial institutions, transport networks, government bureaucracies, or armies. For the study of IR, this entails foregoing the common understanding of technology as merely an instrument of political will to allow for the ways in which sociotechnical assemblages of governance, among which we find the state, summon particular framings of the world and permit or induce certain actions within it. Such a conceptual rearticulation will indeed only become more critical as our societies become ever-more reliant on technologically enabled modes of distributed cognition and representation for their orientation and steering.

Toward Postanthropocentric International Relations

At a time in which we are simultaneously undergoing an ecological awakening to our tight-knit relationship with the natural environment and experiencing an accelerating pace of technoscientific change, our established notions of what it is to be human are not only wavering but increasingly appear to stand in the way of a greater cognizance of our present condition. In a variety of fields of enquiry, previously unquestioned anthropocentric assumptions are being scrutinized and progressively jettisoned. Under such conditions of cognitive upheaval, the capacity to think systemically has never been more vital for the task of effectively grappling with the pressing challenges facing us in the early twenty-first century.

As currently the most sophisticated formulation of systems thinking, CT offers us an array of concepts to speak about the emergence, behavior, and transformations of dynamic systems that cut across the ontological domains we have traditionally employed to carve up the world. Ranging from self-organization and nonlinear feedback loops to evolutionary landscapes and complex adaptive systems, complexity's conceptual toolkit permits the production of illuminating analytical accounts that remain nonetheless sensitive to contingency and the inherent limits to knowledge. And yet for all the insights that CT has already generated in those areas of its application, its greatest contribution may still be to come with the constitution of a generalized ecology of relations that can encompass the manifold processes underpinning global life.

It is necessary at this point to preempt two potential objections to such a proposition. While this complex ecology should strive to examine the tight mesh of relations that cuts across various domains in order to

shed light on the dynamics of the systems thus brought into focus, this is
not tantamount to an argument that boundaries and delineations should be
dispensed away with entirely. On the contrary, one of the essential lessons
of CT is that boundaries do exist and do matter but that crucially they are
always porous, membranes rather than barriers, lines of passage as much
as of demarcation. The boundary is that which permits the perpetuation of
the distinction between two systems (or between a system and its environment) while simultaneously providing the necessary surface of contact for
their co-constitutive relationship. Boundaries therefore become, by virtue of
this very duality, more important rather than less within CT in comparison
with those approaches keen to inscribe such boundaries much more firmly.

Nor does a complex systems approach necessarily entail the dissolution
of agency into concatenations of structural determinations. Human agency
in the world is very real, in a sense more so than ever in the age of the
anthropocene. But agency is always situated and embedded in particular
contexts, realized through the assemblage of material entities rather than an
abstract property of a human nature given once and for all. Here again we
encounter the paradox we met at the outset of our discussion, that in order to
enhance our ability to act in the world, it may be necessary to forsake some
of our cherished sense of human autonomy. The formidable global problems
we presently face require more agency, not less; this is not something that
can be decreed but rather must be painstakingly assembled and embodied.

The loss of our anthropocentric certainties undoubtedly raises thorny
questions about the politics that are to come in its wake, a consideration
of which this chapter has admittedly largely had to forego in favor of a
treatment of the ontological foundations on which they will rest. What new
meanings do representation, sovereignty, or governance take on beyond
anthropos? What reconceptualizations of power and struggle follow from
the incorporation of biosphere and technosphere? These are questions to
which no definitive answers can today be offered. Whether they entail a
new stewardship of "Homeland Earth" (Morin 1999) or a global "Parliament
of Things" (Latour 1993), the form and content of a post-anthropocentric
politics still remain to be invented.

And yet the discipline of IR is not the least promising site for its elabo-
ration. Its neorealist formulation is certainly hopelessly inadequate to the
task with its ontology of black-box state entities whose behaviors are directed by an ahistorical and unevolutive structure and its positivistic method
founded in an outdated conception of science. But the cumulative efforts to
open up the discipline to a range of different theoretical perspectives and
new loci of enquiry over the past thirty years have succeeded in making it

into a much more plural and self-critical field of investigation propitious to experimentation beyond its limited cannon. The globalization debates of the nineties disaggregated the study of global politics from a near-exclusive focus on state actors and the philosophical enrichment of the discipline has led to a sustained interrogation of its foundational categories. So that we can legitimately ask today what the discipline of *inter*-national *relations*, pared down to its essence, is if not the study of the interstitial and relational per se? Therein lies the greatest hope that IR may still provide a fecund conduit for the complex ecology of relations necessary to taking the full measure of the postanthropocentric turn that awaits us in the age of the anthropocene.

Bibliography

Balée, W. L. (1988). Historical ecology: Premises and postulates. In W. L. Balée (Ed.), *Advances in Historical Ecology* (13–29). New York: Columbia University Press.

Bousquet, A, and Curtis, S. (2011). Beyond models and metaphors: Complexity theory, systems thinking, and international relations. *Cambridge Review of International Affairs*, 24(1), 43–62.

Bousquet, A. (2009). *The scientific way of warfare: Order and chaos on the battlefields of modernity*. London: Hurst Publishers.

Capra, F. (1996). *The web of life: A new synthesis of mind and matter*. London: Flamingo/HarperCollins Publishers.

Clark, A., and Chalmers, D. J. (1998). *The extended mind*. Analysis, 58, 10–23.

Cudworth, E., and Hobden, S. (2011). *Posthuman international relations: Complexity, ecologism and global politics*. London: Zed Books.

De Boever, Murray, A., Roffe, J. and Woodward, A. (Eds.). (2012). *Gilbert Simondon: Being and technology*. Edinburgh: Edinburgh University Press.

DeLanda, M. (1994). *War in the age of intelligent machines*. New York: Zone Books.

DeLanda, M. (2004). *Intensive science and virtual philosophy*. New York: Continuum.

Dickinson, W. R. (2000). Changing times: The Holocene legacy. *Environmental History*, 5(4), 545–556.

Dupré, J. (2012). *Processes of Life: Essays in the Philosophy of Biology*. Oxford: Oxford University Press.

Erickson, C. L. (2008). Amazonia: The historical ecology of a domesticated landscape. In H. Silverman and W. H. Isbell (Eds.), *Handbook of South American Archaeology* (93–104). New York: Springer.

Freud, S. (1955). A difficulty in the path of psycho-analysis. In *The Standard Edition of the Complete Psychological Works of Sigmund Freud, Volume XVII (1917–1919): An Infantile Neurosis and Other Works* (135–144). London: Hogarth Press.

Harrison, N. E. (2006). (Ed.). *Complexity in world politics: Concepts and methods of a new paradigm*. Albany: State University of New York Press.

Hayles, K. (1999). *How we became posthuman: Virtual bodies in cybernetics, literature and informatics.* Chicago: University of Chicago Press.

Hollans, J., Hutchins, E., and Kirsh, D. (2000). *Distributed cognition: Toward a new foundation for human-computer interaction research.* ACM Transactions on Computer-Human Interaction 7(2), 174–196.

Hutchins, E. (1995). *Cognition in the wild.* Cambridge: MA, MIT Press.

Hutchins, E. (2005). Material anchors for conceptual blends. *Journal of Pragmatics,* 37, 1555–1577.

Hutchins, E. (2008). The role of cultural practices in the emergence of modern human intelligence. *Philosophical Translations of the Royal Society Biological Sciences,* 363, 2011–2019.

The Economist (2011). The anthropocene: A man-made world, May 26.

Kavalski, E. (2007). The fifth debate and the emergence of complex international relations theory. *Cambridge Review of International Affairs,* 20(3), 435–454.

Kelly, K. (2010). *What technology wants.* New York: Viking.

Kircher, J. (2009). *The balance of nature: Ecology's enduring myth.* Princeton, NJ: Princeton University Press.

Ladle, R. J., and Gillson, L. (2009). The (im)balance of nature: A Public perception time-lag? *Public Understanding of Science,* 18(2).

Latour, B. (1993). *We have never been modern,* Harvester Wheatsheaf, Hemel Hempstead.

Latour, B. (2005). *Reassembling the social: An introduction to actor-network theory,* Oxford University Press.

Latour B. (2009). A plea for earthly sciences. In J. Burnett et al. (Eds.), *New social connections: Sociology's subjects and objects.* Basingstoke: Palgrave.

Latour, B. (2010). A collective of humans and nonhumans. In C. Hanks (Ed.), *Technology and values: Essential readings.* Chichester: Wiley-Blackwell.

Leroi-Gourhan, A. (1993). *Gesture and speech.* Cambridge, MA: MIT Press.

Lovelock, J. (2000). *Gaia: A new look at life on earth.* Oxford: Oxford University Press.

McPherron, S. P., Alemseged, Z., Marean, C. W., Wynn, J. G., Reed, D., Geraads, D., Bobe, R., and Bearat, H. A. (2010). Evidence for stone-tool-assisted consumption of animal tissues before 3.39 million years ago at dikika, ethiopia. *Nature,* 466 (7308), 857–860.

Morin, E. (1999). *Homeland Earth: A Manifesto for the New Millennium.* Cresskill, NJ: Hampton Press.

Nicholson, J. K., Holmes, E., Lindon, J. C., and Wilson, I. D. (2004). The challenges of modeling mammalian biocomplexity. *Nature Biotechnology,* 22(10), 1268–1274.

Oller, D. K., and Griebel, U. (Eds.). (2008). *Evolution of communicative flexibility: Complexity, creativity, and adaptability in human and animal communication.* Cambridge, MA: MIT Press.

Pickett, S. T. A., and Ostfeld, R. S. (1995). The shifting paradigm in ecology. In R. L. Knight and S. F. Bates (Eds.), *A new century for natural resources management* (261–278). Washington, DC: Island Press.

Regan, T. (1983). *The case for animal rights.* Berkeley: University of California Press.

Shaviro, S. (Ed.) (2011). *Cognition and decision in non-human biological organisms.* Open Humanities Press.

Shumaker, R. W., Walkup, K. R., and Beck, B. B. (2011). *Animal tool behavior: The use and manufacture of tools by animals.* Baltimore, MD: The Johns Hopkins University Press.

Simondon, G. (1989). *Du mode d'existence des objets techniques.* Paris: Editions Aubier.

Singer, P. (1975). *Animal liberation: A new ethics for our treatment of animals.* New York: Random House.

Stevens, W. K. (1990). New eye on nature: The real constant is eternal turmoil. *The New York Times,* July 31.

Stiegler, B. (1998). *Technics and time, I: The fault of Epimetheus.* Stanford, CA: Stanford University Press.

Wendt, A. (2004). The state as person in international theory. *Review of International Studies,* 30(2).

White, T. D., Asfaw, B., Beyene, Y., Haile-Selassie, Y., Lovejoy, C. O., Suwa, and WoldeGabriel, G. (2009). *Ardipithecus ramidus* and the Paleobiology of Early Hominids. *Science* 326 (5949), 75–86.

Wolfe, C. (2010). *What is posthumanism?* Minneapolis: University of Minnesota Press.

Chapter 8

The Good, the Bad, and the Sometimes Ugly

Complexity as Both Threat and Opportunity in National Security

Myriam Dunn Cavelty and Jennifer Giroux

Introduction

Security, both national and international, in the 21st century is increasingly defined by and organized around uncertain and unpredictable challenges, better grasped by the concept of risk than the concept of threats. Whereas the security paradigm during the Cold War was informed by threats, defined as problems that are "consciously and actively created by one security actor . . . for another" (Bailes 2007, 2), today, the discourse includes challenges that are myriad and indirect, often unintended, and by definition situated in the future. These "risks," expressed in probabilities of occurrence, exist in a permanent state of virtuality, exemplified by anticipation. Unlike conventional security practices—which are characterized by the principles of prediction, strategy, and hierarchy—most risks (and particularly those with security implications) cannot be predicted, or prevented; rather, they must be managed proactively, highlighting the need for a precautionary approach to governing these risks and the implications for society (Aradau and van Munster 2007). This calls for tailored security practices that are organized around principles of uncertainty, improvisation or "ad-hocery," and decentralization (Williams 2008).

The notion and concept of complexity occupy a multifaceted place in this discussion about risks and security. On the one hand, complexity is conceptualized as a key characteristic of new security challenges, and therefore viewed as *a threat*. In addition, one of the main referent objects in a Western security context and therefore focal points of national security is the complex body of "vital systems" (in the policy world, the term "critical infrastructures" is more commonly used; however, we choose the terms "vital systems" and "vital systems security" to connote a more sociotechnical focus). Vital systems are physical infrastructures, but also assets, services as well as key institutions, such as markets and governmental entities that are crucial to the function and development of society (Collier and Lakoff 2008). They are regarded as "critical" (in the sense of "vital," "crucial," "essential") by the authorities because their prolonged unavailability would, in all likelihood, result in social instability and major crisis. But they are also regarded as complex, consisting of multiple components of varying criticality (Lewis et al. 2011), interacting and overlapping in complex ways and bound together by physical, geographic, and cyber interdependencies (Rinaldi et al. 2001). The criticality and complexity of these systems can even be viewed as a necessity in terms of efficiency and functionality of vital systems. However, scientific observations regarding the behavior of complex systems, like those which are vital, have unveiled new insights and become a powerful driver for conceptualizing new opportune modes of security governance to tackle increasingly complex phenomena. Brought together, the conceptual duality of "the complex"—as threat and opportunity—creates an interesting entry point to examine the interrelationships between these two conceptions.

In this chapter we explore the emergence and evolution of the particular role of "the complex" and by extension complexity thinking (CT) in the vital systems security debate in two subsections, and discuss the implications of this for national and international politics. First, we describe the multifaceted conceptualization of the threat, as perceived by national security actors in a broad sense. In this subsection we describe how the continuing reliance on information technologies for control and maintenance of vital systems compounds complexity, bringing forth an increasing number of networks, nodes, and growing interdependencies in and among them. By their very nature, complex systems contain the risk of large-scale, catastrophic events that are not bounded or localized, but sweeping. With critical, and often hidden, thresholds—or so-called tipping points—and emergent properties, they pose a conundrum for prediction (Scheffer et al. 2009)—particularly as it relates to the behavior of these systems and the way in which complexity feeds into the threat perception.

In the second subsection, we explore how complexity has more recently been seized by the national security community as an opportunity to learn about new modes of politics and governance for complex sociotechnical systems, in particular, *the concept of resilience*—or the ability of a system to resist, absorb, recover from, or adapt to (adverse) changes in condition—that emerges as a key concept within the field of vital systems security and beyond. In other words, resilience has become an approach to risk management "which foregrounds the limits to predictive knowledge and insists on the prevalence of the unexpected" (Walker and Cooper 2011, 6) across the entire range of societally relevant issues. Indeed, one can observe a clear link between the growing popularity of resilience among national security experts and the threat perception that is fed by "the complex." While a world of threats (that are "knowable" and calculable) comes with a feeling of certainty since actions produce particular (knowable, calculable) consequences, a world of risks constantly challenges the predictive capacities of security providers and is troubled by definitional struggles over the scale, degrees, and urgency of risks. Needless to say, if the mere task of "knowing" these challenges is so hard, preventing them seems completely unachievable. In this context, the concept of resilience has become a concept that allows having (or rather regaining) a sense of safety/security even though disruptions of various kinds are seen as inevitable.

Throughout, we particularly focus on the interaction and fusion of human and non-human aspects within the discourse. CT provides the framework in which to situate the interconnection and interaction between the technical (non-human) and social (human) space, while critical security studies help to unearth aspects of the inherently political nature of this interaction. The relations between human and nonhuman systems offer an interesting starting point for challenging traditional conceptions of world politics as well as for rethinking partially outdated concepts of global life, as we show in the concluding section.

Complexity as Threat: System Vulnerabilities and Cascading Effects

Despite the apparent heightened attention nowadays, vital systems security is not a new topic. At its heart is the conceptualization of security threats as problems of *system vulnerabilities*, the degree to which a system (any system) is susceptible to, or unable to cope with, adverse effects. The genealogy of this danger discourse can be traced back at least to the notion of "total war" and the associated methodology of strategic bombing (Collier and Lakoff 2008), which is characterized by an abstraction and depersonalization of the enemy; away from the fighting forces toward networks of productive capacities necessary to engage in full-scale war, including cities and other "vital nodes." Similarly, the threat discourse existed before the complex interdependence of liberal (risk) societies and their growing technological sophistication transnationalized and technologized the types of security problems they face. Looking back, a steady stream of government reports from the 1960s onward warned of the vulnerabilities of a "sprawling, open country knitted together by transportation, power and communications systems designed for efficiency not security" (Brown 2006, 51).

For most of the time, the possibilities of infrastructure discontinuity caused by attacks or other disruptions were inferior security concerns when compared to the superpower antagonism. This changed around the mid-1990s, when a growing concern with information security found a technical vocabulary, a set of analytical tools, and practices of intervention in a longstanding mode of thinking about infrastructures/vital systems as a security problem (Dunn Cavelty 2008). The current episode of vital systems security that we focus on is dominated by the multiple transforming effects of information and communication technologies (ICT). More concretely, the new perspectives that the "cyber-revolution" brought to the problem led to change in the danger discourse in terms of referent object as well as the threat environment.

Below, we continue by first showing how a particular type of (highly complex) referent object is conceptualized in the technical and social domain and then pivot to the corresponding threat discourse. From this, vital system security emerges as an all-encompassing and all-enveloping security focus with substantial bearing on the relationship between government and society, nationally and internationally.

The Increasingly Complex, Interdependent Body of Vital Systems

The vital system security discourse was never static as its technical aspects were constantly evolving. Most importantly, changes in the technical substructure changed the referent object in substantial ways. In the 1970s and 1980s, the debate started to focus on those parts of the private sector that were becoming digitalized and thus connected to the government networks where classified information resided—complementing the "old" Cold War images of built physical infrastructures as critical objects. The growth and reach of computer networks into more and more aspects of life changed this limited referent object in crucial ways. In the mid-1990s, it became clear that key sectors of modern society, including those vital to national security and to the essential functioning of (post)industrialized economies, had come to rely on a spectrum of highly interdependent national and international software-based control systems for their smooth, reliable, and continuous operation. The referent object that emerged from this was the totality of critical (information) infrastructures that provide the way of life that characterizes our societies (Dunn Cavelty 2010). This meant a move away from (only) military-state assets toward private-economic assets—a shift which was helped along by the privatization and deregulation of many parts of the public sector since the 1980s and the globalization processes of the 1990s. Large parts of vital systems were thus put in the hands of private enterprise, which at the same time meant a move away from the classic national security actors as the ones mainly or predominantly in charge of protecting and securing them. Vital system security became essentially conceptualized as a "shared responsibility."

The fusion of physical objects with ICT compounded and transformed the complexity of vital systems—and continues to do so with the "smartification" of refrigerators, houses, electricity grids, and so on. Bridged and interlinked by information pathways, the body of critical infrastructures is interconnected and highly complex. Spatially, critical infrastructure systems spread over more and more territory. Continuing reliance on information technologies for their control and maintenance brings forth an increasing number of networks, nodes, and growing interdependencies in and among these systems (Rinaldi, Peerenboom, and Kelly 2001). On a technical level, information or virtual systems serve as the underbelly of physical (critical) infrastructures in that they are increasingly responsible for operations and functioning. For instance, supervisory control and data acquisition (SCADA) systems are computer systems that monitor and control industrial, infrastructure, or facility-based processes. It is through SCADA systems that cyber incidents, such as the infamous Stuxnet worm (Farwell and Rohozinski 2011), can cause physical damage to the function of vital systems. Furthermore, humans are behind or rather interacting with every network. This human interaction compounds the complexity of the system—altering the management of risks to involve not only the management of the technical dimension but also the human (and, with that, behavioral) dimension.

At a societal level, broad accessibility to ICT has created a new sublayer for virtual interactions and activities—fundamentally transforming daily life. Since the 1990s, technology has increasingly served an critical role for a number of activities that were once only expressed in physical form. Where the technical meets the social is best expressed in cyberspace, a complex ecosystem in its own right, where the daily virtual interactions of billions of people interact and overlap with databases, resources, and networks—such as those supporting critical infrastructures and vital services. What emerges from these interactions is an image of modern vital systems in which it becomes futile to try to separate the human from the technological. Technology is not simply a tool that makes life livable: rather, technologies become constitutive of novel forms of "a complex subjectivity," which is characterized by an inseparable ensemble of material and human elements (Coward 2009, 414). From this ecological understanding of subjectivity, a specific image of society emerges. Society becomes inseparable from vital systems, and even more, society becomes in itself a critical infrastructure. In vital systems security, society is a way of life provided by the uninterrupted substructure of technology.

Complex Threat Dimensions

The salience of vital systems as a focal point of the current national security debate of Western states was supported by the confluence of two interlinked factors that are reinforced and changed by the conceptualization of the protection-worthy as outlined above: the perception that (a) modern societies are exposed to an ever-increasing number of potentially catastrophic vulnerabilities due to complexity (Furedi 2008), which, (b) can be willfully exploited. This threat perception was influenced by the larger strategic context that emerged after the Cold War. Of course, the influence of globalization is notable here where dynamic geostrategic conditions took shape, characterized by more numerous areas and issues of concern, and smaller, more agile and more diverse adversaries. As a result of the difficulty in locating and identifying enemies, the focus of security policies partly shifted away from actors, capabilities, and motivations to general vulnerabilities of the entire society. In this respect, the global complex interdependence of societies and their growing technological sophistication grew, as did the security spectrum, shifting from issues that were "localized" or national to those that are transnational and/or have a technological component. The combination of vulnerabilities, technology, and transnational issues brought vital systems to center stage, particularly because they were becoming increasingly dependent on the smooth functioning of all sorts of computer-related applications, such as software-based control systems.

  More specifically, the threat discourse in vital system security consists of an inward-looking narrative about one's own vulnerability plus an outward-looking narrative about nondeterrable threats. The inward-looking narrative links complexity with vulnerability. The very connectedness of infrastructures poses dangers in terms of the speed and ferocity with which perturbations within them can cascade into major disasters. There is widespread fear in the policy community that vital systems could be severely damaged by a single catastrophic event or a complex chain of events, man-made or not. Such fear met (at least partial) reality, for example, during the 2011 Tohoku earthquake-tsunami disaster in Japan, which brought to light the devastating impacts of systemic interdependency between interacting social, ecological, and technical systems.

The outward-looking (and more traditional national security) narrative sees an increasing willingness of malicious actors to exploit vulnerabilities in complex systems without hesitation or restraint. Because vital systems combine symbolic and instrumental values, attacking them becomes integral to a modern logic of destruction (Coward 2009, 408–09) that seeks maximum impact. Again, it is the cyber-moment that elevated the discourse to another urgency level through a change in the (interlinked) temporal and the spatial dimensions of the threat. It reformulates space into something no longer embedded into place or presence. Laws of nature, especially physics, do not apply in this nonspace/place—there are no linear distances, no bodies, no physical copresences. Actors are represented by symbols, and the effects of their actions manifest through this nonplace, occurring anywhere and instantaneously.

Combined, this conceptualization results in two noteworthy characteristics of the threat representation. First, the protective capacity of space is obliterated; there is no place that is safe from an attack. Second, the threat becomes quasiuniversal because it is now everywhere—and nowhere at the same time. Threats or dangers are no longer perceived as coming exclusively from a certain direction—traditionally, the "outside"—but are system inherent. The threat is networked and complex—and the threat *is* the network and *is* complexity. In addition, attempts to add substance to threat estimates fail as an irredeemable consequence of the complex object which is threatened and that which threatens. Threats/risks to the complex body of interdependent vital systems are situated in an uncertain future, which is changed by our actions in the present. Threats become unpredictable and in essence unknowable. Complexity manifests as an epistemological breakdown: it is linked to the fact that most of the intellectual tools used to probe the pervasive uncertainties underlying vital systems—mainly based on standard risk management techniques—inevitably fail because they strive for fixity and certainty, which are unattainable (Ramsden 2008, 57).

Complexity as Opportunity: The Governance of the Unpredictable

In this section, we turn to the other side of this discussion where we address what it means to move to a perspective that seeks to understand the nature of system, its effects and interdependencies, and build and foster systems, as well as systems thinking, that can adapt and change in the face of adverse events (Tweed and Walker 2011, 938). The "systems perspective" and complexity thinking overall are obviously closely related to the debate about vital systems security. To note, studies have examined the behavior and performance of technical systems and focused on the effects of cascades, or events that have ripple effects across a system, and surprises, or unexpected events that arise out of interactions within the system that produce new, unforeseen phenomenon (Bonen 1981; Hughes 1987; Mitleton-Kelly 2003; Geels 2004; Lei et al. 2010; Lewis et al. 2011).

It is a more recent development, though, that the national security community has become aware of the potential benefits of complexity thinking. Inspired by studies that examined the mathematical properties of nonlinear, unstable systems, complexity science was used from the 1970s onward as an alternative perspective to analyze how societies maintain order, regulate, and adapt to changing conditions (Parsons 1964; Easton 1967). For instance, natural disaster preparedness and hazard relief research used the systems theoretical perspective to understand how crisis-affected communities cope and adapt to large shocks, whereas the psychology field used it to look at how trauma or adversity influenced the development of children and adolescents. Holling's (1973) path-breaking work showed how a complex systems framework could be used to analyze the characteristics, process, and adaptive behavior of complex social and political systems, research that has since inspired studies in international relations (IR) as well as political engagement and action (e.g. Zolo 1992; Urry 2003; Geyer and Rihani 2010).

A commonality among most of the aforementioned work is the way in which the authors have distinguished between the different types of systems. On one end of the scale, there are ordered systems. They include those that are structured around a set of rules or laws and are characterized by predictability (cause-and-effect relationships) and stability. On the other end are chaotic systems, which are turbulent and in a constant flux. Somewhere in between the two extremes, we find complex (adaptive) systems, which "are characterized by diverse agents that interact in a dynamic network that is open to the environment," resulting in a system that evolves and adapts over time (Lei et al. 2010, 383). These are systems whose behavior can, in principle, by understood and also, within limits, governed. However, complexity is inherently a matter of perceptions. Whereas most technical-scientific studies assume that there is an objective reality to different system states (a system either *is* ordered, complex, or chaotic), others that abolish the concept of objective reality also dissolve the idea of intrinsic complexity, meaning that complexity is not a property of an object, but rather depends on the observer. This means that "reality" is approachable only through social definitions. Individuals do not respond to reality directly, but through socially constructed thought frameworks. In theoretical terms, this means that complexity, if perceived by decision makers or other influential actors to be a problem, will influence the threat perception of key actors and their subsequent actions. In IR or political sciences more generally, this is an important distinction, because it changes the role of complexity from something naturally given to something that in itself is inherently political.

Overall, the complex-systems perspective provides a lens through which to view, appreciate, and understand the complex interaction between humans and nonhuman systems that render unpredictable consequences. Questions about the governance of systems of any kind can therefore directly be informed by the insights of complexity studies—and they have been. This is the focus of the first subsection below. Closely related is the concept of resilience, which provides the complementary framework for dealing with the surprises, disruptions, and cascades that are bound to occur (Brunner and Giroux 2009). It has become one of the trendiest concepts in modern security discourse—as a result of complexity thinking permeating many different aspects of modern security. Discussions on resilience stress the ability of system flexibility—expressed in the capacity to quickly adapt to change—and adaptability, which allows a system to respond, reorganize, and renew despite being challenged by extreme shocks and adverse events. Moving from security to resilience has interesting implications for the political relationship between the governor and the governed. This is the focus of the second subsection.

Governing Complex Systems: Promises and Limitations

From a governance perspective, the management of multilevel (internal and external) complexity imparts considerable challenges. Overall, the current political period seems to have dispersed power, most notably away from nation-states. Embedded in a world complete with interdependencies, transnational phenomena, and accelerated complexity, nation-states have diminished capacity to mobilize and control physical (and virtual) borders, communication and financial systems, and the movement of goods and people. As a consequence, it is often concluded that static, state-centric models of government are poorly equipped to handle this environment as they are predominantly inflexible—hindered by hierarchy and bureaucratic structures that limit the flow of information, engagement of multiple actors, and ability to change and adapt quickly. CT can assist with informing the future development of governing systems. In effect, governance theory and complexity theory (or complexity thinking) render many similarities and synergies. Mainly, both view social organization as a changing system of actors who are constantly interacting and shaping the internal environment as well as being affected by factors and influences in the broader external environment. In a complex systems perspective, the integration of multiple levels, actors (agents), and sectors creates some advantages such as flexibility, resource maximization, and other adaptive traits. Comparably, complex governance systems integrate a variety of stakeholders at the microlevel who maintain varying independent goals, responsibilities, perceptions, and—in some cases—autonomy (Rhodes 1996; Czempiel and Rosenau 1992; Pierre and Peters 2000).

From the systems perspective, understanding how to facilitate collaboration and encourage organic management without controlling it is significant. Axelrod and Cohen (1999) argue that the goal of complex governance networks is to achieve a balance between two thresholds of control (where there is too little connectivity) and autonomy (where there is too much connectivity). This space is referred to as an opportunity for governance bodies to explore and exploit. Exploitation activities can be things like implementation, selection, and refinement; whereas exploration involves activities such as information gathering and synthesis within a network, learning, experimenting, and maintaining sufficient resources. Balance between these two areas is an important element to creating or maintaining adaptability within complex systems. Along this logic, in order to progress governance in the direction that it can increase resilience and meet today's demands, systems (society, networks, etc.) need to identify ways of building a culture of adaptability. There are three guiding principles to this (Snowden 2008; Snowden and Boone 2007).

First, the ability to govern will be enhanced by the *unraveling of hierarchy* and the creation of networks that are comprised of small, self-forming groups. Referred to as "fine granularity," Snowden argues that in order to become more adaptable, organizations need to decentralize. This means increasing the connectivity of relevant actors. This shifts the focus away from trying to control the environment and predict events, to building capacity within societies and learning to live with and potentially shape change. Additionally, networks should be created in an organic manner; forced mandates that bring together actors that have not naturally come together can result in ineffective outcomes as the network may not understand or invest in the relationships. States can, however, create opportunities for multiple stakeholders to develop partnerships more naturally by bringing them together under the banner of key issues. Disaster trainings or roundtables, for example, can provide a core activity for relevant public and private actors to naturally come together to address a security/vulnerability concern. Through this process relationships are forged and networks developed. Though this increases the complexity, it also presents the opportunity to build adaptive qualities.

Second, the sharing and exchange of information through multiple connections will increase in the 21st century due to the rapidly changing advances made in information communication technology where people can produce and transfer information in the physical or virtual space. This flow of information funnels through and between networks creating what Snowden (2008) calls "distributed cognition" where intelligence gained within the complex adaptive systems enables "diverse networks to contribute to decision-making and system design." From a crisis management perspective, complexity and uncertainty (especially in disaster systems) call for coordinated communication channels between agencies and relevant stakeholders. This involves having a shared idea of general protocol during a crisis as well as knowledge of capacity throughout the crisis management chain (i.e., disaster response members, law enforcement, journalists, etc.). Also, disasters are typically known for amplifying chaos and disrupting communication flows so contingency plans are an important element in the system knowledge ecosystem.

Finally, "disintermediation" is ultimately about bringing the agents that operate at the top closer to those that operate on the bottom. Currently, governing bodies continue to cling to hierarchal structures that prevent them from spotting patterns and making decisions based on contextual familiarity. Yet there are some encouraging developments underway that illustrate attempts by states to interact more closely with the local level. Fusion intelligence centers in the United States aim to bring federal agencies together with local and regional officials in the spirit of sharing information and enhancing all around network knowledge and relationships.

These three principles are also particularly relevant to the vital systems/national security debate, where the decentralization of power from the state means that public administration becomes a process carried out by multiactor structures and interactions. Most applicable to this discussion is the emergence of a network approach to governance that has led to the formation of self-governing structures—namely, public-private partnerships—that encourage and provide a platform for collaborative efforts between state and nonstate actors that together fulfill the delivery of public services (Sørensen and Torfing 2007). This type of network approach assumes that modern governance occurs as a collective of public and private institutions and actors who possess different levels of authority, knowledge, and influence. This shifts the focus from top-down control to partnership facilitation where the state is responsible for shaping "framework conditions in such a way that cooperation operates smoothly even without constant oversight" (Dunn Cavelty and Suter 2009, 5). Though this signifies a greater increase in power dispersion across the nation-state, governments undertake the function of defining partnership tasks, responsibilities, and imposing minimum regulations without distorting the ability of the network to organize from the bottom up. In other words, through this lens governance becomes a shared process, ultimately creating greater complexity in the administration of public goods. Through this metaprism, exploration activities—such as information sharing—are significant contributors to the overall robustness of the network.

Quite obviously, such ideas come with considerable challenges for government, particularly in the national security domain, where there is a "fundamental tension between the dual needs for institutional stability and change" (Duit and Galaz 2008, 319–20). Historically, states achieved order through control that flowed from the top down. In complex adaptive systems, it is the absence of hierarchy and primary control that allows order to emerge from the interaction between the agents. In the field of security, often seen as a fundamental need of human beings and whole societies, the outsourcing of essential functions in the field of vital system security to self-regulating networks that are not subject to government oversight is quite problematic. The problem of unclear allocation of responsibilities is also broadly discussed in the general literature on governance. Advocates of the network approach argue that the government is responsible for coordinating and stimulating networks, but not for the direct fulfillment of functions. However, many authors point out that in real life, expectations of the state are really much higher (Posner 2002).

The dissonance between the logic of providing the necessary level of security and the logic of self-regulation or self-organization is also felt in an additional area. Complex adaptive systems are not immune from catastrophic and disturbances events; in fact, the significant variation and unpredictability within complex systems produce inevitable fluctuations that encourage cascading tendencies, which, under a security perspective, are almost always undesirable, because they can (and often do) have catastrophic consequences. This is where the concept of resilience comes in—and how we can explain why the concept of resilience has become a key (and buzz) word in the security domain (Bara and Brönnimann 2011).

Resilience and the Certainty That Things Will Go Wrong

Resilience is commonly understood as the ability of systems—consisting of infrastructures, government entities, businesses, and society—to adapt to adverse events and to minimize the impacts of such events. While resilience is by no means a new concept, its current rise indicates a shift in security thinking that naturally flows from what we discussed above: while defensive, deterring, or protective measures aim to prevent disruptions from happening, resilience accepts that certain disruptions are inevitable (Brunner and Roth 2012). If resilience is a core concept, security does not refer to the absence of danger or efforts to eliminate them—but rather the ability of a system (including society) to quickly and efficiently reorganize to rebound from a potentially catastrophic event. Resilient behavior thus covers the entire range of "shock" responses of complex systems, including at the individual (e.g., trauma), organizational (e.g., business continuity), societal (e.g., community coherence), national (e.g., critical infrastructure protection), and international (e.g., globalization) levels. Despite the diversity of academic backgrounds as well as the nonuniformity of theoretical approaches, almost all resilience research is ultimately devoted to the same overarching question: How do systems whose internal structures and processes are characterized by high levels of uncertainty or ignorance adapt to external influences with the potential to change major characteristics of the system or to destroy the system altogether?

In the vital systems debate, resilience is also on the rise. Early documents defined protection as the main goal of CIP policies, whereas the focus of more recent policy papers has shifted toward resilience as the main purpose of CIP (Suter 2011). The shift from protection toward resilience is the result of broader reflections on how to best protect vital systems and mitigate impacts of potential failures (Homeland Security Advisory Council 2006), which surfaced in response to events like Hurricane Katrina, which clearly showed that traditional protection policies are too limited in their scope (Scalingi 2007). For risk management in vital system security, this shift means that protection is no longer the only goal of these practices; rather, risk management should also enhance the resilience of vital systems. The move from a rather technical focus that sees vital systems as technical systems to a focus that focuses on society more broadly is a rather small one. Increasingly, states have begun to place more emphasis on enhancing *societal* resilience. As Goldstein states, this can be defined as building up the "community's ability to regain equilibrium and return to normal" (Goldstein 2011, 360). Since it can be assumed that any large-scale event in the developed world will in some ways also damage vital systems, the vital systems security debate and the general catastrophe debate of the West begin to fuse.

Resilience approaches privileged self-organized governance from within the system rather than by hierarchically superior actors outside the system. For example, from a resilience perspective, the responsibility for protecting disaster-prone communities should primarily be located at the level of the community itself and only supplemented or supported by other actors on higher levels. In recent research, the role of ICT in enhancing this resilience has received more systematic attention. In particular, recent cases (Giroux and Roth 2012) have shown the novel coordination and behavioral characteristics that can emerge when disaster strikes, the resourceful, adaptive attributes of communities in today's postdisaster environment, and the growing role that crowdsourcing and new media tools play in such contexts. In many crisis situations, the convergence of people, material, and information can be observed. New information technologies foster three different forms of convergence: First, materials such as software programs or satellite imagery converge and are able to facilitate the coordination of crisis mitigation and recovery. Second, additional human resources can be mobilized in crisis situations which do not have to be physically at the location of the crisis, but can theoretically be anywhere in the world. These human resources can be utilized for example to coordinate relief efforts, analyze satellite imagery, or fulfill language translation tasks. Finally, useful information from the cyber zone can converge around a crisis. Particularly useful is information that can guide the behavior of the agents in the crisis zone. In sum, new information technologies such as crowd-sourced online maps have the potential to open new opportunities to enable collaboration in crisis situations and overcome coordination problems. The application of these technologies can activate additional valuable resources and speed up information collection and dissemination in complex emergencies. Thereby it can function as an important tool to increase systemic resilience (Dunn Cavelty and Giroux 2011).

Though collaborative action is often depicted as an alternative model of governance that bypasses state institutions, governmental actors actually play an important part in said governance—be it as facilitator, supporter, or multiplier. While governments are increasingly calling for the more resilient societies, the relationship between self-organizing crisis management and state actors is not straightforward and probably even carries risks for the latter, as outlined in the last subsection. One the one hand, emergence behaviors in crisis situations can support and complement governmental action. On the other hand, state actors only have limited means to steer emergence at the community level, since resilience is by definition achieved through self-organization. Moreover, the ambivalent influences which powerful nonstate agents could potentially bring to bear in emergent processes within complex crisis systems are often overlooked. However, since it appears illusive that states will (re)gain control over critical infrastructure in the near future that is mostly in private hands today, there are few alternatives for state actors but to develop strategies that treat social stakeholders as partners.

If resilience is a goal of system behavior, then fostering self-organization becomes the key goal for security policy. How this can be done in a systematic way is a different and altogether underresearched topic. Due to its popularity, differing intellectual traditions, and perhaps the differing degrees of theorization in each discipline, the incorporation of resilience into security policy and decision making within the private and public sectors has often occurred in an *ad hoc* and normative manner. It may well have become the "pervasive idiom of global governance" (Walker and Cooper 2011, 144) but the ambiguous nature of the concept, and its nonsystematic incorporation into the protective and regulatory landscape addressing public and private sector risk and security, raises several issues concerning the effectiveness, longevity, meaningfulness, and operationalization of policy and practice based on resilience approaches. Much more research is needed to understand the mechanisms and consequences of resilience thinking in an age of complexity.

Conclusion

Traditional approaches to the study of IR based on concepts such as equilibrium, stability, predictability, centralization, and linear causality are generally at odds with complex, nonlinear phenomena that the world seems to be confronted with. Rightful questions about the applicability of the physics and mathematics to social systems aside, the CT literature has placed within our grasp a set of very powerful intellectual tools and concepts. New concepts, such as emergence, become conceivable, and new methods, such as nonlinear computer modeling, suggest themselves as fruitful modes of study. The field of vital system security, a security issue with all-encompassing tendencies, is particularly well suited to study multiple complexity practices in politics.

The complexity paradigm turns one's attention to the concept of the inherently unpredictable situation—a situation unpredictable in itself, not just by virtue of the limits of its observer. This resonates well with the general postmodernist/poststructuralist account in which no determination is possible. The new sciences confirm the message that the observer and the observed cannot be detached from each other and that observation itself is an ontological event. Additionally, the complex is assigned a specific epistemological meaning: it shows the limits to knowledge due to complexity and unpredictability. The positivist-empiricist idea that a trained observer can encapsulate the amazing complexity of the world into grand theoretical projects through a variety of rigorous procedures is an antithesis of current circumstances. The complexity turn also has methodological consequences since viewing the current environment as so interactive as to inhibit the tracing of causal sequences disputes the framing of hypotheses that link independent and dependent variables. More attention must be given to processes, which is also the remedy proposed by some constructivists to overcome the agent-structure problem, or behavior, which is the focus of large-scale computer-based modeling efforts.

To summarize, the attention given to complexity as both a threat and an opportunity in security politics has several theoretical and practical consequences. First, the disciplinary distinction between "the international" and IR and the noninternational, or not-IR becomes untenable. When moving to a systems perspective, global life is not defined by borders but by multifaceted networks, in which power takes various forms. Furthermore, questions about how the concept of complexity is used, seized upon, and instrumentalized in the political realm move to center stage. In addition, it calls for a specific mindset in both government and society. On the one hand, complex contexts require interactive—and specifically more democratic and multidirectional—communication in order to generate the most innovative ideas. Also, dissent and diversity should be encouraged, because they advance the emergence of well-forged patterns and ideas. As the outcomes are unpredictable in a complex context, policy makers should focus on creating an environment from which positive things can emerge, rather than trying to bring about predetermined results and possibly missing opportunities that arise unexpectedly.

On the other hand, a political discourse of uncertainty is needed in order to generate legitimacy for the possibility of failure. In a world of complex systems, there can be no security in the absolute sense. In fact, the opposite is true: incidents are deemed to happen, because they simply cannot be avoided. Public policy must more actively recognize and communicate that some policy measure could be successful but that others will result in failure due to unintended consequences brought on by the interactions within and between complex systems. The "freeing" of the policy designing process to be one that plans for success as well as failure can potentially render unintended consequences that are beneficial to complex systems management

(Little 2011, 14). However, even though we must expect disturbances in vital systems in the future, we must not expect outright disasters. Some of the disturbances may well turn into crises, but a crisis should and can be seen as a turning point rather than an end, where the aversion of disaster or catastrophe is always possible. If societies become more fault tolerant psychologically and more resilient overall, the likelihood for catastrophe in general and catastrophic system failure in particular can be substantially reduced. Such wishes for future behavior have a bearing on our lives as political subjects, on power distribution and responsibilities.

Bibliography

Aradau, C., and van Munster, R. (2007). Governing terrorism through risk: Taking precautions, (un)knowing the future. *European Journal of International Relations*, 13(1), 89–115.

Axelrod, R., and Cohen, M. D. (1999). *Harnessing complexity: Organizational implications of a scientific frontier.* New York: Free Press.

Bailes, A. J. K. (2007). Introduction: A world of risk. In *SIPRI Yearbook 2007: Armaments, Disarmament and International Security* (1–20). Stockholm: SIPRI.

Bara, C., and Brönnimann, G. (2011). *Resilience: Trends in policy and research.* Zurich: Center for Security Studies.

Bonen, Z. (1981). Evolutionary behavior of complex sociotechnical systems. *Research Policy* 10(1), 26–44.

Brown, K. A. (2006). *Critical path: A brief history of critical infrastructure protection in the United States.* Washginton: George Mason University Press.

Brunner, E., and Giroux, J. (2009). *Examining resilience: A concept to improve societal security and technical safety.* Zurich: Center for Security Studies.

Brunner, E., and Roth, F. (2012). *Roots of resilience:A historical perspective on resilience and civil defense in Switzerland.* Zurich: Center for Security Studies.

Collier, S. J., and Lakoff, A. (2008). The vulnerability of vital systems: How "critical infrastructure" became a security problem. In Myriam Dunn and Soby Kristensen, *The politics of securing the homeland: Critical infrastructure, risk and securitisation.* London: Routledge.

Coward, M. (2009). Network-centric violence, critical infrastructure and the urbanization of security. *Security Dialogue,* 40(4–5), 399–418.

Czempiel, E. O., and Rosenau, J. N. (1992). *Governance without government: order and change in world politics.* Cambridge: Cambridge University Press.

Duit, A., and Galaz, V. (2008). Governance and complexity—Emerging issues for governance theory. *Governance,* 331–335.

Dunn Cavelty, M. (2010). Cyber-security. In Peter Burgess, *The Routledge companion to new security studies* (154–162). London: Routledge.

Dunn Cavelty, M. (2008). Like a phoenix from the ashes: The reinvention of critical infrastructure protection as distributed security. In Myriam Dunn Cavelty and Kristian Søby Kristensen, *Securing the Homeland: Critical Infrastructure, Risk, and (In)Security* (40–62). London: Routledge.

Dunn Cavelty, M., and Giroux, J. (2011). Crisis mapping: A phenomenon and tool in complex emergencies. *CSS Analyses*, 103.

Dunn Cavelty, M., and Suter, M. (2009). Public-private partnerships are no silver bullet: An expanded governance model for critical infrastructure protection. *International Journal of Critical Infrastructure Protection*.

Easton, D. (1967). *A systems analysis of political life*. New York: Wiley.

Farwell, J. P., and Rohozinski, R. (2011). Stuxnet and the future of cyber war. *Survival: Global Politics and Strategy*, 53(1), 23–40.

Furedi, F. (2008). Fear and security: A vulnerability-led policy response. *Social Policy & Administration*, 42 (3), 645–661.

Geels, F.W. (2004). From sectoral systems of innovation to socio-technical systems: Insights about dynamics and change from sociology to institutional theory. *Research Policy*, 33(4), 897–920.

Geyer, R., and S. Rihani, S. (2010). *Complexity and public policy*. London: Routledge.

Giroux, J., and Roth, F. (2012). *Conceptualizing the crisis mapping phenomenon: Insights on behavior and the coordination of agents and information in complex crisis*. Zurich: Center for Security Studies.

Goldstein, B. E. (2011). Conclusion: Communicative resilience. In B. E. Goldstein (Ed.), *Collaborative resilience: Moving through crisis to opportunity* (359–372). Cambridge: MIT Press.

Gross, M. J. (2011). Stuxnet Worm: A Declaration of Cyber-War. April. http://www.vanityfair.com/culture/features/2011/04/stuxnet-201104.

Holling, C. S. (1973). Resilience and stability of ecological systems. *Annual Review of Ecology and Systematics*, 4, 1–23.

Homeland Security Advisory Council. (2006). *Report of the critical infrastructure task force*. Washington, DC: Department of Homeland Security.

Hughes, T. P. (1987). The evolution of large technological systems. In W. E. Bijker, T. Parke Hughes and T. J. Pinch (Eds.), *The Social construction of technological systems: New directions in the sociology and history of technology* (51–82). Cambridge: MIT Press.

Lei, T. E., Bekebrede, G., and Nikolic, I. (2010). Critical infrastructures: A review from a complex adaptive system perspective. *International Journal of Critical Infrastructures*, 6(4), 380–401.

Lewis, T. G., Mackin, T. J., and Darken, R. (2011). Critical infrastructure as complex emergent systems. *IJCWT* 1(1), 1–12.

Little, A. (2011). Political action, error and failure: The epistemological limits of complexity. *Political Studies*, 60, 3–19.

Mitleton-Kelly, E. (2003). Ten principles of complexity and enabling infrastructures. In E. Mitleton-Kelly (Ed.), *Complex systems and evolutionary perspectives on organizations: The application of complexity theory to organizations* (23–50). Oxford: Elsevier.

Parsons, T. (1964). Evolutionary universals in society. *American Sociological Review,* 29, 339–357.

Pierre, J. B., and Peters, G. (2000). *Governance, politics and the state.* Basingstoke: Macmillan.

Posner, P. L. (2002). Accountability challenges of third-party government. In. L. M. Salamon (Ed.), *The tools of government: A guide to the new governance* (523–551). Oxford: Oxford University Press.

Ramsden, J. J. (2008). An introduction to complexity. In J. J. Ramsden and P. J. Kervalishvili (Eds.), *Complexity and security* (55–70). Amsterdam: IOS Press.

Rhodes, R. A. W. (1996). The new governance: Governing without government. *Political Studies,* 44(4), 652–667.

Rinaldi, S. M., Peerenboom, J. P., and Kelly, T. K. (2001). Complex networks: Identifying, un-derstanding, and analyzing critical infrastructure interdependencies. *IEEE Control Systems Magazine,* 21(6), 11–25.

Sanger, D. E. (2012). Obama order sped up wave of cyberattacks against Iran. *The New York Times.* June 1.

Scalingi, P. (2007). Moving beyond critical infrastructure protection to disaster resilience. In J. A. McCarthy, *Critical thinking: Moving from infrastructure protection to infrastructure resilience* (49–72). Washington: George Mason University.

Scheffer, M., et al. (2009). Early warning signals for critical transitions. *Nature,* 461(3).

Snowden, D. (2008). *Everything is fragmented—Complex adaptive systems at play.* December, http://www.kmworld.com/Articles/News/News-Analysis/Everything-is-fragmented%E2%80%94Complex-adaptive-systems-at-play--51363.aspx.

Snowden, D., and Boone, M. (2007). A leader's framework for decision making. *Harvard Business Review,* http://hbr.org/2007/11/a-leaders-framework-for-decision-making/ar/1.

Sørensen, E., and Torfing, J. (2007). *Theories of democratic network governance.* New York: Palgrave Macmillan.

Suter, M. (2011). *Resilience and risk management: Exploring the relationship and comparing its use.* Zurich: Center for Security Studies.

Tweed, F., and Walker, G. (2011). Some lessons for resilience from the 2011 multi-disaster in Japan. *Local Environment,* 937–942.

Urry, J. (2003). *Global complexity.* Cambridge: Polity.

Walker, J., and Cooper, M. (2011). Genealogies of resilience: From systems ecology to the political economy of crisis adaptation. *Security Dialogue* 14(2), 143–160.

Williams, M. J. (2008). (In)security studies, reflexive modernization and the risk society. *Cooperation and Conflict* 43(1), 57–79.

Zolo, D. (1992). *Democracy and complexity.* Cambridge: Polity.

Chapter 9

Complexity and Stability in Human-Environment Interaction

The Transformation from Climate Risk Cascades to Viable Adaptive Networks

Jürgen Scheffran

Complexity Thinking in International Relations

During the 1980s complexity thinking (CT) emerged as a new paradigm in the scientific world. CT offers a rich framework for analyzing and handling complex problems and opens the possibility of integrative approaches from the micro to the macro level of the earth system. In a complex system, the self-organization of individual components can lead to new emerging patterns, which do not exist in the individual units and thus are more than the sum of its parts. Complex systems often tend to generate surprises, react sensitively to parameter variations, and are unpredictable. Uncertainties open a range of possible futures and offer the freedom of choosing alternative action paths.

Initially driven by the natural sciences, CT also began to transform the social sciences. It was remarkable that the decade that established complexity science ended with the chaotic demise of the Cold War. In 1989, various events brought about the dramatic breakdown of the socialist world system, an event of global and historic dimensions that hardly anyone expected or predicted. CT in international relations reached a turning point. The transformation of a globalized international system and the redistribution of power in an emerging multipolar structure continue. The structurally simple and highly organized East-West conflict was followed by a period of disorder and instability that challenged the dominant concepts in International Relations (IR). The positive consequences of the new era came under pressure by countering trends and violent conflicts. Today's international landscape is quite fractal, involving an increasing diversity of actors and factors that interact with each other in a highly dynamic and complex way. Rapidly changing conditions are indicative of unstable processes where seemingly minor events and even individuals can change the course of history. When everything is connected to everything, changes in one part of the world could have significant impacts elsewhere.

Over the last decades human-environment interactions contributed to the shift of the global coordinates. Irrespective of when the limits to growth take effect, the continued expansion of human activities in the anthroposphere transforms the whole earth system into a new geological epoch, the anthropocene. One of the most intricate global challenges is climate change, a highly complex nexus between the natural and the human world. Facing this problem, humanity has the choice between a slippery slope of risk cascades of environmental destruction, poverty, and violent conflict, or a transformation of the socioeconomic system into a more sustainable and peaceful world, involving the formation of viable and resilient networks enhancing international cooperation.

All these phenomena can be expressed in terms of the relationship between the complexity and the stability of systems, an issue that is at the core of complexity thinking. When systems are not able to adapt to changing circumstances, they may become unstable beyond certain tipping points, thus losing essential qualities that define their identity, in the worst case their existence. When systems are not adequately complex to handle the challenges in their environment they risk failure and instability, while adaptive complexity improves the chances for survival. With climate change and other global problems more "tipping points" may arise in the future which could turn into existential threats. Alternatively, new complex networks could emerge that are viable, resilient, cooperative and thus more sustainable.

Several questions are relevant in this context: Are complex systems more stable or unstable? How will environmental changes affect the evolution of the international system? Will climate change undermine the stability of societies, and which regions are most vulnerable? How do complex systems switch between equilibria? Will humanity be able to realize the transition from "negative complexity" to "positive complexity"? Will institutions evolve that are able to manage this complexity and its transformation?

Addressing these questions, this chapter will focus on the interplay between complexity and stability which can be observed in many fields of international relations. CT is useful in understanding possible transitions between pathways and active transformation processes in international relations. IR theory is not yet developed enough to handle these complex challenges. Linear systems models, rational choice optimization, and static two-player games were the modeling paradigms of the Cold War but reach their limits in this new environment. CT is challenging the dominant rationalist, realist, and reductionist IR framework even though there is still a long way to go to develop useful tools and move them beyond the academic realm into the day-to-day world of policy making (Geyer and Pickering 2011).

The concepts, language, and methods of complexity theory are slowly making their way into IR (Bousquet and Curtis 2011). Although the meaning of complexity often remains vague, and concepts are lacking clarity (Geller 2011), several CT approaches to IR have been undertaken (Alberts et al. 1997; Cedermann 1997; Elhefnawy 2004; Mesjaz 2006; Harrison 2006; Kavalski 2007). CT "eschews the flaws and limitations of previous instantiations of systems theory and offers an array of conceptual tools apposite to analysing international politics in the twenty-first century" (Bousquet and Curtis 2011, 43). In great demand are practical tools that are adequate to represent the uncertainty and complexity of IR, the adaptive nature of human decisions, and its bounded rationality. The representation of international political landscapes needs models that analyze the nonlinear dynamic interaction across multiple levels of decision making, from local to global.

In the following the complexity-stability interplay will be conceptually analyzed, with a reference to both terms and the relevance of tipping points, cascades, and social networks. Several historical cases of instability and transformation will be used to point to the relevance of these aspects. Climate change will be assessed in more depth, based on an integrated framework of human-environment interaction. Finally, the conditions for a sustainable transformation toward more resilient and viable systems and networks will be considered, with a view on the role of CT and transdisciplinary science.

The Relationship between Complexity and Stability

Conceptual Issues

To understand the relationship between complexity and stability, a short introduction to the meaning of both terms is helpful. Although complexity is one the most frequently used terms, there is no common agreed definition. Numerous meanings of complexity have been identified and discussed (Casti 1979; Scheffran 1983; Abraham et al. 1990). In one or the other way complexity expresses the difficulty to describe, understand, or explain something. Critical issues are to select an appropriate language for understanding and explanation, to identify essential features, to decompose a system into units or construct it from units, and to find the shortest possible model description of an object that contains the "essential" features. A description that is too simple may fail to represent the essential features and thus produce errors, while a description that becomes too complex is difficult to handle and may be a waste of resources. As Albert Einstein has put it: "Make things as simple as possible, but not simpler." This leads to the concept of adaptive complexity, focusing on what an adequately complex representation of an object is that is adaptive to the context and circumstances.

Also unclear is the concept of stability which is rooted in the natural sciences but is relevant in the social sciences as well. In general terms, stability means that "minor disturbances will not be magnified into a major disturbance, but on the contrary, dampened so as to have only a small and disappearing impact" (Ter Borg 1987, 50). A stable system will be able to maintain its essential attributes that determine its identity and core complexity while other features can still change. If magnification processes exceed dampening mechanisms, instability could lead to the breakdown of essential attributes. In case of instability a qualitative change of systemic conditions results, like a transition from peace to war, from conflict to cooperation, or from environmental destruction to sustainability. Thus, the stability concept is relevant for the study of transitions and transformation processes.

Two related concepts are viability and resilience. For viability it is essential to stay within boundaries within which a system can exist (Aubin and Saint-Pierre 2007). To avoid crossing limits of catastrophic change, control and regulation mechanisms are required. Resilience is the ability of a system to cope with or compensate for external shocks and surprises (Holling 1973). Social resilience implies that a community is able "to withstand external shocks and stresses without significant upheaval" (Adger et al. 2002).

Common elements of complexity and stability are the "essential features" of a system that determine its identity. The relationship between complexity and stability has been studied since the 1970s, initially for ecological systems (May 1972) and more recently for socioeconomic systems (Haldane and May 2011). A prominent question has been whether an increasing system complexity will lead to more stability or instability. In reality there are numerous complex systems that are pretty stable: biological organisms, ecosystems, societies, networks, and technical systems. This is in contrast to the observation that a randomly constructed or modified complex system is often dysfunctional because the parts of a system do not fit together. In biological evolution, many mutations are harmful to organisms and selected out in the evolutionary process. In a few cases, however, mutations can lead to an innovation that improves the fitness of the organism. Thus, in the evolutionary process unstable complex systems tend to disappear, while those with better fitness remain. As a consequence, complex systems that went through such a selection process are more stable against experienced events. A new and unforeseen "disturbance," however, may endanger a system and force it to adapt to changing conditions. As a result, complex structures evolve that are more adequate to the environmental conditions.

Each scientific discipline investigates transitions from the simple to the complex: from nuclear particles to atoms (physics), from atoms to molecules (chemistry), from molecules to cells and ecosystems (biology), from consumers to firms (economy), from citizens to states (political science), and from single agents to social networks (social science). For successful adaptation more attributes are added that improve a system's fitness through innovations. If a disturbance exceeds the adaptive mechanisms, the system may get "out of control." If complex systems fail to adequately respond to changing circumstances, this may lead to a loss of essential attributes, even a breakdown of complex structures, moving down the complexity ladder to more simple systems. Unstable systems that cannot adapt will disappear, while stable ones survive that are adequately complex to deal with the changing environment. Thus, systems generate an adaptive level of complexity to stabilize their existence.

Not only do complex systems adapt to a certain environment; they also develop mechanisms to modify and control their environment. This can be observed for many organisms, most evidently human beings. As complex systems design more complex control mechanisms, these may become too complex to handle, an issue that is known for complex technical devices such as nuclear reactors. Keeping control systems as simple as possible and as effective as necessary is a major challenge that is also relevant for an increasingly complex system of international relations. Human beings can construct their environment and select action paths according to their values, capabilities, and rules which are subject to a social learning process. If limits are reached and resources become scarce, new strategies and innovations are required to ensure survival under more difficult conditions. Thus, the complexity and stability of human societies need to be adjusted to the natural environment. It is important to understand that stability in international and domestic politics may not depend "on the existence of a *unique* equilibrium around which patterns of political behaviour can be coordinated" but on "multiple simultaneous equilibria" (Ayson 2012). International institutions can be regarded as four types of political equilibria which are related to three successive levels of stability (preservation of a unique political equilibrium;

transition between unique equilibria; oscillation between multiple simultaneous political equilibria).

Tipping Points, Cascades, and Conflicts in Complex Social Networks

The complexity-stability relationship is particularly relevant in transition processes that change the qualitative structure of systems. The processes occur when systems break down or new ones are being formed. Methods of nonlinear dynamics have been used to describe transition phenomena, such as self-organization or micro-macro phase transitions. In this context, seemingly minor events on a microscale could lead to major qualitative changes on a macroscale. Transitions often occur beyond tipping points when the dynamics of change accelerate and there is a qualitative switch of behavior. Tipping points imply "that events and phenomena are contagious, that little causes can have big effects, and that changes can happen in a non-linear way but dramatically at a moment when the system switches" (Urry 2002, 8). Often the switching results from triggering events, such as natural disasters, mass migrations, or social movements, and leads to cascading sequences, such as when an action taken by one actor provokes more intense actions by other actors. A self-reinforcing chain reaction could increase the possibility of social cascades when individuals follow the actions of other agents. If the choices and actions of others influence our own decisions, tipping points in social interaction that undermine the stability of the whole system may become more likely. Collective transitions into a qualitatively new social structure can be found in many social contexts, from voting patterns to the stock market. Cascades and catastrophic events are shaped by institutional responses in one or the other way. Crises are major drivers of policy formation and related responses and represent complex adaptive systems (Lehmann 2011).

Conflict may be seen as a special form of social instability which emerges from incompatible actions, values, behavioral rules, and priorities of agents who fail to reduce their differences and tensions to tolerable levels. Conflicting actions may undercut each other's values and provoke responses generating further losses. A conflict escalates if actions by conflict parties aggravate the conflict tension and intensity which corresponds to an inherently unstable cascading interaction that cannot be easily contained. If unresolved, conflicts consume a considerable amount of resources, pushing conflict parties toward extreme actions, such as the use of violence, until the capability to act by some actors is exhausted or destroyed, if not replenished by some processes. Conflict resolution may help to reduce the conflict tension and stabilize the interaction by involving actors in learning and negotiations until agreement is reached. Cooperation is a process in which actors adjust their goals and actions to achieve mutual benefits. The transition from conflict to cooperation requires adaptation toward common positions and mutually beneficial actions that stabilize the interaction (Axelrod 1997; 1984; Scheffran and Hannon 2007). Whether this succeeds depends on the governance capacity of societies to manage conflicts.

Various methods and tools have been developed to study the complexity and stability of interaction between systems and agents and their relevance in IR and related fields of environmental, energy, and security policy (Helbing 1995; Scheffran 2006a). These include system dynamics, dynamic game theory, agent-based modeling, and social network analysis. Particularly relevant for CT in IR are adaptive networks that are dynamically switching in response to changing internal and external conditions. Understanding the emergence of collective behavior and the evolution of cooperation is a dynamic field of current interdisciplinary research. Of great interest is the dynamic spread of processes across a social network, such as the diffusion of diseases or social behavior patterns like technical innovations and social practices (Kempe et al. 2005). Social networks evolve through interaction processes, such as conflict, cooperation, competition, and coalition formation among a large number of participants (Flint et al. 2009; Maoz 2010). In this process connective complexity is an important indicator for network stability. A crucial phenomenon in social networks is path dependency (Kominek and Scheffran 2012) where social actors are locked in certain pathways of action that are self-enforcing and hard to change individually. When agents follow other agents or organizations, path dependency has a magnifying effect, leading to a collective dynamics (Granovetter 1978; Schelling 1978; Dodds and Watts 2004).

Historical Cases of Instability and Transformation

Human history was shaped by numerous social transformation processes, including wars, revolutions, and the collapse of civilizations. In one or the other way the processes can be described as the interplay of complexity and stability, as demonstrated by more recent events.

Security Dilemmas, Cycles of Violence, and Chaotic Regime Change

Many conflicts have been influenced by the "security dilemma" where threats to security of one agent provoke reactions that threaten the security for other agents, contributing to a "cycle of violence." This inherently unstable interaction had dramatic consequences a hundred years ago when the network of nations and alliances drifted into a cascade of events leading to World War I (Vasquez et al. 2011). In its aftermath the conditions were prepared for World War II, which was then followed by the bipolar East-West conflict. During the Cold War, strategic stability was a prominent concept in international security, focusing on two stability dimensions (Schelling 1960). Arms-race stability was designed to control the nuclear arms race and strengthen mutual cooperation of the two super powers through arms control and disarmament. The concept of crisis stability aims at reducing the motivation for the use of violence and the pressure for quick and preemptive actions, such as through force structures that minimize preemptive advantages (e.g., of first strikes) and technical instability of weapon systems against error or failure.

While the bilateral East-West conflict appeared to be structurally simple (which is debatable), the 1980s ended with the chaotic breakdown of the Cold War (Scheffran 1989). The rather static socialist system was not stable against the complexities of its time, and when Mikhail Gorbachev tried to adapt and reform the system, the inherent contradictions and incompatibilities went out of control and triggered a wave that removed the socialist system. The momentous events in 1989 were an expression of systemic instability and on November 9, 1989, reached a tipping point in world history when minor events led to the "fall of the wall," leading to a cascade of events that fundamentally transformed the international system.

Post–Cold War Era of Instability and Fragility

The end of the Cold War resulted in a world (dis)order with ever-growing complexity and instability across multiple levels of international relations (Scheffran 2008a). While military forces dominated the East-West conflict, the concepts of security and stability were expanded by environmental, economic, social, and human dimensions. The hostile relationship between the former superpowers was replaced by a relationship based on arms control, political dialogue, crisis management and verification. However, the unipolar dominance of the United States provoked resistance from Russia and China and attracted criticism from European allies, notably in the Iraq war of 2003 and its aftermath. Nuclear and missile proliferation continued, and new arms races emerged, including outer space. Conflicts in the Balkans, in Africa, the Middle East, and other parts of the world provoked foreign military interventions. New technologies accelerated a revolution in military affairs (Neuneck 2008).

Due to globalization, in conjunction with rapid developments in computing, communication, and transportation, changes in one region may have significant impacts in other regions. Accordingly, individuals and small groups can have huge effects, as demonstrated by the 9/11 terror attacks and the recent cases of whistle blowers who distributed large amounts of sensitive information to the public. Environmental degradation, poverty, and hunger affect the living conditions in many parts of the world. Terrorism provides a justification to keep the cycles of hatred and violence alive. Especially vulnerable are societies on the edge of instability, such as states in transition from authoritarian to democratic regimes or states lacking legitimacy and ability to protect citizens from harm. Human insecurity and personal instability could trigger societal and political instability, and vice versa. The marginal impact of environmental change could undermine the ability to solve problems and further dissolve state structures, possibly leading to their collapse. Particularly critical is the situation in fragile and failing states with social fragmentation, weak governance structures, and inadequate management capacities (Milliken and Krause 2003; Rotberg 2003; Starr 2008).

Credit Crunch and Financial Collapse

The economic crisis of 2008 demonstrated the instability of the increasingly complex and interconnected world economy. Driven by reckless lending practices of financial institutions and short-sighted human behavior, local fluctuations and individual reactions accumulated collectively and moved the global financial system to the brink of collapse. Once a critical boundary was passed, self-enforcing mechanisms were triggered, creating losses of trillions of dollars. Long-term investment and regulatory policies were unable to handle the significant short-term local fluctuations. In Europe the economic crisis was followed by the Greek credit crunch where the interaction between rating agencies and governmental responses created an explosive situation.

Food Riots and the Arab Spring

An expression of the inherent instability in the international system is the series of protests and uprisings in the Arabic countries of North Africa and the Middle East during 2011. Among the various factors contributing to instability was the increase in the price of food, partly caused by speculations on globalized food markets, which added to the local dissatisfaction of people with their autocratic governments (Johnstone and Mazo 2011). Starting with riots in Tunisia, which forced the president to flee, the revolutionary

impulse expanded to Egypt and other countries, accelerated and multiplied
by electronic media and social networks on the internet (Kominek and Scheffran 2012). These facilitated the quick spread of successful experiences to
motivate neighboring agents to join in the protest movement. One example
of collective behavior was the peaceful demonstrations on the Tahrir Square
in Cairo. Although supporters of the regime used violence against the crowd
of demonstrators, the demonstration remained peaceful in its self-organized
resistance, which ultimately was successful in bringing down the regime of
President Mubarak.

From a social network perspective, multiple actors in search of food,
jobs, and political opportunities acted path dependently when they followed
others, leading to a multiplier effect that contributed to a mass movement.
Actors followed behavioral rules moving in the same direction, thus induc-
ing a collective transition which was further strengthened through solidarity
principles and collective group action that resulted in a swarming or cascading interaction. Opposing tendencies such as counterdemonstrations or
police action did not contain the collective action, in some cases even aggravated it because it pressed the demonstrators to stay together and act jointly.
Successes achieved as a result of the demonstrations furthered the process,
such as when political regimes in neighbor countries were overthrown. Due
to the intense correlation, collective behavior could lead to rapid switching
between different alternative modes of behavior, ranging from peaceful mass
demonstrations to active defense when being attacked and a breakdown of
the movement. Although the Arabellion was able to destabilize some of the
regimes, it also provoked violent responses, most strikingly in Syria, which
turned into a bloody civil war. Even in Egypt the initially peaceful revolution
led to a military coup against the democratically elected government that
violated the rights of large fractions of the population for religious reasons.

Risk Society, Nuclear Disasters, and the Sustainable Energy Transition

Natural disasters, environmental problems, and technical accidents can play
an important role in triggering social change. During the 1970s the oil crisis
and the debate on limits to growth initiated a major push toward energy
alternatives and sustainable development. In the 1980s environmental pollution and technical accidents (Bhopal, Chernobyl) found their expression in
the concepts of "normal accidents" (Perrow 1984) and "risk society" (Beck
1986). A vivid example of the cascading potential of disasters and accidents
is the earthquake that occurred in Japan on March 11, 2011. It triggered a
chain of events that were more devastating than the earthquake itself. The

tsunami killed more than 15,000 people and traveled thousands of kilometers across the Pacific. The tsunami, together with the earthquake, caused severe damage to the nuclear power plants in Fukushima and induced a nuclear reactor accident, spreading radioactivity into the atmosphere and the ocean, forcing people to evacuate from the region, not to speak of global long-term radiation effects over many generations.

Indirect consequences affected the Japanese power grid, stock markets, the oil price, financial markets, and the economy in general. The nuclear disaster led to the shutdown of nuclear plants in Japan and provoked opposition to nuclear power in other countries. Although Germany was not directly affected by Japan's earthquake, the shock waves of the nuclear disaster triggered the election of a Green Party prime minister in one of most conservative federal states. Concerns over the risks of nuclear power led to a shutdown of some nuclear power plants and launched an ethics commission of the German government that recommended the accelerated phase-out of nuclear energy and a transformation of the energy system.

Complexity and Stability of Climate Change

The Complexity of the Climate System

Weather and climate are typical examples of complex systems and are role models for CT in other fields. Atmospheric science had played a key role in the discovery of chaos theory when in 1963 Edward Lorenz developed a simplified mathematical model for atmospheric convection, based on three nonlinear deterministic differential equations. The Lorenz equations became a standard model for analysis of complex chaotic systems, including key elements of chaos theory, such as bifurcations, strange attractors, and fractals (Haken 1977).

In the past five decades a huge amount of disciplinary knowledge of the various compartments of the climate system has been assembled, including various atmospheric components, rivers, oceans, polar ice, solar radiation, biodiversity, land cover, greenhouse gas (GHG) emissions, and other anthropogenic factors. This "system of systems" is highly complex and cannot be fully described by listing all the equations and data for each of its components. Even if all factors were known individually, it is still not certain how the different relationships and feedback mechanisms interact with each other. The various parts and connections have adapted to each other in the evolutionary process. Interactions which were not compatible have

been canceled out naturally. Although the world's climate has been rather
stable over recent millennia, palaeoclimatic records show that abrupt climate
changes have occurred. Human interventions have destabilized established
relationships in the rather short time period since the beginning of the
industrial revolution and the advent of the anthropocene era of earth history.

Global warming is a challenge that connects the world's natural and
social systems across spatial and temporal scales. Since every human being
contributes to it and is affected by it, a new level of complexity is reached. By
entering unknown areas of the climate system, with the emission of greenhouse gases humankind undertakes a risky experiment that may undermine
climate stability and have a lasting impact on the entire planet. To understand
and manage the complexity-stability relationship in the context of climate
change, new research approaches are needed that assess the highly complex
and uncertain dynamics. While previous research has addressed the causal
chains from different viewpoints, a systematic approach would reconstruct
the complex tree of future pathways and decision points.

Integrated Framework of Climate-Society Interaction

The implications of climate change can be analyzed in a complex integrated
framework that addresses the connections between climate change, natural
resources, human security, and societal stability (Figure 9.1) (Scheffran 2011;
Scheffran et al. 2012).

1. Changes in the climate system, such as increases in GHG
   concentration, temperature, and precipitation, affect environmental systems and natural resources (e.g., soil, ecosystems, forests, biodiversity) through a sequence of complex
   interactions.

2. Changes in natural resources can have adverse impacts on
   human security, which may provoke human responses that
   affect social systems.

3. Depending on the degree of vulnerability, socioeconomic
   stress increases as a result of water and food insecurity, health
   problems, migration, economic degradation, the weakening
   of institutions, diminishing economic growth, and eroding
   societies.

4. Interdependencies between these factors may lead to societal
   instability that can manifest itself in violent forms such as
   riots, insurgencies, urban violence, or armed conflict.

5. A feedback loop allows human beings and societies to adapt to the changing situation and mitigate climate stress through strategies, institutions, and governance mechanisms that apply technology, human capital, and social capital to adjust the economy and the energy system to altered environmental conditions.

In each of the components, a number of variables and interactions are relevant, such as between temperature and precipitation in the climate system, between water and food as natural resources, between different dimensions of human security, and between different patterns of social instability (protests, riots, rebellions, armed conflicts). Accordingly, there is a vast range of possible combinations and thus pathways which interact in a complex way. This is not a deterministic system because human beings as well as societies can respond in different ways shaped by social behavior, policies, and institutions, all of which are affected by uncertainties (Ratter 2013).

If climate change severely affects the stabilizing mechanisms of systems, they could become unstable and break up. Where the critical thresholds are depends on the vulnerability of each system which is a function of the exposure and sensitivity to climate change as well as the adaptive capacity. According to IPCC (2007, 881), sensitivity is the "degree to which a system is affected, either adversely or beneficially, by climate variability or change." Theoretical and empirical efforts are required to estimate the sign and magnitude of the possible connections and pathways (Figure 9.1).

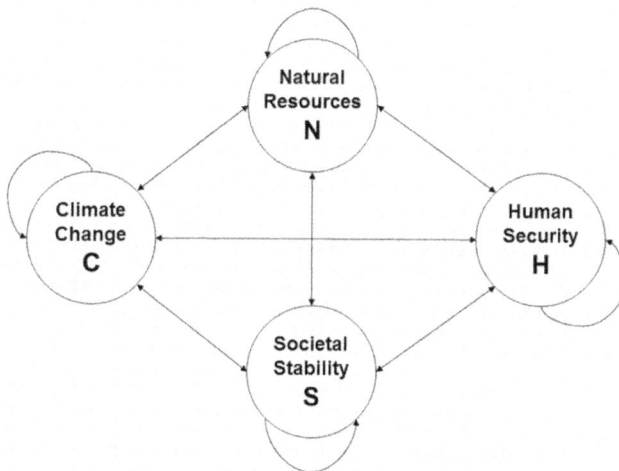

Figure 9.1. Connections and pathways in climate-society interaction (adapted from Scheffran 2011).

242 Jürgen Scheffran

Climate Change and Stability

Climate change can challenge the stability of natural and social systems in multiple ways along the complex pathways mentioned. Depending on the type of systems, disturbances, and responses, various meanings of stability are considered in this context (Scheffran 2011).

STABILITY OF CLIMATIC SYSTEMS, ECOSYSTEMS
AND ECONOMIC SYSTEMS

Article 2 of the UN Framework Convention on Climate Change demands the stabilization of atmospheric greenhouse gas concentrations at levels that "prevent dangerous anthropogenic interference with the climate system." This objective is to be realized in a time frame that guarantees three viability conditions (ecosystems adaptation, food security, and economic sustainability) (Ott et al. 2004; Scheffran 2008b). While the first requires an assessment of the stability boundaries of ecosystems, the last two provide socioeconomic stability conditions that have to be maintained to avoid disruption of society and the economy. Viability conditions for ecosystem and economic stability determine tolerable windows for the admissible speed and magnitude of climate change (Petschel-Held et al. 1999). Over a short time horizon, ecologic, and economic systems would adapt to a slowly changing environment, but with a longer time horizon and more significant changes, they could become unstable. Alternatively, the transition from the fossil energy path to a low-carbon society could be realized (WBGU 2011).

SOCIETAL STABILITY AND FRAGILITY

If climate change undermines societal structures, they may lose credibility and support from citizens, become weak and unable to maintain social order. Climate risks could multiply other problems such as growing populations, inadequate fresh water supplies, strained agricultural resources, poor health services, economic decline, or weak political institutions. Together they could overwhelm the problem-solving capacity of societies, disrupt governments, and lead to societal instability events, including a smaller number of large-scale events (such as wars) and a large number of small-scale events (protests, riots, intergroup violence). Especially at risk are societies on the edge of instability, in particular in failing states that cannot guarantee the core functions of government, such as law and public order, welfare, participation, and basic public services (e.g., infrastructure, health, and education), or the monopoly on the use of force (WBGU 2008). Societal structures that lose credibility and support from the citizens become weak and unstable. Individuals who experience personal losses of life, income, property, job, health, family, or friends, threatening their identity may be more vulnerable to violate established rules. Particularly vulnerable are low-income countries and fragil societies which have little adaptive capacities, for instance in sub-Saharan Africa where about one-third of countries are considered at risk of state failure Wealthier societies are generally in a better position to handle climate impacts because of their higher adaptive capacity. However, developed countries cannot ignore the economic impacts, the migratory pressures, the demands for humanitarian assistance, and may be drawn into climate-induced disruptions in regions that are hardest hit by the impacts. Rapid or drastic climate change could even overwhelm the adaptive capacity of wealthy nations.

RISK CASCADES IN CLIMATE HOT SPOTS

Climate change could simultaneously affect different regions and trigger multiple pathways of instability. Feedbacks and chain reactions between the shrinking availability of resources and violent human responses magnify system fluctuations, possibly leading to catastrophic failure of the whole system. In the worst-affected hot spots, climate change could spread to neighboring states, for example, through cross-border migration, ethnic links, environmental resource flows, black markets, or arms exports. An increase of forced migration could create hot spots elsewhere as a possible nucleus for social unrest. Such spillover effects may contribute to regional instability and expand the geographical extent of a crisis. Due to nonlinear effects, an increase in global temperature above a certain threshold (such as 2°C) may result in disproportionate impacts, such as a reduction of agricultural output in many regions (Hare et al. 2011). Abrupt climate change could induce instabilities, tipping points, and cascading sequences across network connections, and tipping elements in the climate system (Lenton et al. 2007) could trigger tipping elements in social systems. Collective switching of essential system attributes could lead to an increasing or decreasing level of complexity and stability. When climate risk cascades will occur is hard to predict (Onischka 2009). Climate stress may only affect one layer in the causal chain but not be strong enough to penetrate to other levels and thus fizzle out in the causal chain.

STABILITY AGAINST ESCALATING THREATS AND VIOLENT CONFLICTS

While the empirical evidence for climate-induced conflicts is still debated (see the reviews Scheffran et al. 2012; Theisen et al. 2013; Hsiang et al. 2013), there is reason to believe that in the future rising temperatures and changing climate could add to the multiple threats and conflicts of today's multipolar world. They could affect different security dimensions and provoke "security dilemmas" with increasing threat perceptions and a competitive force buildup. Acting as a "threat multiplier" could have various consequences: "military intervention, refugee flows, military coups and revolution, massive violent repression of the opposition (e.g. massacres), social unrest, famine, civil war, etc." (WBGU 2008: 43). In the most affected states the erosion of social order and state failure could be aggravated, leading to a spiral of corruption, crime, and violence. Power vacuums could be filled by nonstate actors such as private security companies, terrorist groups, and warlords. If the degradation of natural resources puts the survival of people at stake or increases resource competition, this could provoke the use of force to protect key resources against competitors. To avoid situations in which rational actions generate unreasonable collective outcomes, rules, regulations, and institutions are required to achieve the benefits of cooperation and maintain social order. To stabilize the interaction, actors could move toward mutually beneficial solutions by resource sharing and risk management. Whether climate change will fuel a vicious cycle or a transition toward cooperation and sustainable peace depends on the human and societal responses and pathways (Figure 9.2).

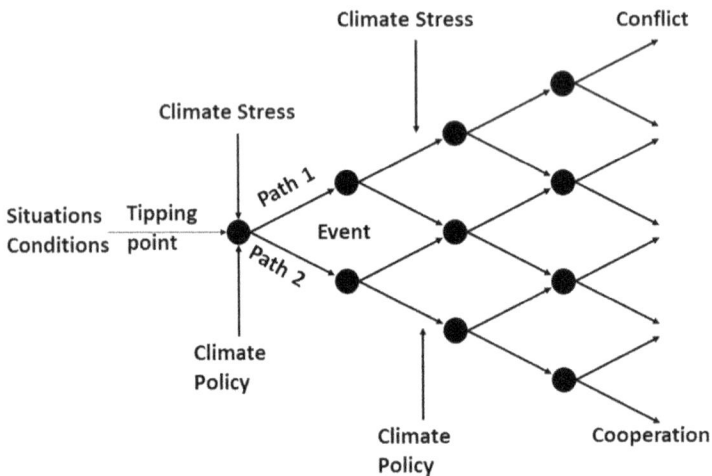

Figure 9.2. Future climate pathways, tipping points and cascades between conflict and cooperation.

From Climate Instability to Environmental Viability and Social Resilience

Toward Adaptive Complexity and Stability

Stabilizing human-environment interactions is becoming a major challenge in IR that requires the integration of CT into global governance. Climate change is affecting the balance between complexity and stability of natural and social systems. To survive destabilizing consequences and avoid tipping points and cascading breakdowns, affected systems need to adapt to the changing circumstances to ensure their viability. Concepts of adaptive complexity and stability influence the multiple decision points and adjust the actions along the causal chain to protect human security, develop social livelihood, and strengthen societal resilience.

Various measures can support the adaptive capacity of ecosystems and their value to humans, including establishment of nature reserves, sustainable land use, preservation of endangered species, and protection of terrestrial carbon stocks. Within limits, ecosystems can be managed to adjust to climate change. To be sustainable, consumption of natural resources should not exceed the natural carrying capacity for these resources, given by their limited regenerative capacity and ability to absorb pollution.

To some degree, social systems have the ability to cope with the magnitude of climate change and develop possible alternative action pathways and human responses. To succeed it is relevant how fast and adequate the responses are compared to the speed and intensity of climate change. Some responses could help to diminish harm and develop new opportunities; others may cause additional problems (maladaptation). A key question is to which degree of climate change societies can adapt and how effective and creative they are in developing coping strategies that are complex enough to deal with the challenges. One task is to translate environmental change into new social and political rules, structures, and institutions that avoid or minimize social instability. Rules and regulations that guarantee a peaceful coexistence of citizens are characteristic of a stable society which in turn is important to satisfy human needs. Concepts of resilience and viability can strengthen the social capability of people in their effective, creative, and collective efforts to handle the problems of climate change (see, e.g., Adger 2003). In a resilient social environment, actors are able to cope with and withstand the disturbances caused by climate change in a dynamic way that preserves, rebuilds, or transforms their livelihood. Key resilience strategies include the building of networks, the cultivation of diversity, and the maintenance of flexibility.

Innovative Approaches to Adaptation, Viability and Capacity Building

Climate change is not only a threat but also offers opportunities for constructive social change. Societies can create new pathways and coping strategies that support a sustainability transition (WBGU 2011):

- New capabilities are required to manage disasters, including emergency planning and decision-making structures. Global information systems for early warning could help with timely responses to extreme events and crises.

- Arms control, nonproliferation, and disarmament would reduce the destructive potential of military forces (especially weapons of mass destruction) that could be used in conflicts. Regional security concepts would establish crisis prevention, conflict resolution, and confidence building to *stabilize fragile and weak states threatened by climate change.*

- Adaptation and mitigation allow societies to develop technology, physical, human, and social capital to sustain human livelihood under changing climatic conditions, for example, by utilizing natural resources more efficiently, growing and producing new types of natural resources, and providing a sustainable energy supply.

- Innovative social mechanisms and institutional processes, including participative concepts, stakeholder dialogues, mediation, and adaptive governance, support people in regions affected by climate change in their creative efforts to protect their livelihoods.

- Human migration as an adaptive response to climate change (Black et al. 2011) is not simply a threat, but could also create opportunities. Migrant networks can facilitate the exchange of knowledge, income, and other resources across regions to strengthen adaptive capacities and resilience against climate change (Scheffran, Marmer, and Sow 2012).

Conflict Resolution, Cooperation, and Collective Action

Since sustainable development strategies often fail due to their inability to consider social interaction, it is essential to understand the collective behavioral changes in a sustainability transition. There are numerous agents involved, acting according to their interests, capabilities, and rules. Multi-agent settings and social networks are relevant when multiple regions, countries, businesses, or citizens are affected by climate change and respond to it. At the global level of decision making, main actors are governments of nation-states or groupings among them. At local levels, citizens and consumers are key players who affect or are affected by global warming. The multilevel process between local and global decision making is connected via several layers of aggregation, with each layer having its decision procedures for setting targets and implementing actions (Figure 9.3). To address social dilemmas, new rules, norms, and innovations, as well as social networks, need to evolve (Ostrom 2000).

A challenge for regional and global governance structures is to develop institutional frameworks and legal mechanisms that avoid the tragedy of the commons and ensure that the cumulative emissions of all human beings will not exceed critical limits. Innovative strategies are also needed to mitigate conflict and facilitate cooperation to improve common security. Climate change could help to unite the international community in a dynamic and

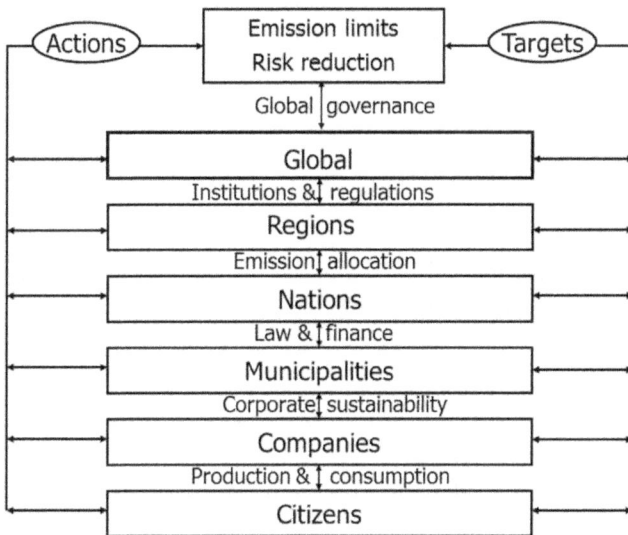

Figure 9.3. Multilevel decision making and interactions on climate change (adapted from Scheffran 2008b).

globally coordinated climate policy (Ipsen et al. 2001). The transition can be described as the formation of coalitions that acquire capabilities from individuals to generate joint values (Scheffran 2006b).

In Lieu of a Conclusion: Towards Transdisciplinary Sustainability Science

To address the complex challenges of climate change, transdisciplinary approaches in education and research could merge natural and social sciences as well as systemic and agent-based approaches (Pohl and Stoll-Kleeman 2007). Transdisciplinarity creates sustainable structures between science and the living environment and offers a framework for scientific collaboration beyond disciplinary boundaries. Transdisciplinary sustainability science is dynamic, self-regulating, dissipative, and network-oriented (Oswald Spring 1992). It is dialogic, works simultaneously with experts and decision makers (top down), and empowers people (bottom up). Integrated concepts such as "consilience" (Wilson 1998) or "sustainable peace" use a holistic socioecological framework for the entire life cycle of goods and services. They take care of the sensitivity to change in a constructive way and rely on anticipatory learning, engaging people with their diverse knowledge, and practical experience in the human lifeworld. The argument of this chapter has been that the transdisciplinarity of CT offers IR innovative ways for addressing the pressing challenges of global life.

Bibliography

Abraham, N. B., Albano, A. M., Passamante, A., and Rapp, P. E. (Eds.). (1990). *Measures of complexity and chaos*. New York: Springer.

Adger, W. N., Kelly, P. M., Winkels, A., Huy, L. Q., and Locke, C. (2002). Migration, remittances, livelihood trajectories, and social resilience. *Journal of the Human Environment* 31(4), 358–366.

Adger, W. N. (2003). Social capital, collective action, and adaptation to climate change. *Economic Geography*, 79(4), 387–404.

Alberts, D. S., and Czerwinski, T. J. (Eds.). (1997). *Complexity, global politics and national security*. Washington, DC: National Defense University Press.

Aubin, J.-P., and Saint-Pierre (2007). An introduction to viability theory and management of renewable resources. In Jürgen Kropp and Jürgen Scheffran (Eds.), *Decision making and risk management in sustainability science* (43–80). New York: Nova Science.

Axelrod, R. M. (1984). *The evolution of cooperation.* New York: Basic Books.

Axelrod, R. M. (1997). *The complexity of cooperation: Agent-based models of competition and collaboration.* Princeton, NJ: Princeton University Press.

Ayson, R. (2012). The complex stability of political equilibria. *Political Science,* 64(2), 145–161.

Beck, U. (1986). *Risikogesellschaft. auf dem Weg in eine andere Moderne.* Frankfurt: Suhrkamp.

Black, R., Bennett, S. R. G., Thomas, S.M., and Beddington, J. R. (2011). Migration as adaptation. *Nature,* 478, 447–449.

Bousquet, A., and Curtis, S. (2011). Beyond models and metaphors: Complexity theory, systems thinking and international relations. *Cambridge Review of International Affairs,* 24(1), 43–62.

Casti, J. (1979). *Connectivity, complexity and catastrophe in large-scale systems.* Vienna: International Institute for Applied Systems Analysis.

Cederman, L-E. (1997). *Emergent actors in world politics: How states and nations develop and dissolve.* Princeton University Press.

Dodds, P. S., and Watts, D. (2004). Universal behavior in a generalized model of contagion. *Physical Review Letters* 92(21), 218701 (1–4).

Elhefnawy, N. (2004). Societal complexity and diminishing returns in security. *International Security,* 29, 152–174.

Flint, C., Diehl, P., Scheffran, J., Vasquez, J., Sang-hyun, C. (2009). Conceptualizing conflictspace: Towards a geography of relational power and embeddedness in the analysis of interstate conflict. *Annals of the Association of American Geographers,* 99(5), 827–835.

Geller, A. (2011). The use of complexity-based models in international relations: A technical overview and discussion of prospects and challenges. *Cambridge Review of International Affairs,* 24(1), 63–80.

Geyer, R., and Pickering, S. (2011). Applying the tools of complexity to the international realm: From fitness landscapes to complexity cascades. *Cambridge Review of International Affairs,* 24(1), 5–26.

Granovetter, M. (1978). Threshold models of collective behavior. *The American Journal of Sociology,* 83(6), 1420–1443.

Haken, H. (1977). *Synergetics.* Berlin/Heidelberg/New York: Springer.

Haldane, A. G., and May, R. M. (2011). Systemic risk in banking ecosystems. *Nature* 469, 351–355.

Hare, W. L., Cramer, W., Schaeffer, M., Battaglini, A., and Jaeger, C. (2011). Climate hotspots: Key vulnerable regions, climate change and limits to warming. *Regional Environmental Change,* 11(S1), 1–13.

Harrison, N. E. (Ed.). (2006). *Complexity in World Politics: Concepts and Methods of a New Paradigm.* Albany: State University of New York Press.

Helbing, D. (1995). *Quantitative Sociodynamics—Stochastic methods and models of social interaction processes.* Boston: Kluwer.

Holling, C. S. (1973). Resilience and stability of ecological systems. *Annual Review of Ecology and Systematics.* 4, 1–23.

Hsiang, S. M., Burke, M., Miguel, E. (2013). Quantifying the influence of climate on human conflict. *Science 341* (13 September).

IPCC (2007). *Climate change 2007—Climate change impacts, adaptation and vulnerability.* Intergovernmental Panel on Climate Change. Geneva: Cambridge University Press.

Ipsen, D., Rösch, R., and Scheffran, J. (2001). Cooperation in global climate policy: Potentialities and limitations. *Energy Policy* 29(4), 315–326.

Johnstone, S., and Mazo, J. (2011). Global warming and the Arab spring. *Survival,* 53, 11–17.

Kavalski, E. (2007). The fifth debate and the emergence of complex international relations theory. *Cambridge Review of International Affairs,* 20(3), 435.

Kempe, D., Kleinberg, J., and Tardos, E. (2005). Influential nodes in a diffusion model for social networks. In L. Caires, et al. (Eds.), *ICALP 2005, LNCS,* vol. 3580, 1127–1138, Heidelberg: Springer.

Kominek, J., and Scheffran, J. (2012). Cascading processes and path dependency in social networks. In, Hans Georg Soeffner, *Transnationale Vergesellschaftungen.* Wiesbaden: VS Verlag für Sozialwissenschaften.

Lehmann, K. (2011). Crisis foreign policy as a process of self-organization. *Cambridge Review of International Affairs* 24(1), 27–42.

Lenton, T. M., Held, H., Kriegler, E., Hall, J. W., Lucht, W., Rahmstorf, S., and Schellnhuber, H-J. (2008). Tipping elements in the earth's climate system. *Proceedings of the national academy of sciences of the United States of America* 105(6), 1786–1793.

Maoz, Z. (2010). *Networks of nations: The evolution, structure, and impact of international networks, 1816–2001.* New York: Cambridge University Press.

May, R. M. (1972). Will a large complex system be stable? *Nature,* 238, 413–414.

Mesjasz, C. (2006). Complex systems studies and the concepts of security. *Kybernetes* 35, 3–4.

Milliken, J., and Krause, K. (2003). State failure, state collapse and state reconstruction: Concepts, lessons, and strategies. In Miliken, Jennifer (Ed.), *State failure, collapse and reconstruction,* 753–774. London: Blackwell.

Neuneck,, G. (2008). The revolution in military affairs: Its driving forces, elements, and complexity. *Complexity* 14(1), 50–61.

Onischka, M. (2009). *Definition von Klimarisiken und Systematisierung in Risikokaskaden.* Diskussionspapier, Wuppertal: Wuppertal Institut für Klima, Umwelt, Energie.

Ostrom, E. (2000). Collective action and the evolution of social norms. *Economic Perspectives,* 14(3), 137–158.

Oswald Spring, Ú. (1992). Ecodevelopment: What security for the third world? In Elise Boulding (Ed.), *New agendas for peace research. conflict and security reexamined* (121–126). Boulder, London: Lynne Rienner.

Ott, K, Klepper, G., Lingner, S., Schäfer, A., Scheffran, J., and Sprinz, D. (2004). *Reasoning goals of climate protection—Specification of art.2 UNFCCC.* Berlin: Federal Environmental Agency.

Perrow, C. (1984). *Normal accidents: Living with high-risk*. Princeton, NJ: Princeton University Press.

Petschel-Held, G., Schellnhuber, H. J., Bruckner, T., Toth, F. L. and Hasselmann, K. (1999). The tolerable windows approach: Theoretical and methodological foundations. *Climatic Change*, 41(3–4), 303–331.

Pohl, C., and Stoll-Kleemann, S. (Eds.). (2007). *Evaluation inter- und transdisziplinärer Forschung: Humanökologie und Nachhaltigkeitsforschung auf dem Prüfstand*. München: Ökom.

Ratter, B.M.W (2013). Surprise and Uncertainty—Framing *Regional Geohazards* in the Theory of Complexity. *Humanities 2*, 1–19.

Rotberg, Robert I. (2003). Failed states, collapsed states, weak states: Causes and indicators. In Robert I. Rotberg (Ed.), *State Failure and State Weakness in a Time of Terror* (1–25). Washington, DC: Brookings Institution Press.

Scheffran, J. (1983). *Complexity and stability of macrosystems with applications* (in German). Diploma Thesis, Physics Department, University of Marburg.

Scheffran, J. (1989). *Strategic defense, disarmament, and stability*. PhD Thesis, University of Marburg, IAFA Publication Series No. 9.

Scheffran, J. (2006a). Tools for stakeholder assessment and interaction. In Susanne Stoll-Kleemann and Martin Welp (Eds.), *Stakeholder dialogues in natural resources management* (153–185). Heidelberg: Springer.

Scheffran, J. (2006b). The formation of adaptive coalitions. In Alain Haurie, Shigeo Muto, Leon A. Petrosjan, and T. E. S. Raghavan (Eds.), *Advances in Dynamic Games* (163–178). Springer/Birkhäuser, Heidelberg.

Scheffran, J., and Hannon, B. (2007). From complex conflicts to stable cooperation. *Complexity*, 13(2), 78–91.

Scheffran, J. (2008a). The complexity of security. *Complexity*, 14(1), 13–21.

Scheffran, J. (2008b). Preventing dangerous climate change. In Velma I. Grover (Ed.), *Global Warming and Climate Change*, 2 vols. (449–482). Hamilton, Ontario: Science Publishers.

Scheffran, J. (2011). The security risks of climate change: Vulnerabilities, threats, conflicts and strategies. In Hans Günter Brauch, et al. (Eds.), *Coping with global environmental change, disasters and security* (735–756). Berlin: Springer.

Scheffran, J., Marmer, E., and Sow, P. (2012). Migration as a contribution to resilience and innovation in climate adaptation: Social networks and co-development in Northwest Africa. *Applied Geography* 33, 119–127.

Scheffran, J, Brzoska, M., Brauch, H. G., Link, P. M., and Schilling, J. (Eds.). (2012a). *Climate change, human security and violent conflict: Challenges for societal stability*, Berlin, Springer.

Scheffran, J., Link, P. M., and Schilling, J. (2012b). Theories and models of the climate-security link. In Jürgen Scheffran, et al. (Eds.), *Climate change, human security and violent conflict* (91–132). Heidelberg: Springer.

Schelling, T. C. (1960). *The strategy of conflict*. Cambridge, MA, Harvard University Press.

Schelling, T. C. (1978). *Micromotives and macrobehavior.* New York: Norton.

Schweitzer, F. (Ed.). (1997). *Self-organization of complex structures: From individual to collective dynamics.* London: Gordon and Breach.

Starr, Harvey (Ed.). (2008). Failed States. Special Issue. *Conflict Management and Peace Science* 25(4).

Ter Borg, M., and Tulp, M. (1987). *Defence technology assessment—Improving defence decision making.* Amsterdam: Nederlandse Organisatie voor Technologisch Aspectenonderzoek.

Theisen, O. M., Gleditsch, N. P., and Buhaug, H. (2013). Is climate change a driver of armed conflict? *Climatic. Change* 117, 613–625.

Urry, J. (2002). *Global Complexity.* Cambridge: Polity Press.

Vasquez, J. A., Diehl, P. F., Flint, C., and Scheffran, J. (Eds.). (2011). Forum on the spread of war, 1914–1917: A dialogue between political scientists and historians. *Foreign Policy Analysis* (Special Issue) 7, 139–141.

WBGU. (2008). *World in transition—Climate change as a security risk.* London: Earthscan.

WBGU. (2011). *World in transition—A social contract for sustainability.* Berlin: German Advisory Council on Global Change.

Wilson, E. O. (1998). *Consilience.* New York: Knopf.

Conclusion

Complexifying IR

Disturbing the "Deep Newtonian Slumber" of the Mainstream

Emilian Kavalski

Only after we are clear about the shape of our dream will we have a chance of attaining it: not merely a "science," but a powerful, parsimonious, and perhaps even elegant science of international politics.

—Ronald Rogowski (1968, 418)

As Roger Beaumont (1994, 145) has quipped, there is something quite paradoxical implicit in any attempt to "conclude" the observation of complexity—the reason being that the sequential unfolding of uncertainties, dilemmas, and contingencies works against focusing analysis and drawing neat conclusions. This sentiment echoes James Rosenau's own chagrin at the expectation that edited collections should have a concluding chapter "that ends on an upbeat note, celebrates the realization of common themes, ties all the contributions into a coherent whole and thus demonstrates the wisdom of collecting the essays between the same covers." As he put it, "to write an Epilogue is to strain for what may be a misleading sense of closure. It amounts to having the last word, just like superpowers do" (Rosenau et al. 1993, 127–28). Sharing Rosenau's repulsion towards the privilege of editorial "superpower," this conclusion drafts a hesitant outline of some of the themes zigzagging across the analyses of the preceding chapters. The following remarks, therefore, are not *the* authoritative version of a concluding chapter that "ties all the contributions into a coherent whole," but just one of many possible versions.

Thus, rather than "impose an outlook," this concluding chapter illustrates *a* perspective on the preceding discussions. My hope is not dissimilar to that of Rosenau's—that "readers [do not] mistake [what follows] for conclusions shared by all the contributors."

If anything, this volume should have made clear that the perception of complexity does not automatically imply a "'defeatist' attitude" (LaPorte 1975, 328). Instead, as the preceding chapters reveal, complexity thinking (CT) not only calls for (as well as suggests) new ways of thinking about and doing international relations (IR), but it also insists that the discipline needs to rethink many of its core beliefs if it is to maintain its relevance. In this respect, IR's "scientific" credentials have long concerned proponents and detractors. As the contributions in this volume reveal, establishing the scientific validity of the input of CT to IR appears to be one of its key hurdles. As Ronald Rogowski's claim in the epigraph suggests, the hankering after an "elegant science of international politics" has virtually become a "dream" to which his and subsequent generations of IR scholars have succumbed. Belying this dreaming is a question whether IR's social scientific inquiry can ever approximate that of the natural sciences. Perceiving the natural sciences to be "exact science," cohorts of IR students have been developing "powerful" and "parsimonious" models for the explanation and understanding of international politics. Take the "balance of power," for instance. Its aim is to ascertain the existence of a particular regularity in world affairs—parity between adversaries. Borrowing the notion of equilibrium from the natural sciences, the balance of power explains international order as a regulating mechanism motivated by the natural desire of states for survival.

In this way, IR has tended to propound explanations premised on assumptions of predictability rooted in the conviction that international life is a closed system, changing in a gradual manner and following linear trajectories, which can be elicited through discrete assessments of dependent and independent variables. What IR intends to produce in this way is a nearly mechanistic model of international politics that is perceived to be as rigorous and robust as the one of the natural sciences. In recent years, the simplification and reductionism underpinning this "dream" of a scientific IR have come under severe criticism from different quarters. In fact, some—such as John G. Ruggie—have made the point that the discipline needs to wake up from this "deep Newtonian slumber," if it is to have any bearing on the real world of international politics (Ruggie 1998, 194).

The contributors to this volume have sought to actively add to such a decentering project by advancing the complexification of IR. As the preceding chapters reveal, complexification may entail different things for different authors, but what all of them share is some form of engagement with the complexity paradigm of the philosophy of science. Originating in the natural sciences, CT challenges the Newtonian view of an orderly world and suggests that global interactions occur in a nonlinear fashion. Consequently, the outcomes of such interactions are difficult to infer, let alone to predict. In this respect, the proponents of the complexification of IR have noted that while the "hard" sciences have become increasingly "soft" as a result of their acceptance of the uncertainty and randomness of global life, IR has "hardened" as a result of its suppression of ambiguity, disregard for surprises, and overinvestment in its desire to forecast international developments. Some commentators explain this search for (and commitment to) a predictable worldview of regularities as a "need for psychological closure," reflecting a desire for definitive conclusions in support of preferred theoretical assumptions (Lebow 2010, 259). Others have raised the pertinent question whether "scientific IR" is not premised on "fundamentally misleading notions about science" (Popolo 2011, 23). Thus, the question that emerges is whether things appear perplexing because the ken of the mainstream is askew.

In its response to this query CT exposes that Newtonian IR tends to operate on very little information (usually a few variables); yet, this does not prevent it from jumping to conclusions as if it had knowledge about the whole picture. Such lack of sensitivity to what IR does not know furnishes a model of the world that is rarely stumped. As a result, when the accepted framework for explanation and understanding fails—it faces a question that it cannot answer (for instance, "Why did IR fail to anticipate the end of the Cold War?")—IR reduces its cognitive dissonance by coming up with a question that it can respond to (for instance, "Why did the Cold War end?," answer: "Because the Soviet Union could no longer maintain the balance of power, and therefore, without such capability, it could no longer survive in the international system and had to implode").

The complexified IR suggests that by answering the wrong questions, Newtonian IR enacts a theater of validity to generate explanations far more coherent than the turbulent realities of global life. Therefore, the "incredible rate of failure" of the very frameworks asserting the "law-like regularities" of international politics to anticipate any of the major events of the past twenty-five years should not be surprising (Cudworth and Hobden 2011, 10). The irony of this situation is not lost on some observers, who note that it is the very "commitment to science and scientific methods by international relations scholars" that provides "a major impediment to their practice of science" (Lebow 2010, 259).

Thus, this conclusion offers a brief overview of the current state of the art in the nascent complexification of IR. The focus of the remaining sections is the complexification of the ontology, epistemology, methodology, and ethics of IR. The following remarks are meant to highlight a few trends that have been suggested in the preceding chapters.

The Complex Ontology of IR

When he urged IR to come out of its "degenerating" Newtonian repose, Ruggie (1998, 194) specifically mentioned that the discipline reengages with the *reality* of global life. As he pointed out with chagrin and frustration, "the term 'ontology' typically draws either blank stares or bemused smiles" from the IR community. The contention is that IR is plagued by attention blindness: because of its preoccupation with "reductive theories about '*the logic of anarchy*'" (Booth 2007, 327), it cannot discern the vast and heterogeneous reality of global life. Owing to its reductionism, mainstream IR views reality "not as a continuous flux . . . but as a series of instantaneous 'snapshots' extracted from this flux" (Popolo 2011, 25). Thus, as Lebow (2010, 285) suggests, the dominant accounts of interstate relations miss the "open-ended, nonlinear nature of the social world." He insists that the "confluence and consequences [of international politics] are best envisaged as a complex, nonlinear system," "in which multiple interrelated chains of causation have unanticipated interactions and unpredictable consequences" (Lebow 2010, 93, 77).

The ontology of complexity therefore provokes a reckoning with the multiple possibilities of *becoming* and *becoming-other* inherent in the pervasive ambiguity of global life (Kavalski 2009, 543). This is an important qualification on the earlier suggestion that CT merely models "the ontologicial layers in world politics as interrelated systems" (Harrison and Singer 2006, 26). Such ontological commitment reflects the insistence on "the continuous precipitation of new life and new meaning" (Popolo 2011, 43; see also Deuchars 2010; Connolly 2011). It is therefore not surprising that the application of CT to IR is described explicitly as a "shift from epistemology to ontology" (Yavlaç 2010, 169). The reason for this shift is the understanding of reality as "stratified" between the actual, the empirical, and the real (Yavlaç 2010, 170). This stratification addresses three of the key ontological claims animating the complexification of IR: (i) that the international is emergent; (ii) that the international is irreducible to and much more than its constituent parts; and (iii) that the international is subject to unexpected and (often) radical transformations—that is, small alterations in initial conditions can lead to profound changes in outcomes (Leon 2010, 38; Joseph 2010, 61).

In this setting, CT asserts that the world with which IR engages self-organizes in complex and contingent ways. Yet, what distinguishes this collection is the confrontation with the "ontological issue of the different layering of the social (and natural) world" (Joseph 2010, 65). Conventionally, IR has tended to ignore the fact that international politics both inhabit and are embedded in complex spaces. In this respect, a number of contributors have stressed that one of the greatest ontological boons of complexified IR is the recognition of the "totality" (Yavlaç 2010, 171) of human and nonhuman interactions in global life. It is worth pointing out that such diverse and profound considerations of the complex ontology of international politics are intended not merely as a criticism of mainstream IR, but also as a provocation for reengaging with the ongoing and overlapping interconnections animating global life.

In fact, the radical totality of human and nonhuman interactions has been framed as "posthuman IR" by Cudworth and Hobden (2011). Recognizing the qualitative and quantitative difference between human and nonhuman systems, the "complex ecologism" of "posthuman IR" uncovers that the "world is not divided into territories in which bounded societies of humans live under singular political authority and in the context of discrete natural environments"; instead, global life is "a complex interweave of numerous systems nested, intersected and embedded in each other, all undergoing processes of co-evolution and linked by innumerable feedback loops" (2011, 173, 175). It is for this reason that Dunn Cavelty and Giroux (in chapter 8) suggest that technology is no longer merely a tool for human society, but becomes constitutive of new forms of "complex subjectivities," in which human societies themselves are perceived as critical infrastructures.

In fact, these explorations might remind some readers of Harold Lasswell's (at the time mischievous, but today—with the benefit of hindsight—oracular) question: "[W]hen shall we extend the protection of the Charter of Human Rights to 'machines' and 'mutants'?" (Lasswell 1965, viii). Such inquiry into the subjectivity of nonhuman systems intimates that not only human relations, but all kinds of relations in global life, are marked by uncertainty. Bousquet (in chapter 7) reinforces this point with his insistence that "we [humanity] are merely a particular manifestation of a wider material continuum in which we are deeply entangled." As Ford, however, presciently reminds us (in chapter 3), "all complex adaptive systems are not, as it were, created equal." The ideational input distinguishes human/sociopolitical systems from all others and allows them both purposefulness and reflexivity of agency in global life. Yet, Ford stresses that CT also makes possible the comprehension of "the very cognitive frameworks that *separate* us from nonhuman linearity" (emphasis in original). Echoing this ontological commitment, the complexified perspectives on IR approach world affairs as overlays of complex interactions "between people and each other, their products, their activities, nature and themselves" (Yavlaç 2010, 172). In fact, such complexified ontology echoes the insistence of Harold and Margaret Sprout (1971) that the IR conversation should be moving "toward a politics of the planet Earth."

An Epistemology for the Complexity of IR

As it can be expected, the inclusive ontological purview of the complexity paradigm presents a number of analytical challenges. Yet, as indicated by the proponents of CT included in this collection, assertions about the appropriate ways of describing the world emerge from the ontological assumptions of what the world is like (Joseph 2010, 65). Thus, on a metatheoretical level, the problem stems from the realization that we can never be fully cognizant of the underlying mechanisms and processes of global life, because this will imply "knowing the not knowable" (Kavalski 2007, 448). Some proponents of CT explain that the contingency of our knowledge reflects "the critical importance of non-observables and non-systematic factors." Others, draw attention to the constraining effects of "blind variations (almost guesses) in knowledge" (Harrison 2006, 187). Such statements should not however be taken as an indication of the impossibility of providing robust IR interpretation "rooted in non-linearity and confluence" (Lebow 2010, 6–7). In this respect, as demonstrated by the preceding chapters, the acknowledgment of the limits of our knowledge can become a very productive analytical point of departure.

In this setting, the suggestion is that CT provides a "genuine Epistemic Revolution," which renders the Newtonian paradigm "obsolete" (Popolo 2011, 3–6). In fact, Ernst Haas (1983, 24–26) has long argued that the IR literature needs to learn from the "evolutionary epistemology" of global life. What he had in mind is the emergence of IR scholarship that

> must be open, unspecifiable ahead of events in terms of substance, and as unpredictable as evolutionary adaptation . . . [The inference is that there] is no fixed "national interest" and no "optimal regime." Different perceptions of national interest, changeable in response to new information or altered values, will result in different processes and in a variety of regimes that will be considered rational by the actors—at least for a while.

What is revolutionary about CT's contribution to IR is not only its debunking of the common wisdoms of "scientific IR," but also its dedication to "'uncertain knowledge," where uncertainty is regarded and accepted as an intrinsic quality of nature and not as a result of imperfect knowledge" (Haas 1983, 29). The suggestion is that by focusing mainly on stable equilibrium configurations, the study of IR has remained consciously ignorant of a whole "new species" of discontinuous intuition (Holt et al. 1978, 203; Phillips and Rimkunas 1978, 259–72). Thus, by painting itself into the Newtonian corner, the disciplinary mainstream has, on the one hand, evaded the need to recognize that there are dynamics which are not only unknown, but probably cannot ever be meaningfully rendered comprehensible, and, on the other hand, has stifled endeavors that can engage in thoughtful deliberation and productive management of the discontinuities, complexity, and nonlinearity of global life.

According to the contributions included in this volume, there are several important features underpinning such an approach to knowledge. First, the contingency of both global life and our ability to know it makes it impossible to construct predictive explanations of outcomes. Lebow is quite emphatic when he asserts that "[v]ariation across time, due to the changing conditions and human reflection, the openness of social systems, and the complexity of the interaction among stipulated causes make the likelihood of predictive theory—even of a probabilistic kind—extraordinarily low" (Lebow 2010, 265). Thus, the proponents of CT ascertain that, due to its overreliance on predictive theories, mainstream IR "must be totally discarded" (Yavlaç 2010, 170). A further reason for such rejection is the observation that the production of knowledge by Newtonian approaches has also limited "what is open for debate" (Joseph 2010, 53). For instance, due to the preoccupation with interstate relations, the discipline produces foot soldiers for this or that theoretical approach to international anarchy rather than students genuinely interested in observing the complex patterns of global life.

Second, the unwillingness to engage with the unpredictable becoming of global life reflects the patterns of linear causality that still seem to inform the disciplinary mainstream. The issue of "complex causation" (Lebow 2010, 10) aims to enhance sensitivity to the unintended consequences of international interactions. Such effects defy the conventional focus on purposive behavior. In fact, it is "chance, confluence, and accident that often play a determining role" in global life, rather than intentionality (Lebow 2010, 258). The complexification of IR thereby intends to supplant reductive explanations by considering the "conjuncturally determined" patterns of world affairs (Yavlaç 2010, 171).

Third, the proponents of complexification critique the way in which mainstream IR has theorized international developments by focusing on major events. Richard Ned Lebow indicates that the bias toward events thinking belies the predisposition "to think of big events as having big causes" (Lebow 2010, 266). For instance, the origins of war are usually attributed either to singular events or to the resolve of specific individuals, rather than "the result of nonlinear confluences" (Lebow 2010, 262). The suggestion therefore is that the dynamics of global life are "characterized by unintended consequences, interaction effects, and patterns that cannot be understood by breaking the system into bilateral relations" (Jervis 1991/1992, 42). Thus, the focus on both spatially and temporally proximate causes underpins the blindness to the complex interactions of global life, which turns the disciplinary terrain into a frozen expanse of accidents. The complexification of IR outlined by the preceding chapters evinces that "mainstream IR cannot talk about underlying processes, only about systems and units," which is why the chapters included in this volume advocate the abandonment of the "talk of levels of analysis in favor of complex, layered assemblies of social relations" (Joseph 2010, 64–65).

The resultant complexified epistemology of IR intends simultaneously to rethink and reinvent the study of world politics. Interestingly, most proponents of CT tend to be in agreement that this needs to be done through the "demystification of science" (Lebow 2010, 286). Such demystification entails the rejection of the Newtonian "scientific fallacies" (Popolo 2011, 22) of the discipline and accepting "the fact of *epistemological realism*: namely, that all beliefs are socially produced, so that knowledge is transient, and neither truth values nor criteria of rationality exist outside of historical time" (Wight and Joseph 2010, 13). It is also worth pointing out that while assisting the explanation "of our chaotic and unordered world," CT is idiosyncratically self-reflexive about its own epistemological investments in a specific understanding of the international and readily concedes that "knowledge sometimes has the effect of accelerating disorder" (Lebow 2010, 3).

The Methodology of Complexified IR

The ontological and epistemological assumptions of complexified IR underpin how it examines world affairs. Commentators have noted that CT has already spawned a variety of innovative approaches ranging from agent-based modeling and computer simulations to scenario building and intuitive judgment (Harrison 2006, 189–90; Kavalski 2007, 447). The proponents of CT frame this development as "methodological pluralism," which makes possible the "direct observational access" of the patterns of international affairs (Kurki 2010, 141). In this way, the methodology of complexity assists with gaining a deeper understanding of "our own human experience" (Popolo 2011, 34).

Like most commentators, the contributors to this volume acknowledge that the complexity of global life demands approaches resting on "intuitive judgment," "gut feel," and "speculative thinking" (Bradfield 2004, 35; Cederman 1997, 10). The suggestion is that in some sense "we create our own consciousness of complexity by seeking it out" (LaPorte 1975, 329). For instance, by insisting on the "plausibility of alternative worlds," counterfactual analysis lays bare the "contingency of our own world" (Lebow 2010, 17). Such production of "imaginary constructs" simultaneously allows for the examination of "judgments of possibility" and draws attention to discontinuities of the past in anticipation of future transformations in global life (Cederman 1997, 22). Thus, Harlan Wilson asserts that the "analytical complexity" of studying the complexity of global life has to reflect the interdependence of conceptual factors, variables, and components, which relate in systemic ways (in LaPorte 1975, 282). The bulk of CT research in IR promotes agent-based modeling (ABM) and computer simulations—which rest on mathematical algorithms and data sets—as tools for grasping the complexity of global life (Axelrod 1997; Cederman 1997; Pil-Rhee 1999; Rosenau 2003). Both chapter 1 and chapter 4 offer excellent demonstrations of the value added from employing ABM in the study and practice of IR. At the same time, chapter 5 cautions against the uncritical application of ABM as a one-size-fits-all approach to the complexity of global life.

At the same time, CT investigations take issue with the rational-choice paradigm and its failure to account for the pervasiveness of adaptive behaviors in global life (Axelrod 1997, 4). For some, "the linear hegemony" of rationalist causal thinking represents an "intellectual attempt to control" the study of politics by imposing a conceptual framework that is "blatantly untrue" about the patterns of international interaction (Brown 1995, 144). For others, it "restricts" interpretation by "structuring perceptions of reality" and inhibiting "creative thinking" (Bradfield 2004, 37). In a less radical mood (but equally forcefully), Robert Jervis (1997, 91) demonstrates that the acknowledgment of the complexity of global life renders the methodological apparatus of rationalism useless by "confounding standard tests of many propositions, and undermining the yardsticks or indicators for the success of policies."

Thus, in contrast to the linear perceptions of change in mainstream IR—that is, changes in variables occur, but the effect is constant—the complexification of IR suggests that "things *suffer* change" (Richards 2000; Kavalski 2007). The contention is that the unpredictability of the emergent patterns of international life need to be conceptualized within the framework of *self-organizing criticality*—that is, their dynamics "adapt to, or are themselves on, the edge of chaos, and most of the changes take place through catastrophic events rather than by following a smooth gradual path" (Dunn Cavelty 2007, 99). As the preceding chapters reveal, change in global life entails the possibility of a "radical qualitative effect" (Richards 2000, 1). Thus, when it comes to the trends, patterns, and behaviors of actors and systems in global life, there are infinitesimal amounts of possibilities; yet not all of them are likely—in fact, very few are (Kavalski 2012a). The methodological value of CT for IR is to help identify those that are more likely. Therefore, the alleged arbitrariness of occurrences that mainstream IR might describe as the effects of randomness (or exogenous/surprising shocks) could (and, in fact, more often than not do) reflect ignorance of their interactions.

The Ethics (and Practice) of Political Action under Complexity

The cognitive patterns of the complexification of IR demand meaningful engagement with the self-organizing ambivalence of global life. In this setting, the contention is that ethically oriented political action requires both the acknowledgment of and responsible adaptation to the turbulent reality of international interactions (Rivas 2010, 217). For instance, Lebow (2010, 47) indicates that "ethical beliefs and expectations" inform our "understandings of the world and how it works." The ethos of political action under complexity therefore demands acceptance of living with "the fundamental principle of uncertainty whilst moving away from the very modern idea [that] the role of reason [is to provide] certainty for decisions on human action" (Popolo 2011, 215). Such a framing also suggests the emancipatory potential embedded in and emerging from the "explanatory critique" of complexified IR (Wight and Joseph 2010, 23).

   Normatively speaking, the ethics of political action under complexity demands the development of relevant knowledge about the minimal conditions for resilient and sustainable living. Thus, in summarizing the ethical implications of CT, it can be inferred that the ethos of political action discussed in the preceding chapters hinges on three principles: (i) *precautionary principle*—stressing the need to develop "the art of working with uncertainty"; (ii) *humility principle*—recognizing that "action escapes the will of the actor"; and (iii) *resilience principle*—developing the adaptive capacity to "expect the unexpected as the norm" (Cudworth and Hobden 2011, 184).

   Such consideration of the ethical underpinnings of the complexification of IR suggests that political action does not occur in a vacuum, but in idiosyncratic and dynamic spatiotemporal contexts (Rivas 2010, 225; Patomäki 2010, 149–54). At the same time such investigations contribute actively to the conversation on what being free under the conditions of complexity might mean. The following sections briefly tease out some of the policy and normative implications implicit in the ethics of political action under complexity. Such suggestions are underpinned by the key ontological position of the complexification of IR—that the "international" encompasses the global life of human/sociopolitical and nonhuman/biophysical interactions. As Ernst Haas reminds us, "ethical choices have evolutionary consequences" (Haas 1975, 843). Thus, for Booth, while "the state of nature" is no longer just a fictional narrative but "the most pressing of practical issues," there has been insufficient attention to the policy and ethical choices demanded of decision making in such a complex context (Booth 2007, 327).

Improvisation

By recognizing the pervasive uncertainty of global life, the complexification of IR furnishes the disciplinary inquiry with "concepts to act with" (Geyer and Rihani 2010). In terms of policy formulation, CT calls for an urgent change in both the structures of and ideas about decision making—or, to use "the language of complexity, it requires changes in both institutions and internal models" (Harrison 2006, 192). More often than not, such emergent capacities for political action have been associated with the concept of *improvisation*. Alfonso Montuori (2005, 237–55) points out that improvisation is usually conceived as an exception, "as making the best of things, while awaiting a return to the way things should be done." As he demonstrates, however, improvisational policy making is neither deterministic nor arbitrary; instead, it reflects an ability "to make *choices* in context, which in turn affect the context." Thus, the choice to improvise does not indicate an inability to conduct "business as usual," but recognition that it is the cognitive patterns of "business as usual" (in particular, the belief in "the one correct way of doing things") that are accountable for the current predicaments of global life, such as climate change.

Let's take the experience of surfers (probably one of the most obvious socioecological relationships out there) as an example. Surfers go out into the ocean expecting to ride a wave whose size, speed, strength, and timing are completely unknown to them. In the ocean, they spend significant time (quite literally) *dancing* with the rhythm of the water. In this dance, the surfers learn to distinguish between the different ripples of the water and read which one is likely to be an "ankle buster" (a small wave), an "awesome" (a nearly perfect wave), or a "cruncher" (an impossible-to-ride wave). Premised on their interpretative dancing with the unpredictable motion of the ocean, surfers decide whether they are going to take off or back down from a wave. Their fitness, in terms of adaptation to the movements of the ocean, allows surfers to make decisions that are crucial to their ability to catch and ride the wave. Yet, while waves are similar to each other, they are never exactly alike, and surfers never know—regardless of whether one is a "kook" (a newbie) or a "boss" (a pro)—how the ride is going to proceed and whether it is going to be successful at all. The acceptance of the normalcy of failure is part of the decision making of surfers. In essence, each ride is an improvisation combining the individual skills of the surfer and the unpredictable shape, motion, and breaking point of the wave (Kavalski 2012b).

Yet, it is this inherent insecurity of surfing that underpins its appeal. Having accepted unpredictability as a constituent ingredient of the surfing experience, surfers not only learn to live with it, but also gain the freedom to respond creatively to such uncertainty. In terms of policy making, the suggestion is that leaders need to develop a surfer-like ability to revel in ambiguity by perfecting the capacity to make decisions based on incomplete and constantly changing information, rather than try to control, constrain, and simplify the indeterminacy of global life. In this setting, policy heterogeneity—the simultaneous maintenance of diverse decision-making strategies (alongside the willingness and capacity to develop new ones) to address the contingencies of unintended changes in global life—reflects the demand for resilient modes of policy making. Improvisation, therefore, acknowledges the randomness of the decision-taking process, but it is "randomness for a purpose" that draws on behavioral versatility and policy experience to construct an appropriate response for a particular moment in time (Neubauer 2012, 11). The ability to generate a multitude of potential solutions through combinatorial process is a key feature of improvisation's adaptive capacities (Vermeij 2008, 35).

Thus, rather than reducing uncertainty, the ethics of improvisation demands political action capable of continually imagining global life other than what it currently is. In this respect, and paraphrasing Haas, rather than an inflexible steering of the ship of state, a policy maker has to have a surfer-like capacity for "zigging and zagging" through the turbulent reality of global life in which "old objectives are questioned, new objectives clamor for satisfaction and the rationality accepted as adequate in the past ceases to be a legitimate guide to future action" (Haas 1976, 184–93). At the same time, it cautions that even if adapting appropriately, improvisation is not boundless. It can be quickly undone by external surprise. For instance, going back to the surfer's metaphor, the unexpected appearance of a shark riding the same wave infuses the decision-making context with emotions ranging from panic to an adrenaline-fueled exhilaration. At any rate, such surprises (and the emotions that they provoke) impact on the surfer's investment in a successful ride (from the one prior to the appearance of the shark). Hence, while those who are afraid of sharks most probably should not go into the ocean, the knowledge that sharks inhabit the same waters and, thereby, are not unlikely to be encountered when surfing encourages an awareness that assists in the development of a capacity to respond appropriately when confronted with rapid change and surprises.

The Art of Acting Politically

The discussion of improvisation above backstops the normative suggestion of the complexification of IR—namely, that the capacity to respond to the contingent interaction of global life requires learning the *art of acting politically*. The proposition is that such investigation responds to the query posed by Sir Alfred Zimmern, the first holder of the title of professor of international politics at Aberystwyth, "How could we get the interdependent but chaotic world to work together?" (Zimmern 1934). The suggestion here is that in lieu of a precommitment to particular models, responding to the turbulence, surprises, and unplanned occurrences defining global life demand strategies embedded in nonlinear intuition (Eoyang and Holladay 2013; Goldstein 1994; Olson and Eoyang 2001). In other words, ethical political action requires responsible creative adaptation that addresses the complex interactions of global life while maintaining the coherence and continuity of socioecological systems. The contention is that decision making under the conditions of complexity engages individuals as conscious subjects in a responsible and sustainable interaction with their environment.

Normatively speaking, the complexity of global life confronts IR with the "political effects of agents that are not conventionally perceived as 'political'" (Prins 1995, 819). Hence, the "threats," "dangers," and "insecurity" emanating from nonhuman systems are not conventionally perceived as *intentional*—that is, there is no conflict of wills between distinct (and opposing) strategic actors (Wæver 1997, 230). For instance, the so-called "Frankenstorm" Sandy which hit the East Coast of the United States in the days prior to the 2012 presidential election provided one such instance of the political effects of such "nonpolitical" agents. The question is: How can we all participate meaningfully in something that can plausibly, but still only vaguely, be called international politics populated by actors whose subjectivity lacks "agential intentionality" (Cudworth and Hobden 2011, 140–168)?

While this question does not have a singular and definitive answer, a crucial feature of the responses suggested by CT demand an ethos willing to accept and engage with the ambiguity of global life.

Thus, as Edgar Morin suggests, the recognition of complexity has important effects on the ethics of political action: (i) its "multiplication of alternatives" creates favorable conditions for innovative strategies; (ii) its randomness underscores the increasing significance of individual decisions, which can lead to irreversible and unpredictable changes for the entire process. Thus, just because an action is irreversible does not mean that it should not be undertaken. Instead, acknowledging this "ethical complexification," the *art of acting politically* engages in an "ecology of action," which Edgar Morin calls "living life"—that is, "not just living," but "knowing how to resist in life" by "daring the acceptance to risk" (Morin 2004, 43–44; 2006, 143). In other words, the ethics of resilience suggests that "the search for a single 'optimum' strategy may neither be possible nor desirable. Any strategy can only be optimal under certain conditions and when those conditions change, the strategy may no longer be optimal" (Mitleton-Kelly 2003, 14). Said otherwise, while global life keeps on asserting its complexity, our policy making seems to be invested in stringent models insisting on staying the course. Hence, perhaps ironically, the development of more adaptive decision making has been hampered by the criticism of (what is perceived by electorates and mainstream media as) "flip-flopping." Policy fluctuations responding to the continually changing circumstances of global life are marked by "the lack of absolute [decision-making] control over the outcome of the actions undertaken by the actors" (Adler 2005, 44). Thus, changes in policy rather than "flip-flopping" indicate such adjustments to alterations triggered by the interwovenness of global life.

Policy making under complexity, therefore, calls for "a higher level of reflexivity" and indicates that contingent events bring about opportunities for developing new governance skills and norms (Whiteside 1998, 652). Since political action takes place in a self-organizing context, policy makers need to accept that their decisions will have unpredictable and (oftentimes) unintended outcomes. The complexity of global life demands intellectual flexibility "in order to avoid a dogged, single-minded pursuit of an effect that is no longer important or even obtainable in the evolutionary system of strategic interaction . . . Flexibility requires error, tolerance, and avoidance of over-control" (Sakulich 2001, 38). Decision making free from the aspiration to control change rests on a choice to generate "desirable pathways" in the face of rapid and fast alterations and pervasive uncertainty and risk (Cudworth and Hobden 2011, 181). Therefore, the claim here is that the *art of acting politically* under complexity attests to the ethical choices demanded

by a decision-making "dancing to the rhythms of global life." Such normative understanding borrows from what John Keats has termed the poetry of
"negative capabilities"—the "capabilities of being in uncertainty, Mysteries,
doubts without any irritable reaching after fact and reason"—which demonstrate an ability to think "under fire," live with ambiguity, remain "content
with half-knowledge," and engage in a nondefensive way with change, while
resisting the impulse (merely) to react (Keats 1970 [1818], 43).

In short, the recognition of the complexity of global life demands
thoughtful action framed by an ethics of adaptation.

> The goal is to anticipate the form adaptation is likely to take
> under specified conditions, but this is not to say that adaptation
> is a predetermined process to which decision makers unknow-
> ingly succumb. Societies are not like cats which automatically
> adjust their distance from a blazing fireplace in such a way as to
> stay warm without getting burned. Some do get too close to the
> fires of world politics and wither, while others remain too remote
> from them and freeze. In other words, societies can engage in
> maladaptive as well as adaptive behavior, and the resulting move-
> ment back and forth between the extremes of the adaptive scale
> suggests the central role played by human choice. Such choice is
> no more random than is any human choice, but it grows out of
> historical, cultural, and other immediate and remote factors. The
> point being made here is simply that choice is part of adaptation
> and not precluded by it. (Rosenau 1970, 386)

In fact, it can be argued that such ethics recover the injunctions of some of
the founders of IR who argued that the "realization of the complexity [of
world politics] should make for a more tolerant and broad minded attitude
to foreign policy" (Gettell 1922, 330). Thus, the reference to the *art of acting
politically* reveals that the study and practice of IR should not aim at reducing (and controlling) the complexity of global life, but by acknowledging
its interwovenness develop adaptive capacities for tolerating and working
with change.

Conclusion

It has become expected of policy makers, pundits, and scholars to refer to
a whole raft of global problems—from the economic downturn to climate
change—as complex. While the complexity of these issues is indeed stag-

gering, the term "complexity" is used, more often than not, merely as a descriptor of the intricate nature of these challenges. The contributions to this volume have demonstrated that complexity is not an accidental word, but a key to the understanding and explanation of global life. It is for this reason that the contributors have consciously positioned themselves within the small but resilient oeuvre intent on complexifying IR.

A key feature of this literature is its rejection of the linear reductionism dominating the IR mainstream. In fact, some proponents of CT have suggested that such pandering to a truncated representation of the reality of global life has turned IR into a "miserable science" (Geyer and Rihani 2010, 73). As I have sought to demonstrate in this concluding chapter, at the heart of this misery is IR's conception of "science," which has no space for the uncertainty and randomness of global life. This ambiguity was not lost on the so-called fathers of the discipline. For instance, Hans Morgenthau was well aware of "the inevitable gap" between "the science of political science" (or what he also called "good—that is rational" international politics) and the fact that the "political reality" of world affairs "is replete with contingencies and systemic irregularities" (or what he labeled, international politics "as it actually is") (Morgenthau 1973, 8).

It seems that IR has forgotten Morgenthau's injunction that reality is far more complex than his account suggested. As the contributions to this volume evidence, CT provides a much-needed corrective to the "deep Newtonian slumber" dominating the mainstream of IR. While exposing the "scientific fallacy" of the discipline, CT demonstrates that "an alternative understanding of IR" is "not only possible, but also necessary" (Yavlaç 2010, 168). A critical feature of this alternative understanding is the open, nonanthropocentric ontology of complexified IR. It asserts that "thinking beyond the human condition can allow us to fully appreciate history as becoming, as the nonlinear process which fully reflects the nature of the vortex of time" (Popolo 2011, 28–29). At the same time, the complexification of IR offers nonlinear engagements with the turbulent dynamics of global life involving the coincidence, extensive connectivity, and interaction between highly coupled human and natural system, rapid technological change, and a whole host of social, political, and economic institutions (Kasperson 2008). As the contributions included in this volume indicate, while such complexification frames the future as uncertain and the present as irreversible, it nevertheless stringently refuses to securitize them.

Thus, going back to the query with which this concluding chapter began (Is IR a science?) the CT perspectives outlined in the preceding chapters suggest that it is much more pertinent to respond to the following questions: "What kind of science?" and "Science to what ends?" The contributions to this volume provide distinct yet veritable paths through which these issues can be interrogated. It is expected that to the buffs of the complexification of IR this collection makes available superbly researched accounts of the diversity of CT perspectives and issues. To the neophytes, the analyses on the preceding pages offer rarely comprehensive and insightful glimpses into the diverse perspectives, experiences, concepts, practices, and issues of the complexification of IR. In other words, the conversations included in this collection try to chart the turbulent waters of a complex and uncertain global life. Most poignantly, perhaps, they; reveal that the cognitive crisis in the conventional study of IR becomes the beginning of its complexification.

Bibliography

Adler, E. (2005). *Communitarian international relations*. Cambridge: Cambridge University Press.

Axelrod, R. (1997). *The complexity of cooperation: Agent-based models of competition and collaboration*. Princeton, NJ: Princeton University Press.

Beaumont, R (1994). *War, chaos, and history*. Westport, CT: Praeger.

Booth, K. (2007). *Theory of world security*. Cambridge: Cambridge University Press.

Bradfield, R. (2004). What we know and what we believe. *Development*, 47(4), 35–42

Brown, C. (1995). *Serpents in the sand: Essays on the nonlinear nature of politics and human destiny*. Ann Arbor: University of Michigan Press.

Cederman, L-E. (1997). *Emergent actors in world politics: How states and nations develop and dissolve*. Princeton, NJ: Princeton University Press.

Connolly, W. E. (2011). *A world of becoming*. Durham, NC: Duke University Press.

Cudworth, E. and S. Hobden (2011). *Posthuman international relations: Complexity, ecologism and global politics*. London: Zed Books.

Deuchars, R. (2010). Deleuze, DeLanda and social complexity: Implications for the "International." *Journal of International Political Theory* 6(2), 161–187.

Dunn Cavelty, M. (2007). Securing the digital age: The challenges of complexity and IR Theory. In Johan Eriksson and Giampiero Giacomello (Eds.), *International Relations and Security in the Digital Age* (85–105). London: Routledge.

Eoyang, G. H., and Holladay R. J. (2013). *Adaptive action: Leveraging uncertainty in your organization*. Stanford, CA: Stanford University Press.

Gettell, R. G. (1922). Influences on world politics. *The Journal of International Relations*, 12(3), 320–330.

Goldstein, J. (1994). *The unshackled organization: Facing the challenge of unpredictability through spontaneous reorganization*. Portland, OR: Productivity Press.

Geyer, R., and Rihani, S. (2010). *Complexity and public policy*. London: Routledge.

Haas, E. (1975). Is there a hole in the whole? *International Organization*, 29(3), 827–876.

Haas, E. (1976). Turbulent fields and the theory of regional integration. *International Organization* 30(2), 173–212.

Haas, E. (1983). Words can hurt you; or who said what to whom about regimes. In S. Krasner (Ed.), *International Regimes* (23–59). Ithaca: Cornell University Press.

Harrison, N. E. (2006). Complex systems and the practice of world politics. In Neil E. Harrison (Ed.), *Complexity in world politics: Concepts and methods of a new paradigm* (183–195). Albany: SUNY Press.

Harrison, N. E., and Singer, J. D. (2006). Complexity is more than systems theory. In Neil E. Harrison (Ed.), *Complexity in world politics: Concepts and methods of a new paradigm* (25–42). Albany: SUNY Press.

Holt, R., Job, B., and Markus, L. (1978). Catastrophe theory and the study of war. *Journal of Conflict Resolution* 22(2), 171–208.

Jervis, R. (1991/1992). The future of world politics: Will it resemble the past. *International Security* 16(3), 39–73.

Jervis, R. (1997). *System effects: Complexity in political and social life.* Princeton, NJ: Princeton University Press.

Joseph, J. (2010). The international as emergent: challenging old and new orthodoxies in international relations theory. In J. Joseph and C. Wight (Eds.), *Scientific realism and international relations* (51–68). Basingstoke: Palgrave Macmillan.

Kasperson, R. E. (2008). Coping with deep uncertainty: Challenges for environmental assessment and decision making. In G. Brammer and M. Smithson (Eds.), *Uncertainty and risk: Mutlidisciplinary perspectives* (337–347). London: Earthscan.

Kavalski, E. (2007). The fifth debate and the emergence of complex international relations theory. *Cambridge Review of International Affairs* 20(3), 435–454.

Kavalski, E. (2012a). Waking IR up from its "deep Newtonian slumber." *Millennium* 41(1), 137–150.

Kavalski, E. (2012b). Acting politically in global life: Security and its logic of resilience. In D. Walton and M. Frazier (Eds.), *Contending views on international security* (87–102). New York: Nova Science.

Keats, J. 1970[1818]. In R. Gittings (Ed.), *The letters of John Keats.* Oxford: Oxford University Press.

Kurki, M. (2010). Critical realism and the analysis of democratisation: Does philosophy of science matter? In J. Joseph and C. Wight (Eds.), *Scientific realism and international relations* (129–146). Basingstoke: Palgrave Macmillan.

LaPorte, T. (Ed) (1975). *Organised social complexity: Challenge to politics and policy.* Princeton, NJ: Princeton University Press.

Lasswell, H. D. (1965). *World politics and personal insecurity.* New York: Free Press.

Lebow, R. N. (2010). *Forbidden fruit: Counterfactuals and international relations.* Princeton, NJ: Princeton University Press.

Leon, D. (2010). Reductionism, emergence, and explanation in international relations theory. In J. Joseph and C. Wight (Eds.), *Scientific realism and international relations* (31–50). Basingstoke: Palgrave Macmillan.

Mitleton-Kelly, E. (2003). *Complex systems and evolutionary perspectives on organizations.* Oxford: Pergamon.

Morgenthau, H. (1973 [1948]). *Politics among nations: The struggle for power and peace.* New York: Knopf.

Morin, E. (2004). The ethics of complexity. In Bindé (Ed.), *The future of values* (43–46). New York: Berghahn Books.

Morin, E. (2006). Realism and utopia. *Diogenes*, 39(209), 135–144.

Montuori, A. (2005). The complexity of improvisation and the improvisation of complexity. *Human Relations* 56(2), 237–255.

Newbauer, R. L. (2012). *Evolution and the emergent self: the rise of complexity and behavioral versatility in nature*. New York: Columbia University Press.

Olson, E. E. and Eoyang, G. H. (2001). *Facilitating organization change: Lessons from complexity science*. San Francisco, CA: Jossey-Bass/Pfeiffer.

Patomäki, H. (2010). Exploring possible, likely and desirable global futures: Beyond the closed vs open systems dichotomy. In *Scientific realism and international relations*. In J. Joseph and C. Wight (Eds.) (147–166). Basingstoke: Palgrave Macmillan.

Phillips, W., and Rimkunas, R. (1978). The concept of crisis in international politics. *Journal of Peace Research* 15(3), 259–272.

Pil-Rhee, Y. (1999). *The dynamics and complexity of political systems*. Seoul: Ingansarang Press.

Popolo, D. (2011). *A new science of international relations: Modernity, complexity and the Kosovo conflict*. Farnham: Ashgate.

Prins, G. (1995). The definition of global security. *American Behavioral Scientist*, 38(6), 817–829.

Richards, D. (Ed.). (2000). *Political complexity: Non linear models of politics*. Ann Arbor: University of Michigan Press.

Rivas, J. (2010). Realism. for real this time: Scientific realism is not a compromise between positivism and interpretivism. In J. Joseph and C. Wight (Eds.). *Scientific realism and international relation* (203–227). Basingstoke: Palgrave Macmillan.

Rogowski, R. (1968). International politics: The past as science. *International Studies Quarterly*, 12(2), 394–418.

Rosenau, J. N. (1970). Foreign policy as adaptive behavior: Some preliminary notes for a theoretical model. *Comparative Politics* 2(3), 365–387.

Rosenau, J. N. (2003). *Distant proximities: Dynamics beyond globalization*. Princeton, NJ: Princeton University Press.

Rosenau, J. N., Der Derian, J., Elshtain, J., Smith, S., and Sylvester, C. (1993). *Global voices: Dialogues in international relations*. Boulder, CO: Westview Press.

Ruggie, J. G. (1998). *Constructing the world polity: Essays on international institutionalization*. London: Routledge.

Sakulich, T. J. (2001). *Precision engagement at the strategic level of war: Guiding promise or wishful thinking*. Maxwell AFB, AL: USAF Center for Strategy and Technology.

Sprout, H., and Sprout, M. (1971). *Toward a politics of the planet earth*. New York: Van Nostrand Reinhold Co.

Vermeij, G. J. (2008). Security, unpredictability, and evolution: Policy and history of life. In *Natural security: A Darwinian approach to a dangerous world* (25–41). Berkeley, CA: University of California Press.

Yavlaç, F. (2010). Critical realism, international relations theory, and Marxism. In J. Joseph and C. Wight (Eds.), *Scientific realism and international relations* (167–185). Basingstoke: Palgrave Macmillan.

Wæver, O. (1997). *Concepts of security.* Copenhagen: Copenhagen University Press.

Whiteside, K. H. (1998). Systems theory. *Policy Studies Journal*, 26(4), 636–656.

Wight, C., and J. Joseph (2010). Scientific realism and international relations. the international as emergent: Challenging old and new orthodoxies in international relations theory. In J. Joseph and C. Wight (Eds.), *Scientific Realism and International Relations* (1–30). Basingstoke: Palgrave Macmillan.

Zimmern, A. (1934). Comments, *Hackney Gazette*, January 22.

Contributors

Antoine Bousquet is a senior lecturer in international relations at Birkbeck, University of London (UK).

Erika Cudworth is a reader in sociology and politics at the University of East London (UK).

Myriam Dunn Cavelty is the head of the New Risk Research Unit at the Center for Security Studies, ETH Zurich (Switzerland).

David C. Earnest is an associate professor of political science and international relations at Old Dominion University (USA).

Christopher A. Ford is the Republican chief counsel for the U.S. Senate Committee on Appropriations. The views expressed in Dr. Ford's contributions to this volume are entirely his own, and do not necessarily represent those of anyone else in the U.S. Government

Erika Frydenlund is a doctoral student at the Graduate Program in International Studies, Old Dominion University (USA).

Jennifer Groux is a senior researcher at the New Risk Research Unit at the Center for Security Studies, ETH Zurich (Switzerland).

Stephen Hobden is a senior lecturer in international politics at the University of East London (UK).

Emilian Kavalski is an associate professor of global studies at the Institute for Social Justice, Australian Catholic University (Sydney).

Mark Olssen is a professor of political theory and education at the University of Surrey (UK).

Jürgen Scheffran is a professor of climate change and security at the University of Hamburg (Germany).

Colin Wight is a professor of international relations at the University of Sydney (Australia).

Index

Western modernity; *see* modernity
Westphalian system; *see* system
Whitley, Richard, 57, 70–72, 77; *see* adhocracy
Wieseltier, Leon, 92, 109
Wilson, E.O., 97, 109, 248, 252; *see* consilience
Wilson, Harlan, 261
Wittgenstein, Ludwig, 161
Wolfe, Cary, 175–176, 188, 191, 201, 207
world history; *see* history
world politics, 1–2, 4–8, 12, 19, 143, 162, 173, 178, 180, 186, 256, 260, 267, 269; *see* International Relations
as a complex system, 6–11, 15, 18, 169–184, 231, 235, 250, 253–269
"inside/outside and around" of, 1, 4–6, 16
world war; *see* war

yardstick, 261

Zimmern, Alfred, 265, 272
zone, 3, 57, 60, 118, 123, 222

www.ingramcontent.com/pod-product-compliance
Lightning Source LLC
Chambersburg PA
CBHW031411270326
41929CB00010BA/1409